Near-Death Experience
in
Ancient Civilizations

T0273931

"A groundbreaking exploration that masterfully connects ancient after-life beliefs with the cross-cultural consistency of near-death experiences. Gregory Shushan's meticulously researched work is a must-read for any-one interested in the intersection of history, spirituality, and human consciousness."

JEFFREY LONG, M.D., AUTHOR OF *EVIDENCE OF THE AFTERLIFE*

"Gregory Shushan, the undisputed leading scholar of historical NDEs, presents spellbinding cases from five diverse cultures to arrive at his con-cept of the universal, cultural, and individual features of NDEs—sure to become a fundamental way to conceptualize these fascinating experi-ences. This book is a must-read."

JANICE MINER HOLDEN, PH.D., PRESIDENT OF THE INTERNATIONAL
ASSOCIATION FOR NEAR-DEATH STUDIES

"In this major opus of research and scholarship, Gregory Shushan takes his readers on a panoramic vista of ancient texts and traditions dealing with what are today called near-death experiences (NDEs). This makes for fas-cinating reading, and Shushan explores it all, from his own unique perspec-tive, in this reader-friendly account. A magnificent tour de force."

STANLEY KRIPPNER, PH.D, AUTHOR OF *A CHAOTIC LIFE*

"Gregory Shushan shows the seminal importance of near-death experi-ences in shaping afterlife concepts in disparate societies around the globe. Only someone with Shushan's comprehensive grasp of transcultural spiri-tual beliefs could document so persuasively how near-death experiences have influenced human society through the centuries and continue to challenge our own thinking today about death and what may follow."

BRUCE GREYSON, M.D., AUTHOR OF *AFTER*

"Gregory Shushan offers here a learned comparative vision of the history of religions to plumb the depths of the idea that religious beliefs of the dead and the afterlife do not come from wish-fulfillments, denials, or simple dreams but from consistent and constant experiences of the disembodied soul or spirit."

JEFFREY J. KRIPAL, PH.D., AUTHOR OF *HOW TO THINK IMPOSSIBLY*

"Gregory Shushan's work on near-death experiences is detailed, rigorous, and compelling. His thorough analysis makes it clear that reductive approaches are inadequate to fully understand the pervasiveness of these experiences. His exploration encourages fresh perspectives on this universal human phenomenon, regardless of one's stance on NDEs. A must-read for anyone interested in the subject."

DIANA WALSH PASULKA, PH.D., AUTHOR OF *HEAVEN CAN WAIT*

"This book is a treasure. Shushan's analysis and comparison leads to the conclusion that there is an experiential basis underlying the afterlife beliefs of many ancient cultures."

JEFFREY MISHLOVE, PH.D., HOST AND PRODUCER OF
NEW THINKING ALLOWED

"A crucially important contribution to NDE studies, this book firmly places reported near-death experiences as the source of many of the world's afterlife beliefs. It ushers in a new era of research in this enigmatic experience and, in doing so, becomes essential reading for anybody who seriously wishes to dig deeper into the true significance of the NDE."

ANTHONY PEAKE, AUTHOR OF *THE NEAR-DEATH EXPERIENCE*

"In this seminal, thoroughly researched study of five distinct ancient civilizations, Gregory Shushan argues compellingly that near-death experiences have shaped and informed afterlife beliefs throughout human history. A carefully argued, groundbreaking contribution to the fields of near-death studies, religion, psychology, anthropology, and beyond."

STEPHEN E. POTTHOFF, AUTHOR OF
THE AFTERLIFE IN EARLY CHRISTIAN CARTHAGE

Near-Death Experience
in
Ancient Civilizations

The Origins of the
World's Afterlife Beliefs

A Sacred Planet Book

Gregory Shushan, Ph.D.

Inner Traditions
Rochester, Vermont

Inner Traditions
One Park Street
Rochester, Vermont 05767
www.InnerTraditions.com

Sacred Planet Books are curated by Richard Grossinger, Inner Traditions editorial board member and cofounder and former publisher of North Atlantic Books. The Sacred Planet collection, published under the umbrella of the Inner Traditions family of imprints, includes works on the themes of consciousness, cosmology, alternative medicine, dreams, climate, permaculture, alchemy, shamanic studies, oracles, astrology, crystals, hyperobjects, locutions, and subtle bodies.

Cataloging-in-Publication Data for this title is available from the Library of Congress

ISBN 978-1-64411-868-9 (print)
ISBN 978-1-64411-869-6 (ebook)

Printed and bound in the United States by Lake Book Manufacturing, LLC

10 9 8 7 6 5 4 3 2 1

Text design and layout by Priscilla Harris Baker
This book was typeset in Garamond Premier Pro with Avenir, Gotham, and Ptolemy used as display typefaces

To send correspondence to the author of this book, mail a first-class letter to the author c/o Inner Traditions • Bear & Company, One Park Street, Rochester, VT 05767, and we will forward the communication, or contact the author directly at **gregoryshushan.com**.

For my mother, for nurturing in me a sense of wonder, curiosity, and lifelong intellectual and creative inspiration; and for my father, for providing the balancing counterweight of pragmatism and skepticism, and unwittingly planting the seeds of confidence and aspiration.

Contents

Foreword

John Tait

It is a great pleasure to welcome Gregory Shushan's *Near-Death Experience in Ancient Civilizations*, a thoroughly revised and restructured book that builds upon his 2009 *Conceptions of the Afterlife in Early Civilizations: Universalism, Constructivism, and Near-Death Experience*. That publication has sometimes mistakenly been listed as though it were a collected, edited volume, although of course its most striking feature is precisely that it is the work of a single author, presenting throughout an original and systematic exploration of the evidence and of its implications. This consistent breadth of scholarship may be seen in Gregory's 2018 book, *Near-Death Experience in Indigenous Religions*, winner of the Parapsychological Association Book Award. The present revised work shows the same admirable qualities that Gregory's writing has displayed over at least 25 years: he has a special ability to reflect on, to rethink, and to develop his ideas and the questions that he seeks to address. Hence, in part, the appropriateness of a new edition of *Conceptions of the Afterlife*.

That a new edition is called for also offers an indication of the liveliness of the topic of near-death experience (NDE). Almost everyone in modern societies (and not only Western societies) has read or heard of NDEs. Popular attitudes vary from an instinctive urge to condemn any

such experiences as fraudulent or deluded to an unquestioning acceptance, with confusion and agnosticism as the extensive middle ground.
The literature on NDEs is vast. So also is the quantity of material on
the internet. Aside from sensationalist anecdotes and urban myth, many
of the more serious contributions are limited to psychological or medical methodologies, whether seeking to explain the phenomena—or to
explain them away. One thing that is made very clear by Gregory's work
is that no simplistic approach can prove ultimately persuasive. Psychology
or physiology may be relevant, but they do not provide a straightforward
route to an adequate or appropriate understanding of the variety of
human experiences involved in NDEs.

The topic is a kind of anthropological investigation, but one probing
the worlds of people and cultures that have long passed away (the most
recent evidence adduced here is from Mesoamerica, belonging to a range
of dates, the latest in the sixteenth century CE). However, the task is
essentially no more daunting than that faced by many archaeologists. In
fact, for archaeologists, the pitfalls are well known and much discussed,
while the possibilities for work in phenomenology and cognitive archaeology are rich and are increasingly being followed up. The civilizations
that Gregory calls upon in chapters 3–7 are civilizations that have not
had the same kind of direct input into our modern Western cultures as
the Classical world, or as those cultures that incorporate or owe a debt to
Judaism, Christianity, or Islam. Furthermore, they developed in near isolation from one another, and any possible influences that one may have
had upon another must have been marginal and of no significance for
the work attempted here. Two or more of these societies have, therefore,
over the past half century or longer, been used in comparative studies to
investigate a variety of broad cultural questions, such as state formation
and control, the nature of kingship, and the roles of literacy and orality
in societies.

Gregory's investigation encompasses an enormous span of time—just in
terms of the date of the first appearance of the textual sources investigated.
The Egyptian Pyramid Texts were first inscribed in the third millennium

BCE, and Sumerian (and Akkadian) material from Mesopotamia is of similar antiquity. For the present writer, whose own work essentially concerns ancient Egypt, especially of the later periods, it is fascinating to see, in chapter 3, treatment of well-known and much-studied texts viewed from a fresh perspective. The bulk of the textual material that Gregory evaluates from Egypt can be said to comprise compilations of ritual empowerment. The performance of the texts enabled someone to *do* something, whatever incidental benefits they may also have brought. *Who* exactly was conceived as performing (for example) the Pyramid Texts, and what persona and voice they adopted, are complex and fascinating questions. Our surviving material comprises primarily carved and painted inscriptions upon tomb walls or coffins, although the traditions will essentially have been curated upon papyrus rolls housed in libraries.

A Demotic Egyptian narrative composed or compiled some two millennia later than the Pyramid Texts, the first Setna Khaemwese story (Gregory discusses this text, below), still reflected glimpses of this tradition, together with ideas from the *Book of the Dead*. In an episode of the narrative set long before the New Kingdom backdrop of the main story, a prince has seized by stealth and violence a book written by and belonging to the god Thoth, and begins to explore it:

> He fetched the book up out of the chest of gold, and he read out aloud a written formula in it; he took command of the sky, the earth, the Otherworld, and the deserts and the seas; he found out everything that the birds of the sky were saying, and the fish of the deep, and the beasts of the desert. He read aloud another written formula; he saw Re [the sun-god] as he appeared in the sky, together with his Ennead [attendant gods], and the Moon as he rose, and the various stars. He saw the fish of the deep, although there were 21 god's-cubits [about 36 feet] of water above them.

Near-Death Experience in Ancient Civilizations opens up a multitude of questions that resonate with hopes and fears widely felt in the modern world. Because of the broad comparative approach adopted here, readers, whatever their background, whatever their spiritual and religious beliefs, if any, and whatever their preexisting stance on NDEs—whether one of credence or one of outright scepticism—will find challenging ideas and the need to think afresh.

JOHN TAIT is Emeritus Professor of Egyptology and former Edwards Professor at the Institute of Archaeology, University College London. He has edited hieroglyphic, hieratic, demotic, Coptic, and Greek texts, especially on papyrus, and studies Egyptian literary traditions. His numerous publications include Papyri from Tebtunis in Egyptian and in Greek (1977) and Saqqara Demotic Papyri (1983, with H. S. Smith), and he has made several contributions to the work of the Egypt Exploration Society's project for the publication of papyri from Saqqara and the Project for the Publication of the Carlsberg Papyri (Copenhagen). He received his D.Phil from the University of Oxford.

Acknowledgments

I am very grateful to the variety of specialists in various fields who generously gave their time to providing comments and criticisms that have informed and supplemented this research (though, of course, any errors made and any advice I failed to heed are my sole responsibility).

First and foremost, I would like to thank Paul Badham, John Tait, Gavin Flood, and Wendy Dossett, whose perspectives, encouragement, and support were invaluable to the project. I also owe a debt of gratitude to those who reviewed and commented on particular chapters in their early stages of development, including Stephen Quirke, Stephanie Dalley, Martin O'Kane, Maya Warrier, Stephanie Jamison, Xinzhong Yao, Jordan Paper, J. G. Brotherston, Penny Dransart, Karl Taube, Elisabeth Graham, and Mu-chou Poo. Various forms of encouragement, challenges, discussions, and assistance also came from Ruth Whitehouse, Mark Fox, Penny Sartori, Jennifer Uzzell, Daniel Foxvog, Peter Westh, James Cox, Peggy Morgan, Lalle Purseglove, Stuart Hay, Anthony Peake, Richard Grossinger, Cosmo Naut, and the editorial team at Inner Traditions.

Finally, a very special thanks to my patrons who support my work on Patreon: Donnalee Dermady-Minney, The Daily Grail, Mark Gober, Tim Hacker, Janice Holden, Kristofer Key, Sylvia Kezele, Vince Kitowski, Eric Peterson, Sharif Randhawa, Chris Schelin, David Sunfellow, Brandon Taylor, Samantha Lee Treasure, Alex L. Tsakiris, Christopher Turek, Jack VanAken, Edward Zukowski, and those who wish to remain anonymous.

The research for this book was funded by the UK Arts and Humanities Research Council and was further supported by a fellowship from the Centro Incontri Umani, Ascona, Switzerland.

Introduction

In addition to the fact that some consider them to be glimpses of an actual afterlife, there is another important and largely overlooked dimension to near-death experiences (NDEs): their power to influence spiritual and religious beliefs around the world, contributing to the formation of afterlife beliefs across cultures and throughout human history. As such, they have contributed to the world's mystical literature, ritual practices, and art—and therefore to human culture itself. When you start to look at the history of the study of religious and spiritual traditions around the world, I think you'll agree that the lack of recognition of the cultural impact of NDEs is mystifying.

Near-death experiences typically occur during periods of clinical death or near-death, after which an individual, upon resuscitation, reports having had mystical or spiritual episodes. This book compares reports of NDEs with the afterlife beliefs in five ancient world regions:

- Old and Middle Kingdom Egypt (2700–1800 BCE)
- Early Dynastic Sumer and Old Babylonian Mesopotamia (2900–1595 BCE)
- Vedic India (1500–300 BCE)
- Pre-Buddhist China (1100 BCE–220 CE)
- Maya and Nahua/Aztec Mesoamerica (300 BCE–1520 CE)

Each of these civilizations was characterized by a high degree of cultural independence, developing and evolving largely independent of one another. This means that any similarities between them must be due to something other than "diffusion"—that is, the sharing of myths and beliefs from one group of people to another.

This book is not an introduction or simply a rehashing of information easily available elsewhere—either about NDEs or about the afterlife beliefs of ancient civilizations. It is an original exploration—a journey of discovery in which you will participate, piecing together disparate elements from various afterlife belief systems as found in the world's earliest religious texts. Together, we will tease out their individual meanings, analyze their cultural expressions, and reveal their universal truths. Like any voyage that is worth undertaking, this is a complex, multifaceted one, and perhaps sometimes challenging—but it is, I hope, a rich and rewarding experience from preparation to return.

In a sense, our journey to discover the cultural meanings of NDEs mirrors the accounts of afterlife voyages that we will be exploring. Though we will remain in our bodies for the duration, through the pages of this book we'll leave the mundane world behind, traveling through darkness, emerging into light, encountering spirit beings in other realms, having our identity and sense of self challenged, and reaching barriers and limits that we will at least try to traverse before our return.

The first stage of the journey is to reveal step-by-step that there does indeed exist a series of similarities between afterlife beliefs throughout the world, beliefs that transcend culture, time, and context. These similarities are too consistent and specific for "coincidence" to be an adequate explanation. And yet they must be explained somehow, for the implications are profound: that afterlife beliefs are not entirely invented by cultures and that there appears to be some kind of universal factor at work. In order to explain these dynamics, we will unravel the relationships and interactions between the cross-cultural elements *and* the culture-specific elements (the differences)—particularly in determining the extent to which culture influences NDEs, and vice versa. Specifically, we will examine the theory that NDEs have occurred throughout human history and that they have contributed to the formation of belief systems, being drawn upon in the creation of religious otherworld-journey texts.

The material we will be examining is complex—sometimes obscure, sometimes of crystalline poetic beauty, though occasionally disturbing or even just bizarre. The questions we are asking of this diverse material can only be satisfactorily answered by mining the knowledge and ideas from various scholarly disciplines. Bold claims—claims that could rewrite the history of religions and recast the role of extraordinary mystical experiences in human cultures—must be backed up by careful, sound research. For *new* research to be accepted, we must justify each of our assertions, every step of the way, by reference to demonstrable historical facts and to the scholarly work that preceded us. In other words, rest assured—there is a method to my madness.

It is important to make clear from the outset that the descriptions of the afterlife in the ancient texts considered here are rarely portrayed as accounts of personal experiences. They are religious literatures that scarcely mention NDEs—at least not overtly. Writing was put to only limited uses in the earliest of the ancient civilizations, rarely including personal narratives or documentary accounts of local events. In addition, only a small fraction of texts ever survives in the archaeological and historical records, so it's not surprising that personal accounts of such phenomena are rare. However, there is no reason to assume that the texts did not *incorporate* such material. As you will see, this suggestion is not a rhetorical device of the kind used by fringe conspiracy theorists or found in pseudo documentaries about ancient aliens. I'm not "just asking a question" in order to be provocative and imply an unsubstantiated controversial answer. Rather, I am posing a problem that I intend to address methodically and resolve with a cogent, comprehensive theory.

The descriptions of afterlife experiences under consideration occur mainly in sources that held religious meaning within their respective traditions. The specific nature and purpose of each source is noted though the comparison is not within or between genres, but between the content of relevant sources regardless of genre. The fundamental differences between the types of texts (as well as between the varying religious traditions) actually work to our advantage in determining the extent of cross-cultural consistencies. They add a cross-*contextual* dimension that makes the similarities all the more significant. For example, neither the Egyptians nor the Mesopotamians nor the Mesoamericans left behind anything like the relatively cohesive statements of religious philosophy found in the Upanishads of India or the Confucian Classics of China, while the only systematic "practical" guidebook to the afterlife for the periods under consideration (see chapter 2) is the Egyptian *Book of Two Ways*. Only India and China produced texts concerned mainly with our current life on Earth that nevertheless contain relevant passages; and ethnographic material, collected by foreign, external chroniclers, exists only for Mesoamerica.

The texts are discussed in roughly chronological order within each section, though I've taken some latitude to allow for a more coherent flow. In any case, the dates of composition of most of the texts are largely unknown, though most of them are believed to have originated far earlier than the earliest physical examples, meaning that they likely began as oral literature. However, any discussion of conceptual "development" over time is, to some extent, based upon uncertain chronology. Furthermore, it's almost certain that relevant earlier or contemporary literatures (oral or otherwise) that might have supplemented or contradicted our current understanding of the surviving material existed, but have been lost.

With the exception of some of the Chinese and Mesoamerican poetry and songs, the texts were written and read by the elite. The extent to which they represent the beliefs of the general populace is unknown. No belief is universal, even within a given community, and one of the hallmarks of metaphysical thinking is a diversity of both idea and expression.

Although comparing the beliefs of multiple civilizations alongside near-death experience might seem like an overly ambitious undertaking for a single book, the limitation to only a single narrow area of belief makes it workable. The aim is not to compare "religion" or "myth" or "religious experience" in general, nor even "afterlife beliefs" per se, for notions of spirits continuing existence on Earth (that is, ghosts), reincarnation, and funerary beliefs and rituals are excluded (except where particularly relevant). The focus here is rather on just one aspect of afterlife beliefs: the experiences of the disembodied consciousness of an individual following their physical death. These typically involve journeys to other realms (heavens, hells, and intermediate states), encounters with other beings in other realms (ferrymen, judges, divinities, demons, ancestors), undergoing perils and judgment, and ultimate fates (paradise, punishment, annihilation, rebirth, divinization). That is, the kinds of experiences most relevant to NDEs.

There is also the question of accepting as a confirmed "similarity" an occasional (or even single) occurrence of a theme or concept in one civilization, in comparison with its common occurrence in another. One example is the rare Vedic heavenly boat in India, in contrast to the ubiquitous Egyptian sun-barque that sails with the deceased through sky and the underworld. While such instances will be noted, we're not concerned here with how widespread a conception was, but with whether it existed at all. The cross-cultural recurrence of a theme or concept requires explanation regardless of who or how many subscribed to it.

The intention here, then, is not to present a single coherent view of the afterlife experience in each civilization, but rather to follow the evidence wherever it might lead. This includes whatever diversities, apparent contradictions, inconsistencies, variations, and changes over time might be revealed. A synthesized summary of "the Egyptian experience" or "the Chinese experience" might be more easily digestible, though it would result in an overgeneralized misrepresentation of the material as being more cohesive than it really is. Indeed, the difference and diversity are as interesting as the similarity and consistency.

Another point to consider is that ancient languages and texts are not perfectly understood, and their meanings are sometimes unclear. Problems of interpretation can also arise from our incomplete knowledge of a culture's unique systems of symbolism and metaphor. With many of the texts discussed in this book, it can be difficult to ascertain what is symbolic and what is intended to be taken literally. For example, in the ancient Egyptian Pyramid Texts[1], it's stated that "Nut's belly has been impregnated with the seed of the *akh* who is in her." In Egyptian thought, the *akh* is formed by the reunion of two elements of the soul in the afterlife—the *ka* (the animating life force) and the *ba* (the unique self, or personality). Nut is the sky-goddess and mother of the deceased, and of Re (sun-god and creator), and of Osiris (Lord of the Dead, fertility, and regeneration)—all of whom are associated with each other. Nut's womb is the Duat (the netherworld) that gives birth daily to Re *and* the deceased, who is identified with Re. At the same time, the deceased's sarcophagus on Earth was also seen as Nut's womb. Does the passage thus reflect a conceptual metaphor for the ritual of placing the mummy into the sarcophagus? Or is the ritual of placing the mummy into the sarcophagus an enactment of what was believed to happen to the *akh* when entering the netherworld? Or are both text *and* ritual metaphors for a more generalized concept of entering an afterlife realm prior to spiritual rebirth? Despite over 200 years of formal research on Egyptian language, religion, and culture, much remains speculative. The same goes for all the civilizations considered here—though most especially those with no living legacy (Mesopotamia and, to some extent, Mesoamerica, in addition to Egypt).

It's also important to recognize that we are dealing with texts concerned with themes that by their very nature are intangible, abstract, even ineffable. The Dutch historian of religions W. B. Kristensen[2] suggested that the apparent lack of coherence of such texts might reflect the inexpressibility of the mysteries of death and rebirth. While he concluded that it was a "waste of energy" to even try to make orderly sense of them, I take a more optimistic stance here. Presumably the texts made at least some sense to the individuals who created them and to the members of their communities. The content, meaning, and sometimes presentation of many of these works would not have remained consistent for thousands of years if they were random and confused within their cultures.

Still, we must reluctantly admit that a *thorough* understanding of the beliefs of people in past societies is not possible. As the French historian Jean Bottéro wrote concerning the Mesopotamian afterlife, we can only attempt to piece together bits of evidence from various sources "in order to reconstruct a picture that is very likely to reflect only very badly, even mistakenly here and there, the original view on the matter."[3]

Directly examining the original sources rather than using existing summaries has, however, allowed me to look at the material afresh and in greater detail. Relying on what others select as being important, or neglect as unimportant, limits the potential for new interpretations and insights. This has been vital in avoiding oft-repeated past overgeneralizations. Most significantly, it has resulted in a reassessment of the Mesopotamian afterlife, which scholarly preconceptions tell us was strictly pessimistic and lacking judgment. As we will see in chapter 4, this was not actually the case.

On the subject of thoroughness—what to include and what to leave out—it's neither possible nor necessary to consider each and every otherworldly entity, locale, event, and object referred to in the texts. Some deities and places have multiple designations or epithets, and it's sometimes unclear when a new one is being introduced or a familiar one being described further. To avoid undue repetition, only the earlier version of a passage, theme, or motif will generally be considered.

The first chapter looks in some detail at near-death experiences, with particular reference to the comparison of NDEs across cultures and history. The second chapter gives a historical overview of the civilizations to be considered, explains why they were chosen, and shows how, for the eras under discussion, they had little or no cultural contact with each other.

The following five chapters summarize conceptions of afterlife experiences in each respective civilization, highlighting similarities with NDEs. These chapters are mostly descriptive, with discussion and analysis limited to illuminating the meanings of the texts and understanding continuity and change over time.

Through detailed comparisons, chapter 8 shows how the afterlife beliefs in all these civilizations correspond in many ways to NDEs, but that each civilization interpreted and elaborated upon the phenomenon in culturally distinct ways. The relationship between NDEs and afterlife beliefs is examined in depth in chapter 9, where I show the symbiotic nature of the interactions between culture, belief, and extraordinary experience. Finally, to form a fuller understanding of how afterlife beliefs are generated and how they develop over time, various ideas from anthropology, psychology, and philosophy are assessed. Elements of each are integrated into a comprehensive whole, accounting for the similarities and differences—both across cultures and between accounts of NDEs and afterlife beliefs. The metaphysical implications are also explored, including what an actual afterlife could possibly be like in light of all the cross-cultural similarities and differences.

PART I

Mapping the Terrain of Our Journey

Near-Death Experiences

Their Universal, Cultural, and Individual Features

What Is a Near-Death Experience?

According to research by the British neurophysiologist Peter Fenwick, NDEs occur in approximately "10% of people who come close to death, or who survive actual clinical death."[1] Tens of thousands of accounts have been collected by researchers in the nearly fifty years since the study of NDEs became formalized.[2] Reports are found in both technologically advanced civilizations and in small-scale societies, from ancient to modern times, in all parts of the world, appearing variously in religious, literary, anthropological, scientific, and medical literature.

While even the most skeptical of researchers acknowledge that there are a number of typical subexperiences that make up the NDE, they do not always agree on what they are. Various attempts to define the experience by identifying the most consistently recurring elements have not proven wholly successful. The American psychologist Kenneth Ring, for example, defined the core experience as feelings of peace and well-being, out-of-body experience (OBE), entering darkness, seeing bright light, and entering the light—excluding highly recurrent elements such as meeting other deceased individuals and reaching a border or limit.[3] Others have reduced the supposedly universal core to but two elements, though these differ depending on the researcher: the British philosopher of religion Mark Fox suggested simply darkness and light; the American sociologist James McClenon isolated "seeing other beings and other realms"; while the Australian sociologist Allan Kellehear highlighted journeying to other worlds (usually an idealized mirror image of Earth) and meeting fellow spirits.[4] Kellehear also pointed out, however, that the OBE may be taken for granted in almost all descriptions, for NDE'ers do not claim that their experiences occurred in the physical body.

Other commonly reported features are "the subjective sense of being dead," "beautiful colors," hearing others discuss one's own death, a loud noise, feelings of joy, a sense of profound wisdom or universal understanding, heightened senses and clarity, the impression of having an ethereal body, acceleration of time and thought, precognition and clairvoyance, telepathic communication with other spiritual beings, a sense of belonging or that one has returned "home," a life review accompanied by a sense of moral evaluation or self-judgment, being instructed or deciding to return, returning (often reluctantly), and positive effects on the life of the NDE'er.[5]

Perhaps the most useful way of thinking about the experience is that of the American theologian Carol Zaleski, who characterized the NDE as "a catalogue of assorted motifs."[6] To redefine the "core" of the experience as a changeable collection of possible elements, drawn upon differently by different individuals to comprise the overall experience, prevents the imposition of structure and order where none may exist. It also allows for a purely descriptive consideration of the NDE, because we shouldn't judge an account based on its content, or whether it measures up to some hypothetical (and mythical) prototype. Instead, we should judge by its *context*—that is, whether or not the individual was considered to be temporarily dead or near death and reported having undergone various spiritual episodes prior to revival. The nature of those experiences will always vary. In other words, our popular stereotypes about what NDEs are *like* are not always accurate.

The issue of whether the NDE constitutes evidence for survival after physical death is separate from the question of their impact on beliefs, though it is relevant to the metaphysical theories discussed in chapter 11. The most comprehensive attempt to explain the NDE in material-ist terms has been by the British psychologist Susan Blackmore,[7] who claims that it is the hallucinatory result of a combination of psycho-logical and neurophysiological events and processes of the dying brain. Such perspectives have been criticized for a priori reductionism and for being dismissive of the aspects of NDEs that they cannot explain.[8] There are numerous claims of evidential out-of-body experiences, in which NDE'ers report having seen and heard things while clinically dead—and from places or perspectives impossible from the vantage point of their bodies—that were later independently verified. There are reports of chil-dren encountering deceased relatives they had never met and of NDE'ers who discover the death of a friend or relative by meeting them during the NDE. There are even some claims of visions of the future that are later verified.[9] While impressive, such claims are technically anecdotal and without empirical replication in laboratory settings—a criterion for widespread acceptance in the scientific community.

Metaphysical interpretations of the NDE—by which we mean ideas and concepts beyond observable physical reality—have been criticized for a perceived lack of scientific logic and for not being based on evidence gathered in rigorous, controlled testing. However, Fenwick stresses the significance of the fact that NDEs in cardiac arrest cases can occur when the pateint has a flat EEG reading, when there is "no possibility of the brain creating images" and "no brain-based memory functioning," mean-ing that "it should be impossible to have clearly structured and lucid experiences."[10] These arguments have apparently been bolstered by the research of the British resuscitation expert Sam Parnia. He seems to have shown that consciousness can persist when no brain activity is detect-able, actually *during* the period of clinical death prior to revival. One of his cardiac patients accurately described his own resuscitation, which he claimed to have witnessed while out of body, including the sound of a defibrillator machine. This allowed researchers to pinpoint the time of the event as having occurred during his temporary "death."[11] In a study conducted in a Welsh hospital, intensive care nurse Penny Sartori found that only patients who had OBEs could accurately describe the process of their resuscitation.[12]

Whatever the case, in this book we seek neutral ground, adopting the position that whatever their nature, NDEs are part of human experience. This is attested by the fact that accounts of them are found around the world and throughout history. NDEs are not determined by culture, religion, sex, age, or other demographic factors. Though individuals may be influenced by "imagery and metaphor" in popular and religious culture, it has been found that prior knowledge of the NDE actually decreases the likelihood of having one. Nor is there any significant difference between Western NDEs reported before and after 1975, when the phenomenon was popularized and the term coined by the American psychiatrist Raymond Moody.[13] Near-death experiences in children are largely consistent with those of adults, further demonstrating that it is not mainly a matter of cultural conditioning (though, of course, children are not free of cultural influences—even cartoons can feature afterlife and OBE imagery). NDEs also occur in congenitally blind individuals who nevertheless report *visual perception* during the experience.[14]

Near-Death Experiences across Cultures

The issue of universality is controversial in near-death studies, with some researchers emphasizing cross-cultural difference at the expense of similarity. For example, in his assessment of perhaps the earliest Western NDE account that explicitly claims to be factual (that of Cleonymous of Athens in around 310 BCE), the Dutch historian Jan Bremmer writes that the only similarity between the account and modern NDEs is a "feeling of drifting away."[15] This is despite clear references to typical NDE elements such as OBE, meeting deceased relatives, moral evaluation assisted by mystical or divine beings, and clairvoyance.

Likewise, in their study of Chinese NDEs, the physicians Feng Zhi-ying and Liu Jian-xun interpreted some common NDE elements as being inconsistent with the (hypothetical) Western model because the descriptions were influenced by cultural and individual idiosyncrasies. For example, sensations of weightlessness and "feeling estranged from the body" must surely be equated with the OBE. "Unusually vivid thoughts," a feeling that thought has accelerated, a sense of peace and euphoria, and a life review are all standard NDE elements that were reported by their subjects.[16]

Similarly, the American Buddhist and neuroscientist Todd Murphy writes that there is no being of light in Thai NDEs—despite reports of the Buddha appearing as a star and of encounters with "spiritual lights." He also states that Thai NDE'ers do not report feelings of bliss, ecstasy, peace, and the like, but rather "pleasantness, comfort, a sense of beauty and happiness." Rather than seeing these as analogous emotional states, he sees discontinuity. Even encounters with deceased friends and relatives are classed as dissimilarities because they don't specifically *greet* the NDE'ers, but rather *instruct* them. Murphy's conclusion that "accounts of Western NDEs would seem to be useless in helping Thais know what to expect at their deaths" is not supported by the Thai references to OBE, traveling in spiritual form to another realm, life review with moral evaluation, encounters with divine and mystical presences, positive emotions, transcendent feelings and an impression of knowing "all the truths of the universe," visions of the future, deceased relatives, and being instructed to return.[17]

Perhaps most influentially, Zaleski highlighted differences between medieval European accounts of "otherworld journeys" and modern Western NDEs. In descriptions of moral evaluation, the medieval accounts focus more on punishment and the process of judgment, whereas the modern are more concerned with education and rehabilitation. Borders and limits are threatening and perilous in medieval accounts but not in their modern counterparts. Medieval guides are figures of "hierarchical and feudal authority," while the modern equivalents are characterized by "benevolent parental acceptance."[18] However, differences in the way such general thematic elements are experienced, interpreted, or expressed do not invalidate the importance of the similarities. The mechanism of judgment, the nature of the barriers, and the role or character of the guides are clearly shaped by social and cultural contexts; but their common underlying structures remain moral evaluation, borders and limits, and guides. The fact that these elements occur cross-culturally at all, even within these wide variations, is in itself significant—particularly when we consider that the medieval texts also feature OBEs, seeing the body, having an ethereal body, distortions of time, a tunnel or path, other realms, deceased relatives, beings of light, life review, expanded consciousness, "glimpses of heavenly bliss," being sent back to the body, reluctance to return, and subsequent spiritual or moral transformation.

Thus, despite a general thematic consistency, there are clearly cultural differences between NDE accounts. These differences do not negate similarities, nor do similarities negate differences. Both require acknowledgment and explanation.

One interesting recurring difference between cultures is the reason for the return to the body. In the NDEs of some societies, experiencers are usually informed by a deity, being of light, or deceased relative that it is not their time to die, or that they have further responsibilities on Earth. Examples of this type of return are found in contemporary Western accounts, ancient and medieval China, and Native North America. In other societies, the individual chooses whether or not to return. This was common in nineteenth- and twentieth-century Mormon NDEs, as well as in recent Western examples.[19] In still other accounts, NDE'ers return because of a clerical error in the otherworld: the person's "death" was a case of mistaken identity. The spirits accidentally took them in place of someone else with the same name, and they are sent back to the body when this is discovered. Such examples are known from ancient Greece and Rome, early Christianity, and modern Thailand.[20] Nor are such differences necessarily cultural, for *all* types of reasons feature in some societies, including medieval Europe and modern India.[21] Murphy argued that the reason Thai

NDE'ers are not given the choice of whether or not to return is that Thai culture is not as individualistic as Western culture.[22] However, this falsely overgeneralizes the Western NDE, which commonly features a forced, reluctant return. There are also unique or idiosyncratic reasons that don't conform to any generalizations.

The worldwide distribution of these various reasons for return makes diffusion unlikely—for example, that modern Thailand borrowed from medieval Europe, or that the contemporary West borrowed from medieval China. The explanation more likely lies in culturally specific manifestations of a general "return" element. In other words, the *rationale* for the NDE'er's return to the body depends on individual circumstances, though being *instructed* to return—for whatever reason and by whatever being—is widely recurrent (and the return itself is obviously universal).

This is not to rule out the possibility that one account might influence another. Medieval European otherworld-journey narratives are greatly influenced by earlier Christian visionary literature, such as the vision of St. Paul. Their length, intricate detail, and obvious embellishments remind us that they were part of a literary genre as opposed to a historical one.[23] Likewise, nineteenth- and twentieth-century Mormon NDEs are characterized by motifs that reflect and reinforce Mormon beliefs, including guardian angels, an afterlife government, and a socially stratified, highly organized spirit world with buildings, gardens, and Sunday school.[24] Ancient and medieval Chinese NDE accounts have clear Daoist and Buddhist elements, as well as familiar elements of the NDE: OBE, ascending to other realms, deceased relatives, spiritual beings, judgment, being sent back, and positive aftereffects.[25]

All this shows that NDE accounts are written from within a deep cultural immersion and that accounts from connected communities can influence each other. At the same time, the existence of common NDE features (OBE and seeing the body, darkness, being of light, life review, universal understanding, deceased relatives, positive aftereffects) shows that the NDE is a panhuman experience. Furthermore, McClenon points out that some of the earlier medieval European accounts often "do *not* conform to the image of the afterworld that was commonly accepted" at the time—particularly in their descriptions of intermediate states which were written before the idea of purgatory had been introduced.[26] Another example is an early-twentieth-century Zuni NDE featuring encounters with deceased relatives and bright light—motifs that are inconsistent with Zuni afterlife conceptions.[27] This shows that as well as conforming to certain cultural and religious beliefs, NDEs also innovate away from them by introducing new concepts. Likewise, certain themes or ideas that we might expect to find in the NDEs of religious people are not reported at all. For example, neither Hindus nor Western Christians commonly describe salvation, redemption, or reincarnation.[28] NDEs are thus, in part, *independent* of their cultural context.

Differences can also be due to the contexts of the narratives—whether they were written for some religious, political, or other purpose. In the medieval European accounts, for example, "harsh judgment scenes, purgatorial torments, and infernal terrors" were common.[29] This is because the texts they're found in were written for religious and moral proselytizing. The same association can also be found in Chinese examples, in which hellish scenes tend to be prominent in NDEs that are found in religious teachings.[30] In fact, most of the historical NDE accounts were written in times and places that lacked secular contexts for the objective reporting or study of extraordinary phenomena. There was no anthropology or sociology of religion, let alone scientific approaches to religious experience. Nevertheless, the accounts do present the experiences as factual and relating to specific individuals. In other words, they were intended to be accepted as documentary proof of the afterlife.

While negative NDEs are known to occur, they are quite rare and not cross-culturally consistent.[31] The European medieval texts focus more on punishment than their Classical Greek and Roman forebears do, for example, not because more people were having distressing NDEs but simply because they reflect the focus of Christianity at the time. This can also be applied to the relative rarity of contemporary distressing Western

NDEs: the focus of Christianity is no longer as deeply concerned with the threat of hell and eternal punishment.

The life review is another example of a widespread thematic element of NDEs that is expressed in culturally particular ways—what we might call *difference embedded in similarity*. The typical Hindu version of the life review does not feature a panoramic and empathetic experience of all one's memories and actions as in the stereotypical modern Western version. Instead, NDE'rs are read a document outlining their good and bad deeds—just as is done by the god Chitragupta in Hindu mythology.[32] This, incidentally, has serious ramifications for scientific materialist arguments that the elements of NDEs can be explained by the various "special effects" produced by a compromised or dying brain. For example, the British philosopher H. H. Price suggested that a brain function that normally restricts the flow of memory ceases at death, causing memories to flood the consciousness, resulting in a life review.[33] More recently, it has been discovered that there is a burst of brain activity at the moment of death, and scientists have interpreted this as the cause of life reviews.[34] However, a dearth of accounts of such experiences in India—and in small-scale societies[35]—demonstrates that the panoramic life review as such is not universal and therefore is not produced by biological processes in a dying brain. Indeed, the most common types of NDEs in which the "typical" life review occurs are those of nearly drowning or falling from a height, in which the individuals only *believed* they were near death.

Some differences between NDEs are also specific to individuals. In many Thai NDEs, messengers of the afterlife deity Yama, called Yamadutas, take the deceased to be judged in hell. These beings are described in highly individualistic ways, however: as two young men wearing white robes, as three men in turbans, or as one man three times larger than an ordinary human.[36] The famous Swiss psychiatrist and founder of analytical psychology Carl Jung had a highly individualistic NDE in 1944. He recalled floating in space a thousand miles above Ceylon (now Sri Lanka) and encountering a Hindu man dressed in white, sitting in the yoga lotus position at the entrance of a temple hollowed out of a meteor. Though obviously reflective of a mind immersed in the study of myths, symbols, and dreams, Jung's experience also featured the more common thematic NDE elements of OBE, other realms, being of light, border, feelings of being home in the otherworld, cosmic understanding and unity, life review, and a forced, reluctant return.[37]

Still other differences seem to be due to the idiosyncrasies of particular researchers. For example, only the French author Jean-Baptiste Delacour described accounts in which NDE'ers experienced receding landscapes and people in the otherworld. The German philosopher Johann Christoph Hampe is the only researcher to have reported NDE'ers returning to the body by going back the way they had come, effectively having a reverse NDE. It seems a good possibility that Delacour's and Hampe's descriptions can be seen as specifically French and German cultural elements, respectively.

E. B. Tylor, the nineteenth-century British anthropologist, reported NDEs in which experiencers cannot eat food in the spirit realm or they will be unable to return to Earth.[38] There are many examples from the Maori, Dakota Sioux, and other small-scale societies worldwide—and the same idea also appears in ancient Greek myth (such as the *Homeric Hymn to Demeter*). The puzzle of these kinds of extremely specific similarities between only certain societies will be returned to in chapter 8.

Navigating the Similarities and Differences

How have other scholars dealt with the issues of similarity, difference, and universalism in NDEs? Though some have taken more nuanced approaches than others, most have succumbed to the pitfalls of overgeneralizations and simplifications. Bremmer, for example, argued that a lack of accounts of meeting deceased relatives in medieval Western NDEs is a reflection of the "rather cold" personal relationships people had with each other in that era. Evidence for the "coldness" of medieval personal relationships is not provided, though, and deceased relatives actually *are* a highly recurrent feature of the medieval texts. Bremmer also wrote that modern NDE'ers do not experience guides because the afterlife realm is no longer conceived of as being far away.[39] But the afterlife realm is virtually never characterized as being physically near (indeed, the notion of physical location is irrelevant) or easily accessible, and guides *do* feature regularly in modern Western reports, often in the form of relatives or a being of light.

Nevertheless, some NDE elements do seem to correspond to social organization. Only in small-scale societies, for example, is the afterlife realm sometimes located in an earthly locale. The means of getting there also differs, for rather than traveling through a tunnel or speeding though darkness, in small-scale societies the NDE'er typically walks along a road to the spirit realm. This is the case with Kaliai Melanesian NDEs, for example, which also feature culture-specific elements such as ascending a ladder toward a house above and various earthly type places (houses, villages, forests). These descriptions occur alongside typical NDE elements of OBE, darkness, light, deceased relatives, instruction to return and a reluctance to do so, barrier or limit, moral assessment, and other realms.[40] Travel by road is also typical of NDEs of the Chamorro people of Guam and of Native Americans. These also feature other realms, judgment or other assessment of earthly life, guides, barriers, darkness, idealized mirror images of Earth, joy, an encounter with a deity, being instructed to return, and positive aftereffects.[41]

The reason for the absence of tunnels in many non-Western NDEs has been addressed by Kellehear. He suggests that tunnels are associated with industrialization and would thus not feature in the NDEs of people in preindustrial societies. The key issue, he argues, is not why tunnels are more commonly reported in the West, but rather why Westerners often interpret *darkness* as a *tunnel*. The tunnel is simply a symbol of transition—something that leads from one place to another just as a road does.[42] While a compelling argument, architectural tunnels exist in Eastern societies and have the same function—including India, for example, where NDE tunnels are not reported. India also has vehicles which people can drive through tunnels at high speeds. The sensation of speeding through a dark tunnel with a light at the end in order to get from one place to another is thus not limited to the West. Kelleahear also adds that "Western people have grown accustomed to seeing strange new worlds through the dimness of tunnels," including telescopes and microscopes, though these are by no means limited to the West, either. Furthermore, all manner of subterranean structures and passages were built in the ancient world (tombs, temples, divinatory installations, water works, granaries, etc.), though the tunnel motif is variable in ancient NDEs. Kellehear is surely correct, however, that the key factor is not the tunnel at all, but the experience of entering darkness and transition from one realm to another. Even in some contemporary Western NDE accounts, the use of the word "tunnel" is due to limitations of language when trying to describe an ineffable experience, for "shape reflects architecture rather than experience, but it is experience that is being described." In fact, *ineffability* is often cited as a key element of the NDE. Finally, the modern NDE stereotype of traveling through a tunnel has been overemphasized even in the West, and in many reports, the individuals actually speak only of moving through darkness.[43]

A similar but less convincing argument was made by Bremmer, who suggests that the absence of life reviews in ancient and medieval texts was because trains and moving pictures were only invented in the nineteenth century, enabling "people to see a fast succession of scenes."[44] However, this ignores the fact that individuals have been traveling at respectable speeds by horse and boat since prehistory and by chariot and wagon since early antiquity. Furthermore, life reviews are not typically successional, but are often described as all the events of one's life (and associated emotions) occurring simultaneously. Finally, there are indeed reports of unambiguous pre-nineteenth-century life reviews, such as that of British Admiral Francis Beaufort in 1795.[45]

Of greater merit is Kellehear's rather ingenious explanation for the cross-cultural similarities and differences of life reviews. The "sense of self," he argues, "is a social construction of identity" that only came into being with "historic religions" (as opposed to the "archaic" religions of

the present book). This newfound sense of personal individuality created a division between the human and the divine—thereby giving rise
to the notion of separate divine and human realms. Almost by definition, these divisions resulted in a view of the self as flawed and a desire
to become more divine-like. Small-scale societies, on the other hand,
have less distinction between the self and that which is external to the
self, and therefore less distinction between the mundane and the divine,
and between myth and reality. "Anxiety, guilt, and responsibility" are of
the world, not merely of the individual, and "individuals are no more
responsible than the world." Moral behavior is encouraged by laws and
fear of consequences within the social group, not by ideas of heaven and
hell. For example, when told by missionaries that they were sinful and
in need of redemption, the Arunda aboriginal people became indignant
and declared that they were collectively *all* good. Without a sense of individual moral responsibility or guilt, the "life review" concept is culturally irrelevant. In contrast, historic religions stress "the cultivation and
development of the moral self vis-à-vis the divine world and its demands."
The afterlife experiences of people belonging to such traditions are therefore directly linked with conscience—which, again, is itself a result of the
self/divine schism that is linked with identity.[46]

Nevertheless, there *are* examples of judgment or other moral evaluation
in NDEs in small-scale societies, including Native American and Pacific
accounts. These contradict Kellehear's generalization about small-scale
societies because they demonstrate personal moral conscience.[47] When we
look at religious and spiritual ideas about the afterlife, beliefs that postmortem fates are determined by character or moral worth are pervasive around
the world, in both small-scale and archaic societies.[48] As Kellehear himself
pointed out, the life review may also occur in non-NDE contexts in small-
scale societies, such as in dreams and shamanic experiences.

There is also debate about the terms scholars use in their generalizations about NDE elements. For example, Zaleski takes exception to the
term "being of light," arguing that it denies the testimonies of NDE'ers
themselves, who may say they met the Buddha or Jesus. Although

intended to be merely descriptive in a generic way, she asserts that "being of light" is itself a culturally constructed idea, and that imposing it on NDE accounts cross-culturally is therefore inaccurate.[49] However, this argument sidesteps the fact that NDE'ers actually describe a "being of light" in similar ways cross-culturally—even if they do interpret it in culture-specific modes. It also ignores another significant fact: people do not identify the being of light with a religious figure alien to their own belief system—Christians don't claim they encountered the Buddha, and Buddhists don't claim they encountered Christ. This means that there is, in fact, a cross-cultural experience of a "being of light" identified in various ways depending on the NDE'er. As the theologian Oliver Nichelson wrote, Zaleski's argument "is much like saying that the red fruit growing on trees is a function of the imagination because it is called 'apple' by Americans and 'pomme' by the French."[50]

The *Bardo Thödol*, otherwise known as the *Tibetan Book of the Dead* (eighth to eleventh century CE), offers a striking parallel when it states that at death the "Dharma-Kaya of Clear Light" (that is, the Absolute or Ultimate Reality) will be experienced in whatever form will most comfort and calm the individual. As the book's Tibetan translator, Kazi Dawa-Samdup, clarified:

> Thus, to appeal to a Shaivite devotee, the form of Shiva is assumed;
> to a Buddhist, the form of the Buddha Shakya Muni; to a Christian,
> the form of Jesus; to a Moslem, the form of the Prophet; and so on
> for other religious devotees; and for all manners and conditions of
> mankind a form appropriate to the occasion.[51]

In fact, the description of dying in the *Bardo Thödol* so closely corresponds to the NDE that it can effectively be seen as verification that the book genuinely is what it purports to be—a preparation for what happens at death (regardless of whether the dying experience is neurophysiological or spiritual).[52]

It's ironic that Zaleski is concerned about denying experiencer testimony with the term "being of light" when her characterization of NDEs in general is that they're "through and through a work of the socially conditioned religious imagination." This seems to deny the testimonies of NDE'ers altogether—ignoring the fact that they stress the *reality* of the experience. She describes NDEs as "religious storytelling," ignoring similarities between the NDEs of atheists, children, and the blind, and across cultures—including those in her own study. If NDEs are nothing but made-up stories, accounts of them in so many different circumstances must be explained. Zaleski takes great care in outlining the similarities between the modern and medieval narratives, only to largely ignore them and focus primarily on claims of their cultural invention.[53] Similarly, the Buddhism scholar and NDE researcher Carl Becker stresses the similarities between the NDE and the *Bardo Thödol*, though he fails to accommodate those similarities in an argument that NDEs are delusional "mental projections."[54] Because they characterize the NDE as individually *created*, such perspectives actually imply the *impossibility* of the very cross-cultural similarities the researchers themselves identify.

Most would agree that experience can't be entirely separated from culture. We are, after all, products of our societies and we're shaped by the images, symbols, beliefs, and ideas that we encounter from birth to death. In this sense, Zaleski is correct in her claim that it's not possible to fully differentiate between "some original and essential religious experience" and its "subsequent layers of cultural shaping," for they are so intertwined.[55] We might be able to identify common themes between accounts, such as a being of light, but we don't have access to what that "being" might truly be. We can't somehow strip it of any cultural or symbolic expression, because that expression is all we have. This does not, however, mean that there's no distinction between an experience and a person's interpretation of the experience, as Zaleski argues, or that there *is* no experience—only "storytelling." Acknowledging the interdependence of experience and culture in no way suggests that experience is an entirely cultural creation—they're obviously two different things requiring two different words to understand them.

Many kinds of experience originate in phenomena that are *independent* of culture, which are then interpreted in ways that are relevant to the individuals and their societies.[56] Feeling grief at the loss of a loved one, for example, is not a cultural construct, but mourning is expressed differently in different cultures.[57] Bremmer argues along similar lines when he observes that the ancient Greek NDE account of Thespesius of Soli (related by Plutarch around 81 CE) contains elements of Platonism, Pythagorism, and Orphism.[58] However, this demonstrates only that experience can resemble and reflect belief—not that it is *dependent* upon the belief. In fact, in the case of NDEs and afterlife beliefs, the situation seems to be just the opposite: the former can originate in the latter. This is known as the "experiential source hypothesis," which will be discussed in more depth in chapter 9. Readers, however, will see ample evidence of it throughout the book.

To summarize, acknowledging individual and cultural differences in accounts of NDEs, and in the interpretation of them, does nothing to invalidate the actual occurrence of NDEs, or the notion that there's a somewhat consistent *thematic* core to them. As McClenon argues, "Zaleski's data do not demonstrate that NDE accounts are entirely a product of the imagination," but actually the reverse:

> Although European NDEs reveal the effects of cultural shaping, Zaleski's data support the experiential hypothesis because the same universal elements found in modern NDE accounts are present in both Medieval Christian and Asian NDE folklore.[59]

While variations between NDEs cross-culturally are partly due to "the way certain societies emphasize or downplay certain cultural images and symbols," the duration of the experience can also account for differences. The life review may come at a later stage in the dying process, for example, which could account for it being more common in the West, where modern resuscitation technology can revive individuals at later stages of near-death than in preindustrial societies. The circumstances of the trauma might also be important. The life review, for example, seems to occur most frequently in sudden or unexpected "deaths," though it is rare in attempted suicides.[60]

Untangling the Individual, the Cultural, and the Universal

It's clear that NDEs are not merely a matter of cultural and individual *interpretation*, but also one of cultural and individual *perception*. In a sense, there's a creative element to the experience, for NDE'ers unconsciously "clothe" it in symbols and sensations that are personally relevant to them—giving each element form and meaning in real time. The elusive "common core" is simply more general and thematic than is often supposed—consisting of experiences such as moving from one place to another, going to another world, meeting a spiritual being, and so on—which are given lifelike (or *after*lifelike) expression by the individual's mind. Scenes of idealized otherworldly beauty, for example, might be symbolic manifestations of the feelings of joy, peace, and calm typically reported by NDE'ers.[61] This is consistent with the concept of a mind-dependent afterlife as modelled by H. H. Price, as well as with ideas about the afterlife in some of the ancient texts and in Mahayana Buddhism (as will be discussed in chapter 10).

At the same time, attempting to determine exactly which elements are "real" and which are symbolic projections of the NDE'er's thoughts can be speculative. Kellehear writes that while we may be able to determine if "certain structural elements," such as the life review, are specific to certain types of societies, "only if we have strong evidence that these NDE accounts are purely subjective, like dreams, can we link even small details of the NDE content to culture and biography." While this is an important point, it's perhaps an overstatement: an NDE doesn't have to be *purely* subjective (as opposed to partly subjective and partly objective) to embody identifiable cultural and individual elements. As Kellehear himself acknowledged, the implication of his perspective is that all the different worlds and beings encountered in all the different NDEs are actually real (again, more on this in chapter 10).[62]

The health scientist William J. Serdahely has suggested that NDEs are "individually tailored" to give individuals what they need for the most productive "learning experience." That the character of the experience is in part determined by the NDE'er's psychological and emotional states is demonstrated by a woman who had *two* NDEs on two separate occasions—one positive and one negative.[63] Zaleski similarly suggested that the purpose of otherworld "visions" is that they provide "the imaginative means through which one can instill a religious sense of the cosmos" in order to provide orientation in the present life.[64] The notion is not without problems, however (especially in light of Zaleski's earlier arguments about NDEs being "constructed" by culture and religion). What is the process by which the "learning experience" comes about? Is it also created by the individual and their culture, and therefore is it knowledge they already had? Or is it "individually tailored" by some external entity, for some unspecified ultimate purpose? Furthermore, why would such a "learning experience" occur when a person is threatened with the end of life, when presumably there would no longer be a reason to learn anything?

How researchers classify NDE elements also affects how they assess similarities and differences. Zaleski, for example, sees the "bridge" motif in the medieval European accounts as analogous to the "tunnel" in modern NDEs.[65] But they are not actually thematically comparable: the medieval bridge acts as a *barrier* to the ultimate state in the other world, while the modern tunnel is a means of transportation to an apparently intermediate state. The medieval bridge is more aptly classified as a "border or limit" element. The medieval accounts also describe ascent to the otherworld and generally traveling through darkness—and it is these elements that would be analogous to the "tunnel."

Accounts of any kind of experience rely on unverifiable, subjective, individual testimony, and the vagaries of memory. The human mind also has a tendency to create plots or narratives about events when relating them to others. This likely has a profound impact on descriptions of an ineffable experience such as an NDE. Nor do we always know if particular elements were not experienced or were simply not recorded—due, for example, to being forgotten or considered unimportant. As noted earlier, OBEs are not always reported, though NDE'ers do not claim to have traveled to another realm *in* their bodies. Darkness is another element that could easily be left out.

In summary, in the historical and modern Western, Chinese, Japanese, Tibetan, Indian, and small-scale society accounts, NDEs reflect established local beliefs, *and* they share consistent sets of structural similarities. This consistency of reports—and the near-death context itself—distinguishes NDEs from other types of "mystical" experiences, visions, and dreams. Cross-cultural differences can be explained by the fact that NDEs are shaped by culture and by an individual's personality, religious beliefs, and circumstances surrounding their near-death event. Yet, while NDEs are undeniably culturally and individually influenced, and accounts of them are often elaborated or mythologized, they are not entirely culturally constructed. As Kellehear summarized:

> . . . culture supplies broad values and attitudes to individuals and these
> provide individual orientation during an experience. In this way, cul-
> tural influences provide a basis for interpreting NDE content, and
> furthermore are crucial to shaping the retelling of the experience to
> others from one's own culture.[66]

When related to others from a *different* culture, it is likely that even further elaboration and modification occur.

This chapter constitutes a sort of microcosm of themes that will emerge naturally throughout this book. It encapsulates the main questions and issues in relation to the difficulties with comparing belief and related experience in a thorough and meaningful way. The interactions of belief and experience will be further examined in chapter 9. For now, let's turn to the histories and interactions of the ancient civilizations whose afterlife ideas and NDEs we will soon explore.

2

Early Civilizations

Their Nature, History,
and Interactions

The ancient civilizations explored in this book have a very particular and rather special distinction. They are all examples of *"early* civilizations." This is an anthropological term meaning "the earliest form of class-based society that developed in the course of human history."[1] In this usage, despite vast geographical distances and spanning over 4,000 years, the Mesoamerican civilizations are just as "early" as Old Kingdom Egypt, and relative chronology between the two is irrelevant. When recognizably Maya culture first emerged, pharaonic Egypt was in its latest period, firmly under Roman domination; and when Mexico was conquered by Spain, Egypt had been converted to Islam for nearly 900 years.

Though some of the civilizations considered here were made up of collections of city-states (Mesopotamian and Mesoamerican) and others were territorial states (Egypt and China), they are nevertheless characterized by broadly similar social and economic systems. These include wide class division, elite control of resources, and little or no ideological distinction "between the natural, the supernatural and the social."[2] India may or may not be an exception to one or more of these descriptors. The foundational Indian religious texts, the Vedas, do not appear to have emerged from a centralized state society, though the evidence is uncertain. India does, however, share with the others characteristics such as sedentism, agriculture, literacy, and monument building.

All this is important because we need to rule out the possibility that similar ideas about afterlife experiences were a result of diffusion from one civilization to another, and instead show that they developed independently. The American anthropologist Joseph Jorgensen wrote that if the cultures being compared are independent of each other, "one does not have to appeal to prejudice, or to authority, or to one or two possible examples, or to impression, or to polemic to demonstrate the merit of the hypothesis and its validation." Instead, one can reasonably argue that "these relationships are this way because this is the way the world is." Jorgensen concluded that "if the data are independent, the relationship very seldom occurs by chance."[3] In other words, similar ideas between unrelated cultures require a sound explanation, rather than being dismissed as coincidence or as a result of borrowing from one to another.

This is especially important when we consider that some scholars outright deny that similarities exist or are even possible. The French philologist Georges Dumézil, for example, believed that there are similarities between various Indo-European mythologies, but that they're without parallels in the ancient Near East.[4] Since two of our civilizations, Egypt and Mesopotamia, are Near Eastern (and non-Indo-European, as are China and Mesoamerica), the implication is that similarities with the mythologies of the other civilizations should not occur.

The civilizations considered here have therefore been selected according to two criteria: (1) that they emerged largely in a state of cultural independence; and (2) that they produced a religious literature containing descriptions of afterlife experiences prior to periods of significant external influence. For Egypt, this is before the first period of foreign rule, by the Hyksos from the Levant—an era known as the Second Intermediate Period. For Mesopotamia it is prior to the rule of the Indo-European Kassites that ushered in an era of increased internationalism when "it is no longer possible to treat Iraq as though it were isolated—or almost isolated—from the rest of the world."[5] For China it is before the introduction of Buddhism from India, "the last stage during which Chinese civilization may be studied as a relatively self-contained growth."[6] For India it is before influence from the reimportation of Buddhism back from China (and, incidentally, primarily before the Buddha). For Mesoamerica it is before the Spanish conquest and the forced conversions to Christianity.

None of this is to imply that later conceptions are less authentic or less representative of beliefs in general—it is simply that they are more likely to have been influenced by other traditions. The sources under consideration here have no known forebears or previous models upon which they could have been based, which means there can be no claim of diffusion. Nor can there be such claims regarding consistencies with the NDE. For example, if the Maya afterlife conception and an NDE in modern India bear similarities, this clearly demands an explanation; and it would be extremely difficult and highly speculative to construct a chain of connections by which one could have influenced the other.

Most of the world's remaining religious traditions—those that are not considered here—either grew out of earlier traditions, or had enough significant contact with others as to make their relevance to our subject marginal. To illustrate this further, it's worth contrasting our early civilizations with others around the globe:

- Classical Greek religion emerged from Mycenaean religion, which itself emerged from Minoan religion—neither of which left behind any afterlife texts. The Minoans had an exceptionally close relationship with Egypt (as did the later Greeks), and were trading with both Egypt and Mesopotamia from at least the Middle Minoan period (roughly corresponding to the latest Egyptian text we're considering here).
- Roman religion was largely appropriated from Greek religion.

- Judaism arose within the wider Near Eastern cultural milieu, particularly the local Canaanite religion, which itself was influenced by Mesopotamian and very possibly Egyptian religion.[7]
- Christianity and Islam, of course, have their roots in Judaism, as well as incorporating elements of other local belief systems.
- Zoroastrianism seems to have emerged from the same root tradition as the Vedas and was also a Near Eastern religion with extensive connections throughout the ancient Mediterranean.
- Buddhism and Jainism originated in India from within a Vedic context.
- Indigenous Japanese religion (Shinto) was influenced by Chinese Buddhism. Even the earliest relevant Japanese texts such as *Kojiki* and *Nihon Shoki* drew on myths from China, Polynesia, and other regions.
- There are no indigenous Tibetan religious (Bon) texts prior to the introduction of Buddhism.
- There are no texts on Celtic, Norse, or other Western European beliefs that were written prior to Christianity (barring an occasional brief Roman description).
- There is no surviving textual evidence from the Inca civilization of South America.
- Afterlife ideas and NDEs of small-scale indigenous societies in Africa, the Pacific, and the Americas were recorded by foreign explorers, missionaries, and early ethnologists (and are the subject of my book, *Near-Death Experience in Indigenous Religions*).

Another way in which our selection helps us overcome the problem of cross-cultural influence is that each civilization is from a different linguistic group. The ancient Egyptian language is Afro-Asiatic. Sumerian is a linguistic isolate belonging to no known language family. While Akkadian is, like Egyptian, Afro-Asiatic, it derived its script from Sumerian cuneiform and is, in any case, marginal to the study. Chinese is part of the Sino-Tibetan family. Sanskrit is Indo-European. The

Mesoamerican traditions actually have two separate language groups, Uto-Aztecan and Mayan. The degree to which language reflects cultural independence is variable, however. For example, there are some Native American groups with wholly unrelated languages, but nearly identical cultures; but others with closely related languages and wholly different cultures.[8] Indeed, the Sumerians and Akkadians were culturally indistinguishable despite their different language groups.[9]

None of this is to claim that any civilization ever emerged in total cultural isolation, or that there is such a thing as a "pristine" society. Nor do I claim that there was no contact at all between any of the civilizations during the periods under consideration—only that they emerged in as indigenous a context as exists, and have the least possibility, and minimal evidence, of significant influence from the others.

The eminent Canadian archaeologist Bruce Trigger took a similar approach in his cross-cultural comparison of the phenomenon of civilization itself. He considered all the civilizations discussed here, with the exception of India on the grounds of a lack of sufficient information on social structure, economy, and so on. Instead, he chose the Yoruba of Nigeria and the Inca of South America, both excluded here due to the lack of religious texts in their early stages. The same applies to the Olmec, who were apparently subsumed into other Mesoamerican cultures nearly 2,000 years before the Spanish Conquest ending in 1521.

Concerning all these civilizations, Trigger stated that "there is no evidence of historical relations" between them in their formative periods:

> [The] archaeological evidence makes it clear that each of these civilizations evolved separately and largely independently in its own region. . . . If diffusion accounted for major similarities . . . those civilizations that were geographically closest and therefore most easily accessible to one another ought to have displayed the greatest similarities.

In summary, the civilizations considered here were separated from the others by vast spans of time and space. The most extreme example is Mesoamerica and Egypt: there were nearly 8,000 miles between them, across the African continent and the Atlantic Ocean. Temporally, they are separated by nearly 4,000 years, from the earliest Egyptian text to the Spanish conquest. Those in closest geographical and temporal proximity were Egypt and Mesopotamia, with less than a thousand miles between them and roughly contemporary cultural emergence. However, Trigger found far more differences between Egypt and Mesopotamia than between Mesopotamia and Mesoamerica—two of the farthest apart. This means that despite their relative proximity, Egypt and Mesopotamia "can be treated as essentially independent examples of early civilizations"—which is more crucial than "whether or not [they are] totally pristine."[10]

Contact and Continuity

Before proceeding further, it will be helpful to orient ourselves in history by looking at the origins of each of our civilizations, and how they may have related to the others as they developed. Although only the simplest of outlines, this will give us a wide-angle understanding of human cultural and religious development around the world.

Egypt

The Nile Valley was originally populated by immigrants from Northeast Africa and the Sahara around 10,000 BCE. There were further influxes from the surrounding desert areas between 6000 and 5000 BCE. Each of these groups would have had their own traditions and beliefs, though some were likely shared between them. Upper Egyptian (that is, southern) culture gradually subsumed the Lower (northern), and the pharaonic civilization was the eventual result. References to different burial customs in the Pyramid Texts seem to point to a diversity of ethnicities during the Predynastic period,[11] though cultural continuity is seen in archaeological evidence from the earliest artifacts of the Predynastic Badarian period (c. 5500–4000 BCE) through to the Old Kingdom and all subsequent Egyptian history.

Although Egypt was trading with Anatolia, Iran, the Golan Heights, the Red Sea, and Nubia as early as 4500–3300 BCE—at least 900 years before the Pyramid Texts—the only identifiable cultural impact came from Mesopotamia. Scholars of the ancient Near East, however, often infer more influence than is clear from the evidence. One example is that Mesopotamian writing, which appeared around 3500 BCE, "inspired" the idea of writing in Egypt. However, hieroglyphic characters have a long genesis traceable at least back to 4000 BCE—before writing proper in Mesopotamia, and before the appearance of Mesopotamian style art and iconography in Upper Egypt, where the earliest hieroglyphic inscriptions are found.

Nevertheless, if cultural elements such as iconography can be transmitted between civilizations, so can religious beliefs. Samuel Mark, a historian of the ancient world, argues that Osiris was either a Mesopotamian import or a syncretistic Mesopotamian-Egyptian deity. This is based on a common use of the two ideograms meaning "seat" and "eye" to designate both Osiris and the Babylonian deity Marduk.[12] The suggestion is quite speculative, however, for there is good evidence that Osiris evolved indigenously from the Predynastic deity Andjety. While the origins of the gods are obscure, Osiris is attested at least as far back as 2500 BCE and, as we shall see, is prominent in the Pyramid Texts a century later. Marduk, on the other hand, did not rise to prominence until around 600 years later. Furthermore, though both were associated with fertility, Marduk was not an afterlife deity like Osiris. Overall, identifiable influences seem to have been transitory or minor.

Also relevant here is that two gods from Byblos make brief appearances in Egyptian afterlife texts: the apparently minor deity Khay-tau who is found as a "guardian of the celestial gates" in the Pyramid Texts; and the main goddess of the Byblite pantheon Baalat, who has been reduced to the status of a demon in the Coffin Texts.[13] This is unusual because the iconography that Egypt had borrowed from Mesopotamia had disappeared by the Early Dynastic period (2950–2575 BCE), and generally speaking, Egypt was culturally resistant to external influences.

Why these two foreign deities ended up making cameo appearances in Egyptian afterlife texts remains a mystery.

Mesopotamia

The origins of the Sumerians are uncertain, though they likely migrated to Mesopotamia from some unknown area around 5000 BCE. By that time, the region had already been settled by other groups for around a thousand years.

Trade with Iran, Syria, and the Arabian peninsula began in the fifth millennium BCE, then with Afghanistan around 3100 to 2900 BCE. Although the Sumerian language is unrelated to any other known language, Semitic words occur in even the earliest Sumerian texts, which suggests a degree of multiculturalism.

The Uruk period (4000–3100 BCE) saw trade with the Indus Valley, and luxury items of Indian origin have been found in Mesopotamia.[14] All this is well before the date of our earliest relevant Sumerian text, of around 2300-2000 BCE. Some have claimed that Mesopotamia heavily influenced Indus Valley culture, though this is based on the very existence of similarities.[15] As this book attests, however, cultural similarities in and of themselves don't necessarily mean that one was borrowing from another. Notwithstanding their economic contacts, evidence for significant Mesopotamia-India (or vice versa) cultural influence is virtually nonexistent.

India

Like Egypt and Sumer, Vedic civilization seems to have emerged from the interactions and migrations of different human population groups.

The Dravidian civilization originated in the Indus Valley around 2500 BCE. Their archaeological remains include religious installations such as sacrificial altars and purifying baths—alongside more apparently "Vedic" elements, such as representations of a seated figure that may be an early representation of the deity Shiva, as well as phallic-shaped stones (*linga*) like those associated with him in later periods.

Sometime after 2000 BCE, Aryan peoples from Central Asia began to migrate to South Asia, and it seems that they combined with the Dravidians to form Vedic culture. The degree to which the Aryans contributed is debatable, however. The Indian archaeologist B. B. Lal gathered a great deal of compelling astronomical, archaeological, and geomorphological evidence that the earliest Vedic religious text, the *Rig Veda*, is at least as old as 2000 BCE—that is, before the arrival of the Aryan peoples.[16] Most scholars, however, date the text to 1500 BCE and discount Lal's arguments.

Whatever the case, it seems that the Aryan migrants adapted more to the indigenous Dravidian culture, became more "Indianized," than vice versa. Thus, notwithstanding these historical uncertainties, Indian (Dravidian-Aryan) society is understood to have emerged and developed largely from within.[17]

There is evidence for trade between Neolithic India (at Mehrgarh) and Central Asia, Iran, Mesopotamia, and possibly Burma and China.[18] How much cultural impact these connections may have had is unknown. There was no significant contact between India and China until the first to third centuries CE—well after the latest Indian texts discussed here and just after the latest Chinese texts.[19]

The earliest connection between Egypt and Vedic peoples was via the Indo-Aryan kingdom of Mitanni in Upper Mesopotamia during the sixteenth century BCE—approximately a hundred years later than the latest Egyptian and Mesopotamian texts considered here. Mitanni fought with Egypt before forming a political alliance through royal marriages. It's therefore conceivable that there was an indirect exchange of Egyptian and Vedic ideas around the time the *Rig Veda* was written (if we reject the evidence for its earlier composition). However, the presence of Sanskrit words relating to Vedic deities and concepts in Mittani texts—including Mitra, Indra, Varuna, Surya, Nasatya, *Rita* (the precursor to dharma), and *svarga* ("heavenly realm")—shows that Vedic religion was already well developed by that time.[20]

Direct India-Egypt influence is practically impossible for the texts we're considering. Around 200 years separate the latest date for the Egyptian Coffin Texts from the earliest date for the *Rig Veda*. Egypt's highly detailed afterlife descriptions in texts contemporary with the *Rig Veda* (the *Amduat*, for example) bear little similarity to the *Rig Veda's* descriptions, and there is no similarity of type or function of texts, nor any common names. Given that there's no evidence for direct contact between Egypt and India until the Roman period,[21] Egyptian influence on Vedic religion can also be rejected.

China

Chinese civilization emerged from the interactions of diverse cultural groups from various regions, originating as far back as 8500 BCE. Artistic styles and symbolism developed gradually from a number of sources, from both within China and beyond. Clay figurines dating from 4000 to 1000 BCE depict foreign cultural and physical traits, including facial features, beards, earrings, and headgear that might indicate a Central Asian or Iranian origin.[22] At an eighth-century BCE site (Chou-yüan), two figures were found that resemble Hittite figurines from Anatolia.

While extrapolating race from figurines is potentially dubious given the vagaries of both artistic expression and human genetics, it's intriguing that the figures appear to be evidence of shamanism. One of the earlier figures is marked with the same sign used on Chinese oracle bone inscriptions (see chapter 6) that means "ritual meditator" or "shaman." The eighth-century figures are marked with the Old Sinitic sign for "shaman" or "mage," which may indicate itinerant Persian magi working in China.[23] However, while foreign shamanism may have reached China in these periods, it could have encountered a shamanic culture already in place. There would be nothing to support the notion of Mesopotamia or Egypt influencing Persian or Hittite shamanism, which then traveled to China. The same may be said for afterlife beliefs.

There are at least two loan-words to Chinese from the Indo-European Tocharian language, speakers of which are believed to have inhabited northwest China from at least 2000 BCE. The language is, however, closer to the Celtic-Germanic-Greek branch of Indo-European than to the Iranian-Indic branches.[24] All of this means that any significant India-China influence is also unlikely.

Mesoamerica

The Americas were first populated by Siberians who crossed a land bridge at the Bering Strait beginning as early as 30,000 BCE (Siberians themselves originated in Asia and Europe, traveling to Siberia some 38,000 years ago). From the time that the land bridge collapsed in around 10,000 BCE up until the Spanish conquest, trans-Pacific contact with the Americas is generally accepted not to have occurred. If it did, there is little evidence for it and it was unlikely to have resulted in significant cultural influence. There is genetic evidence for interactions between Polynesian and South American peoples from around 1200 CE, though that would not affect our civilizations.

In contrast, there's substantial archaeological evidence attesting to the indigenous development of Olmec civilization around 1200 BCE. It's believed that Olmec religion was the root of all subsequent Mesoamerican religions, including those of the Maya and the Aztec and other Nahua peoples. As the anthropologist and archaeologist Michael D. Coe argued, all these traditions should be seen as parts of a unified, continuous "great religious system"[25] despite any diversity. Although they span wide geographical and chronological expanses, development of these societies was entirely from within the Americas and without known interaction with any external cultures.

Nevertheless, some general parallels between Asian and Mesoamerican cultures *could* suggest survivals from ancient Chinese or Siberian origins. Though highly speculative, the possibility of Central Asian shamanism migrating to the New World cannot be dismissed out of hand—indeed, shamanistic and spirit-beliefs are remarkably similar cross-culturally in these societies even today. Even as cautious a scholar as Bruce Trigger entertained this possibility, stating that if the Shang Dynasty and

Mesoamerican religions "are all derived from historically related shamanistic cults dating back to the Paleolithic period, this might account
for certain similarities among all three."[26] One example is the feathered
serpent deity, which, of course, does not occur in nature (notwithstanding Herodotus's alleged eyewitness account of such animals in Arabia![27]).
This means that the idea of feathered serpents cannot be explained in
terms of observations of an actual animal, so must have some other origin. Whether it's the *same* origin in Old World and New World shamanic cultures is impossible to say with any certainty. Another rather
specific similarity is the practice of placing a jade pearl in the mouth of
the dead.[28]

As will be discussed in chapter 10, there are difficulties with suggesting a common core of shamanic practices across cultures—and especially
of visionary experiences. There are also no linguistic affinities between
Mesoamerica and China, including no shared names of deities. The
minimal amount of evidence for shamanism in Egypt and Mesopotamia
means that these kinds of speculative shamanic diffusion theories cannot
be extended farther than China, or perhaps India.

In short, our civilizations had very little or nothing to do with each other
throughout the periods considered here. While it's just about possible to
posit a chain of connections from Egypt to Mesopotamia to India to
China to Mesoamerica, aside from the lack of evidence, there are nearly
insurmountable problems of chronology due to the different time frames
of the periods we're concerned with.

Nor would it be possible to explain why only particular ideas—such
as afterlife journeys—traveled unaccompanied by further cultural features across such vast expanses of time. In other words, the lack of impact
upon any other aspect of culture makes the notion of influence solely
upon afterlife conceptions extremely unlikely. Diffusion can't specify
how or when concepts traveled from one culture to another, or why some
were adopted and others not. There's no evidence of chronological devel-

opment of beliefs across these cultures and no convincing sequence of transmission. The only evidence for direct trade connections are between Mesopotamia and Egypt, and to a lesser degree between Mesopotamia and India. There is even less evidence for interactions between India and China. With the exception of the two Byblite deities in Egyptian texts, these resulted in no shared deities, rituals, creation myths, funerary practices, and so on.

Global Diffusion

The last remaining hypothesis to address before moving on to the ancient texts themselves is that worldwide similarities can be accounted for by diffusion from a single common origin—an idea sometimes called "grand diffusion." This is usually said to be Africa, where human population groups first originated. Applied to our investigation, the implication would be that the afterlife conceptions of early humans survived for millennia in oral form following migration to other parts of the world, to be eventually written down in culture-specific modes.

The first problem with such a speculation is the assumption that prehistoric individuals even had afterlife beliefs at all. While it's true that burial practices *usually* relate to afterlife beliefs, without the aid of written records, archaeologists can only suggest varying degrees of plausibility that this was really the case. They make such arguments based on ethnographic analogy—the idea that a known behavior or belief in one culture might reasonably help to explain artifacts found in another. But this technique also points out the flaws in overgeneralizing.[29] For example, grave goods—which are usually regarded as offerings that the spirit of the deceased can use in the otherworld—may actually be tributes or memorials to the deceased. They may, alternatively, concern the living rather than the dead, as with the Nankanese of Ghana who place in graves articles belonging to *living* persons so that they will not die. The Ibn of Borneo place knives in graves to symbolize the dead individual being severed from the living.[30]

Conversely, an *absence* of grave goods does not equal an absence of belief. The LoDagaa of Ghana have well-developed afterlife conceptions, though they consume most of the funerary offerings. It's also the case that status, not religion, is often the determining factor for the position in which the corpse is buried, the location and orientation of the grave, and the nature of the grave goods.[31] Finally, even if the *fact* of prehistoric afterlife beliefs could be established, the *nature* of the conceptions is as unknowable as their origins.

The second problem with grand African diffusion theories is that the main migrations out of Africa are believed to have occurred around 75,000–85,000 years ago. This is some 40,000 years before the evolutionary mind-brain development of "cognitive fluidity," believed to be necessary for complex abstract thought, such as afterlife conceptions.[32] While earlier representative art might suggest that abstract thought occurred closer to the time of the African migrations, we are still in wholly speculative territory here.

Chronology is also a problem for the grand diffusion model of the German philologist and Indologist, Michael Witzel. He proposed that hypothetical "early Laurasian shamans" or "spiritual leaders" from around 75,000 years ago are the common source of certain beliefs across the world to this day. These beliefs include the shamanic concept of "birth-death-rebirth." Laurasia was a supercontinent comprising North America, Europe, and much of Asia (excluding India) that broke up in the late Mesozoic, around 200,000,000 years ago. This is an astonishing 199,700,000 years before *Homo sapiens* originated in Africa. Why "Laurasian" cultures would allegedly have more in common with each other than with those of anywhere else is unclear. Witzel's theory revolves around numerous mutually reinforcing, unproven assumptions: the existence of a prehsitoric Laurasian "proto-mythology" from the remote past; that it can be "reconstructed" by projecting the beliefs of historical civilizations onto prehistoric ones across regions and times; and that there was such a thing as a prototypical early Laurasian shamanism.[33]

Furthermore, grand diffusion theories do not account for why only some elements of beliefs, concepts, practices, and other cultural features were transmitted and remained consistent between civilizations, while others changed or were not adopted at all. More specifically, it cannot explain how or why afterlife conceptions spread unaccompanied by creation myths, common deities, names, language, artistic styles, iconographies, and the like. While other traits can be found cross-culturally, including certain mythological motifs (flood myths, for example), they don't have the same overall consistency with parallels in a documented extraordinary experience type (the NDE). Put another way, diffusion cannot explain how afterlife beliefs across such vast stretches of space and time could relate to historical and modern NDEs, which are unsought, unexpected, spontaneous occurrences. A compelling explanation must be able to address the commonality of such experiences worldwide, experienced by individuals of multiple faiths (and those of none), throughout recorded history, in multiple cultural contexts.

Despite being largely discredited as a relic from the nineteenth century, scholars continue to suggest diffusion to explain cross-cultural similarities. The American Indologist Wendy Doniger argues that since there's no such thing as a pristine society, "it is more likely that one culture borrowed the story from the other than that the story was independently created, in parallel, by both cultures."[34] This is certainly the case with the example she uses: Greece and Rome; though it doesn't apply to two wholly unconnected civilizations such as Egypt and Mesoamerica.

The famous French anthropologist Claude Lévi-Strauss also favored diffusion as an explanation, though he did not favor assuming it without evidence. Significantly, he wrote that if diffusion did occur:

it would not be a diffusion of details—that is, independent traits traveling each on its own and disconnected freely from any one culture in order to be linked to another—but a diffusion of organic wholes wherein style, esthetic conventions, social organization, and religion are structurally related.[35]

This is obviously not the case with our civilizations. Ultimately, there's no sound argument that cross-cultural connections could have resulted in a transmission of ideas that could explain the findings that will unfold in this book. The civilizations in question were relatively culturally independent within the boundaries of their general cultural spheres. Even if we were to accept diffusion between any two civilizations (say, China and Mesoamerica), it would not account for similarities with other civilizations. As the Chinese-Taiwanese archaeologist K. C. Chang observed, "universal patterns and separate paths are not mutually exclusive."[36]

As you read the following sections on the afterlife beliefs in each civilization, I invite to you to keep in mind these possible "universal patterns"—especially in relation to near-death experiences. You will then be able to compare notes, as it were, when we embark on the close cross-cultural comparisons in chapter 8. As you seek out these universal patterns, also keep in mind the "separate paths" and enjoy exploring the uniqueness, too. Just like NDEs, the afterlife beliefs in these civilizations have universal, cultural, and individual layers of meaning. It's up to us to try to disentangle them.

PART II

NDEs and the Ancient Afterlife

3

Egypt

Divine Transcendence
and the Cosmic Circuit

Although there is no *direct* evidence for NDEs from the early periods of Egypt, there are parallels in myths and other religious texts. The myth of Osiris tells of how the god died, was resurrected, and became lord of the otherworld. Egyptians viewed Osiris as the first king, and it is possible that the deity was indeed based on an actual historical ruler. If so, it's conceivable that the myth of Osiris might have been inspired by an NDE that this king had sometime in the remote past. While there is no complete narrative of the myth, his story can be pieced together from various texts, including the Pyramid Texts.

From the earliest evidence, the afterlife experience of Osiris served as a model for the recently deceased. Indeed, souls of the dead were actually identified with Osiris in his death and rebirth, and themes such as leaving the body, encountering one's own corpse (which can only happen during an out-of-body experience), traveling through darkness and emerging into light, meeting deceased relatives and a being of light, and positive transformation are all key elements to these writings.

The Pyramid Texts contain the earliest comprehensive descriptions of the Egyptian afterlife. They are ritual spells intended to ensure the survival of souls of the deceased on their journey to join the gods in the divine realm. The texts provide the knowledge and formulas to success-fully negotiate many afterlife perils and obstacles, including demons, caverns, and gates. Originating in the Old Kingdom, they first appeared around 2350 BCE, though some archaic language and references to ear-lier burial practices suggest that some parts date back even earlier.[1] The spells were apparently initially intended for the exclusive use of the king, though after 2200 BCE, they also appear in pyramids of queens.

There is a general continuity of conception between the Pyramid Texts and the Middle Kingdom's Coffin Texts, which began to appear from 2160–1760 BCE. Indeed, there is so much duplication that the texts should not be regarded as completely separate works, but rather as earlier and later versions of a continuous tradition with the same religious functions, revised and expanded over time.[2]

Until quite recently, the Coffin Texts were widely seen by Egyptologists as a "democratization of the afterlife," for these guide-books for the dead were no longer confined to pyramids—they were now painted on coffins that were available to any member of the elite who could afford them. Although there's a paucity of information on popular beliefs prior to the Coffin Texts, however, there's enough to show that people other than royalty conceived of an afterlife. Depictions of funerary rituals in Old Kingdom private tombs, as well as funerary cult evidence as far back as the Predynastic period—including copies of spells found in nonroyal contexts—all show that the afterlife was prob-ably never exclusive to royalty.[3] The Pyramid Texts themselves have ref-erences to spirits with lower status in the otherworld, suggesting that they were not kings but perhaps servants of kings who continued to fulfill their earthly role in the afterlife. The texts refer to souls of the dead who become "clean ones," servants of Osiris; and to others who feed and give life to the "honored ones," presumably souls of a higher status.[4] The very fact that the king becomes a postmortem judge in the otherworld implies the presence of other souls to be judged. Rather than a "democratization of the afterlife," it seems that beliefs merely became increasingly visible in the archaeological and textual record as time went on.

The later afterlife texts of the New Kingdom, such as the *Book of Going Forth by Day* (the *Book of the Dead*) and the *Amduat*, also continue the Pyramid and Coffin Texts tradition. In fact, roughly two-thirds of their content draws upon or even duplicates the earlier texts.[5] Their main innovation is to elaborate upon the existing afterlife conceptions, adding extensive details and lengthy enumerations of regions of netherworlds, types of punishment, names of beings, and so on. They do not significantly supplement or contradict the earlier works for the purposes of the present study.

As the texts were written as generic templates to be personalized for the particular deceased person, references to such individuals from specific copies will be omitted from our summaries.

The Afterlife Experience
in the Pyramid Texts

As mentioned in the Introduction concerning the goddess Nut and the sarcophagus of the deceased, there is a complex and fascinating interaction between text, ritual, and the spatial features of pyramids. The architecture of the tombs mirrors Egyptian afterlife cosmology: in the ritual context, the various passageways and chambers represent the various phases and realms through which the deceased travels.

The spells of the Pyramid Texts were apparently intended to be read in a particular order from one tomb wall to the next, though a logical narrative sequence of a linear afterlife progression eludes us.[6] This is because while the *function* of a spell may be discrete unto itself, its *contents* are often not. For example, a section may be intended to facilitate the transition from one realm to the next, though it can contain references to what the deceased will do or has already done in a different phase. The texts are also extremely repetitive, with similar experiences described for different realms and phases. There are multiple modes of ascent, cleansing, and divinization in nearly every category of text. Whether this reflects the cyclical nature of the afterlife, ritual or architectural restrictions, or simply a lack of concern for linear narrative structure is unclear. Whatever the case, it's clear that the Pyramid Texts cannot be considered a single, cohesive whole, but a body of work incorporating various incantations, ritual formulas, and liturgies from different sources.

All this makes a strict adherence to the ritual order problematic when summarizing the Pyramid Texts' afterlife conceptions. As with NDE'ers trying to describe an ineffable experience, there is a risk of imposing a linear narrative progression where none may have existed. Because of this, our summary will follow the *apparent* intended order of the spells, though different versions of the texts will be consolidated into a composite for more coherent reading. While this may technically violate the integrity of the texts as found in a particular pyramid, they are consistent enough that this does not create a serious concern.

For our purposes, the texts begin with offerings and mummy rituals. Following these are spells for the nourishment of the deceased in the afterlife. Prayers ask Re and Thoth to take the soul of the deceased to dwell with them, to sail on the cosmic waters of the sky in the celestial boat, and to eat and drink as gods do.[7] Re was the creator and sun-god, and Thoth was the god of knowledge, depicted with the head of an ibis or a baboon. In later texts, at least, he was the scribal assistant to Osiris in the judgment of the dead. As far back as the Early Dynastic period (3100–2686 BCE), the word for "god" (*netjer*) was also used for spirits of the dead, and in fact, it is not known which meaning came first.[8] In any case, souls of the dead were associated with the divine from the earliest periods of Egyptian thought.

These spells are followed by the Resurrection Ritual, intended to release the *ba*—the unique self or personality soul—from the body. The first line states that the "deceased" has departed from the body alive, not dead, and should now sit on the throne of Osiris to govern both the living and the dead. They will also govern regions of gods and divinized souls in the horizon, such as the Mounds of Horus, Seth, and Osiris. Horus was the falcon-god associated with kingship, and Seth was the chaos-god and fratricidal brother of Osiris.

In a process known as "member apotheosis," each of the soul's body parts is identified with the god Atum, the source of creation who was associated with the setting sun. Atum is also described as the father of souls of the dead, who brought them into being before the creation of the Earth, people, the gods, and death. There are many references to fathers, mothers, brothers, and sisters in the other realms, though it is not clear if any of them are to be considered earthly relatives of the deceased or if they are all deities. According to one passage, the soul does not have human parents at all, suggesting it instead has a divine or transcendent nature.[9]

Next the soul is warned about "the Great Lake that leads to the *akhs* and the canal that leads to the dead" and is told to avoid being led into the "dangerous, painful" *ba*-house. Souls then ascend with Re, their bones becoming "falcon-goddesses in the sky." Before boarding the sun-boat "on the shoulders of Horus," they will be bathed in the "cool waters of the stars," then raised by the Imperishable Stars. These were literally the circumpolar stars, but also gods and divinized humans. The deceased will then ascend to the earth-god Geb, who is the father of Osiris and thus of the deceased, since they are again mutually identified.[10]

At this point, the soul will be transformed into an *akh*. Translated literally, *akh* means "one who is effective," though its deeper meaning is "the blessed dead" who become "justified" following evaluation of their earthly conduct. It is both etymologically and conceptually related to the word for "horizon," *Akhet*, or "place of becoming akh." Upon entering the horizon, the deceased is a "transfigured spirit that has become one with the light."[11] That the *akh* was considered to have a subtle or spiritual body is evident in the line, "You shall gain control over your body, without impediment."[12]

The soul should then ask Atum for protection against Horus and

Osiris controlling and claiming their hearts and minds. This is despite the fact that the deceased is actually equated with Horus, Osiris, and Seth. There is a further deification of the body parts, which are "completed as every god." The parts of the face are identified as different deities, each referred to as an Imperishable Star—including Anubis, the jackal-headed god associated with embalming and the hall of judgment. Each limb is associated with one of the four sons of Horus—Hapi, Duamutef, Imseti, and Qebehsenuef—who correspond to the four canopic jars that hold the organs of the mummy and deify the cardinal points. Souls are told that they will not die, and that their "identity will not perish."[13]

The deceased will then ascend on the Nightboat with the constellation Orion, which was associated with both Osiris and Sothis, a goddess associated with the star Sirius. Souls are then "encircled by the Duat" in the "undersky," or sky below the Earth. The Dual Ennead—two groups of nine gods—see the souls' entry to the Duat and they say, "Look, Osiris has come as Orion." As Osiris, the deceased becomes a judge among the Enneads and makes their hearts sound. The Enneads show this by taking off their clothes and ferrying the deceased on a causeway called Sound of Heart. They visit Stork Lake, "the drinking place of every *akh*," and the Marsh of Rest, which provides spring water. The Imperishable Stars are again encountered, now in the form of swallows on an island in the marsh, and they give the deceased a "plant of life." The *ba* and *ka* are spiritually purified "to remove the bad that is against you," and the *akh* is clothed. The *akh* will now live a pleasant and happy life in the Duat, for "sadness has ended, laughter has come."[14]

Dangers are also encountered on the journey, including a snake with fiery venom, and monstrous female donkeys and hippopotamuses. Gatekeepers guard the Gates of Horus and Osiris, and souls can pass through only by revealing their identity. Resplendent in divine plumage and clothes, they will then emerge among their "brothers the gods."[15]

The deceased is then introduced to Atum-Re, a composite of both deities, before embarking with them on the circuit through the netherworld, the Akhet, and "the above." The gods announce to each other that the deceased has arrived and has the power of life and death over them, including their hearts and minds. "The *akhs* in the water" will worship the deceased, and the Watchers will dance. The Watchers are mummies that are restored to life as the sun passes through the netherworld.[16]

Osiris is then told that the deceased has surpassed him in weariness, greatness, soundness, and acclaim. A Litany of Identification with Osiris follows, in which various gods and their multiple identities are told that the deceased is Osiris reborn. The "decay" of Osiris and the "efflux" of the deceased—the fluids of the corrupting corpse—are equated with each other, with water, and with the annual inundation of the Nile. Because Osiris is the god of fertility, the inundation, and the dead, there is a conceptual link between death, decay, and rebirth through life-giving waters: It is from death and the netherworld that life emerges. The deceased is commanded, "Raise yourself like Osiris!" before becoming a composite version of the god that incorporates other gods, with the jackal's face of Anubis, the falcon's arms of Horus, the wingtips of Thoth, and a lion's tail—perhaps of the lion-headed rain-goddess Tefnut. Osiris now gives up his throne so that the deceased may rule over those in the Duat, including the other gods.[17]

The next stage of the journey is a return to the cosmic origin point. The soul's emergence from the Duat is described as the birth of a god—conceived by the sky in the Isle of Flame, which was the first matter to arise from the primordial waters, and delivered by the Ennead as the Morning Star. It is now up to the deceased to bring order from chaos and impose Maat on the cosmos. Maat is the deified goddess-principle of cosmic order, truth, balance, and justice.[18]

On the first of the lunar month, the soul ascends from the Duat on a wing of Thoth and in a ferryboat. Crossing the path of the sun known as the Winding Canal, they are guided by Nut, the sky-goddess and mother of the deceased, proceeding "to the eastern side of the sky where the gods are born." The ferrymen announce their arrival when they finally reach Re in the Akhet. Re then guides the deceased to the "sky's dual shrines" to be seated on the throne of Osiris and bathed by Horus's four sons.

There is a further transformation into Nefertem, the deification of the blue lotus from which the sun was born, and into Sia, the deification of intelligence, perception, and wisdom.[19] This acquisition of knowledge gave power over demons and other dangers, and was a prerequisite for divinization. It also helped to socialize newly arrived souls of the dead into the afterlife community, by identifying them to the inhabitants as one of them.[20]

The stars and gods of the Duat are warned that the deceased is "a great god" to be feared and is armed and dangerous. This does not mean that the deceased is no longer subject to perils, however, for new dangers include fire, "traveling in darkness," and "those who are upside down" (that is, denizens of the underworld). Thoth offers protection on the continuation of the journey by decapitating and removing the hearts of enemies.[21]

The deceased is now ferried by Re himself, together with other ferrymen. They proceed through a gate to the Akhet and along a path cleared by Isis, the maternal goddess who was both sister and wife of Osiris. She is accompanied by her sister Nephthys, a protector deity. As a star in the undersky, an immortal *akh* who "cannot truly die," the deceased "will render judgment as a god," "shining as a god," and dressed in a "dazzling garment" in the Marsh of the Beetle. Just as Isis reassembled Osiris after he was dismembered by Seth, Nut now reassembles the bones, limbs, and head of the deceased. Ascending further in the form of the fertility god Min, usually depicted with a prominent erection, the deceased emerges at the voice of Anubis, who brings about a transfiguration into Thoth to allow control of the skies and the gods.[22]

Within the Akhet there are no further obstacles—no ferryman demanding fares, and no barriers to "the White Palace of the great ones at the Beaten Path of Stars"—a possible reference to the Milky Way. The deceased now ferries the Nightboat and must bail the Dayboat alone, before being raised by the clouds to Re. "Four senior *akhs*" leading juvenile deities in braids reveal to Re the deceased's nickname, for even one's own mother does not know one's true identity. This is despite the fact that earlier in the texts, souls had to reveal their identity at the Gates of Horus and Osiris. They are also instructed not to name a god with whom they are identified.[23]

The journey continues to the Marsh of Offerings (referring to the funerary offerings given to the deceased on Earth) to "the god perched on his high tree." It's reached by ferry, by climbing the sunshine, or by striding across the sky. Tefnut arranges plots for the deceased in the Marsh of Offerings and in the Marsh of Reeds. The latter is the deceased's home "among the Imperishable Stars who follow Osiris," where other *akhs* work the land to provide sustenance.[24]

The Akhet is crossed by ascending "the smoke of a great censing," meaning the incense smoke from the deceased's own funeral on Earth. It's also accessed by "a footpath to the sky" and by flight after being transformed into various kinds of birds.[25] The pilot of the sun-boat is told to allow the deceased to navigate the perilous marshes through the Akhet. When they emerge, the deceased will alight in the form of a beetle, and will be nurtured by Isis and nursed by Nephthys and Ipy, a hippopotamus goddess associated with birth. At Stork Mountain, souls will seek their two mothers, "vultures with long hair and pendant breasts," to be nursed by them forever. They will be "purged" in the Jackal Lake by Horus, who will also further release the *ka* from the Duat Lake. The deceased is also bathed by various gods in the Lake of Reeds, in Shu's lakes, the Lake of Tresses, and the Marshes of Turquoise, among others.[26]

Entering the Akhet's Eastern Limit, the deceased "lives on the evolution of every god and eats their bowels when they have come from the Isle of Flame with their belly filled with magic." Consuming and absorbing the power, wisdom, hearts, and *akhs* of both gods and people, the deceased controls even "the controlling powers" and is "senior to the senior ones." As Lord of the Akhet, continuity is the lifetime of the deceased, and eternity is the limit.[27]

Continuing through the Akhet, the deceased is greeted by the Beautiful West, the deification of the setting sun in the direction of the netherworld. Taking the western pathway, however, presents a risk of not returning. The perilous nature of the journey resumes with "apes who sever heads" and other entities, though they're warned that the deceased "has tied his head on his neck" and will pass them peacefully.[28]

In the Spells for Leaving the Akhet, the gods of all four quarters are asked to provide the deceased with the boats used by Osiris to cross to the Cool Waters. More ferrymen are called upon, accompanied by the "unwearying ones" and the Imperishable Stars, who include the "doorkeeper of Osiris"— an "abomination" called Summoner who must be paid a fare. Various beings are greeted and asked to allow the deceased to pass. These include Anubis's daughter Qebehut and "ostrich at the Winding Canal's lip."[29]

Despite the fact that souls of the dead become supreme judges in the otherworld, they are not beyond judgment themselves. In the court of judgment, the deceased is flanked by the gods who form the Dual Maat. Souls who successfully come through the process are referred to as the Herd of Justification. The deceased's innocence is proclaimed, and their "annals" are read aloud by a god. The souls ask that the annals be read truthfully and in their entirety, so it will be known that they were never arrested, put on trial, or even accused. They then stand between two ladders that were made for Osiris, one by Re and one by Horus. Interrogation ensues, regarding purity and divinity. The deceased is asked, "Are you a god of clean places?" before being told by Horus to stand and by Seth to sit. This apparently refers to the spirit rising to stand at the head of the gods in order to be seated in the shrine.[30]

Leading Re on the cosmic circuit in order to "acquire the sky," the deceased's mother now rows the celestial boat. They are joined by the netherworld-gods as they sit and by the sky-gods as they rise. The deceased now transcends the limits of the earth and sky, becomes the moon and Thoth, "the fire in the wind's top," traverses lightning, the Akhet, and the atmosphere between the primordial waters and Earth (deified as Shu), and will "stand up on the eastern side of the hail." Re gives his arm to the deceased, and the text proclaims, *"Akh to the sky! Corpse to the earth!"* The deceased becomes a cloud and a heron, is described as both Brotherly and Sisterly, and is again associated with numerous deities, male and female.

Anubis commands the soul to descend as a star, and at the sky's door it does so, "into the boat like the Sun on the Winding Canal's shores."[31] The journey back down to the Duat has now begun.

New demons are warned to stay away, including a "gored longhorn," the "great black one," and a baboon, described in later texts as "executioner of the damned." Identified now with both Osiris and Re, the deceased enters the sky as "a screeching, howling baboon," descending in a lightning-boat with Re "to the marsh of the two underskies" (north and south). The door of the sky is commanded to open, in a "blast of heat where the gods scoop water." The gods create a path for the deceased, delighting in the spectacle of the ascent. Led now by a cow-goddess "so that Isis may receive him and Nephthys might beget him," the deceased is seated among the gods. The Imperishable Stars and "those in the Akhet" arrive in obeisance. The deceased is now identified with Sobek, the crocodile god and deification of the power of the sun, and will later rest again in the green marshes of the Akhet, making the vegetation there green. He "is lord of semen," who "takes" any woman he chooses (this passage does not appear in the pyramids of queens).[32]

Spells against a reversal of the earthly order in the Duat affirm that the deceased will eat with the mouth and defecate with the anus, will live on dates and offerings rather than urine and excrement, and will breathe through the nose and ejaculate through the penis (this latter passage *does* occur in the pyramids of queens!). The deceased is bathed in the Marsh of Life by Qebehut, perfumed with myrrh, and described as "a bull with sunlight in the middle of his eyes, whose mouth is a fiery blast," who controls gods, cultivates precious stones and trees, and unites the skies.[33]

Various ferrymen are now summoned to transport the transfigured deceased, ascending again from the Duat on a ladder made by Re, with Horus and Seth acting as psychopomps—guides for the dead on their afterlife journey. The Portal of Nu, deification of the primordial waters, is assured that the deceased is not leading gods of chaos but followers of Re. Protectors of the deceased include Grasper of Forelocks, Serpent with Sweeping Head, and Gory All Over, who will lasso, imprison, knife, disembowel, and cook any opponents. Snakes are frequent threats, but there are also centipedes and worms (creatures that might disturb a mummy in a tomb). Finally, yet another ferryman is instructed to fetch a ladder called Salve of Contentment on Osiris's Back for the deceased to ascend with the Sun. The sky is then crossed on reed floats to reach the Akhet "where the sun is."[34]

A Life Review in the
Teaching for King Merikare

Falling between the Pyramid Texts and Coffin Texts is the *Teaching for King Merikare*, an essay on kingship that dates to the First Intermediate Period (2181–2055 BC). It states that the "tribunal which judges sinners" is "not indulgent." The judges "regard a lifetime as but an hour," and they judge souls of the dead based on their "deeds," which are placed before them like a treasure, playing "before their eyes in a single hour, as though it were a biographical film," as Jan Assman put it.[35] Those who have "done no wrong" become godlike for eternity.[36]

Life reviews and moral accountability are also evident in the numerous Old and Middle Kingdom autobiographical funerary texts, which list positive actions and behaviors along with denials of negative ones. They were intended to be recited by the deceased at judgment in the afterlife.[37]

The Afterlife Experience
in the Coffin Texts

Although we've already encountered in the Pyramid Texts most of the themes and ideas found in the Coffin Texts, there are some notable differences. There is no longer an emphasis on a stellar afterlife involving the Milky Way, the Imperishable Stars, and the dead being associated with stars. There's also less focus on ascension and ritual bathing. Instead there is an intensified focus on Osiris, perils, and judgment. Reunions with deceased relatives also become more prominent.

Though there is clearly some ritual significance to the groupings and placements of the spells, as with the Pyramid Texts, our understanding of any intended sequence of events is uncertain. Especially vague is the order of the numerous gates, portals, and paths of the afterlife regions. Our summary will therefore be thematic, synthesizing the various descriptions into a coherent progression, with a focus on divergences from the Pyramid Texts.

The Coffin Texts incorporates the *Book of Two Ways*—a more systematic guide to the afterlife presented in a more linear form. It was accompanied by a map of the otherworld, painted onto the coffins, with drawings of the various pathways and some of the beings encountered on the journey. This text will be considered separately, following discussion about the rest of the Coffin Texts.

Contrary to the Pyramid Texts in which the deceased sails into the eastern Akhet, there is a spell *against* being ferried east. Instead, the god Tekem "opens up the western horizon," Atum opens the "outer door," and Khons, the moon-god, opens the "great door." The deceased is met by "the grey-haired ones," a reference to souls of people who died old, followed by the "silent ones." Deceased relatives, friends, servants, concubines, and associates assemble to greet the new arrival. On the Island of Fire where enemies of the sun dwell in caverns, a soul meets his previously deceased father "to make a doorway into the netherworld."[38]

A Spell for Proceeding to the Gates warns the deceased against going "on the roads of the knife-wielders." It also mentions seven rooms, all with female guardians such as Mistress of the Blessed, "the fiery one," Lady of Punishment, Lady of Life, and "mistress of provisions," Lady of the House of the Horizon.[39]

The deceased assists Re in his fight against the snake-demon Apep, and faces other perils such as crocodiles, vultures, pigs, and beings who "take away a man's soul from him" and "take a woman's heart from her." In a spell to be recited as the deceased "enters into the West," Re is asked for protection against a number of threats including Horus, who binds "evildoers at his slaughterhouse" and destroys souls; the "slayers" who follow Osiris; Guardian of the Lake of Fire who has a dog's face and human skin, captures his victims with a lasso and "lives by slaughter, swallows shades, but is not seen"; Seth, "who takes souls, who laps up corruption, who lives on putrefaction"; and various others who are unnamed, but armed with knives, vats, and fish-traps. The deceased also risks being captured in nets by "fishermen of men," and by Osiris. In a variation of the head-severing apes encountered in the Pyramid Texts, souls of the dead ask "female apes of the sky" to cut off their own heads to allow safe passage.[40]

Also consistent with the Pyramid Texts are spells against experiencing a reversal of the earthly order in the Duat, including walking upside-down, drinking urine, and eating filth and corruption. Impurities such as a street seller hawking excrement must be avoided, for impurity prevents transformation into an *akh*.[41] These types of spells are often found together with spells against dying a second time—that is, annihilation. This reveals the significance of souls being interrogated about what they will eat in the netherworld.[42] In reply, they should describe the abundances of bread and beer in the Marsh of Offerings. They are also interrogated regarding how many fingers they have.[43]

Shu guards a gate leading to a ferry in which the deceased, accompanied by two black storks, will be taken to the Mansion of the Ibis-Faced Ones, and then to the Lotus Barque to obtain bread and milk. There are seven spirit-ferrymen, corresponding to the seven rooms, gates, and female guardians. One of the ferrymen awakens Aken, a vulture-god, who will bring a boat built by Khnum, another god of creation and of the Nile. Each part of the boat is identified with a particular body part of a god.[44]

The portal to the Beyond is guarded by Anubis, and it is followed by a further three portals. The first was created by Sekhmet, the aggressive lion-goddess, and is 50 cubits long, wide as the horizon, filled with blue flame, and overseen by the Swallower of Myriads. The second is overseen by Seth, "He who is in the great flame." The third is personified as a goddess, streaming fire as she descends from the sky. In this portal, the deceased encounters Thoth.[45]

Rowed toward the Marsh of Reeds on a path called the Power of Earth, the deceased escapes the "place of execution," crosses the Sacred Place, and proceeds over a waterway with Osiris. The Marsh of Reeds is enclosed by an iron wall and has "secret ways and portals" through which the deceased is ferried. At the first portal is a gatekeeper; at the second are the Sisterly Companions (Isis and Nephthys) who try to seduce the deceased, but will "cut off the nose and lips of whoever does not know their names." At the third portal, "the air enters and is cut off." The gatekeeper of the fourth portal stands with a corn measurer "wherewith to measure a man's excrement." These and the following three portals each greet the deceased, saying, "Come be a spirit, my brother, proceed to the place of which you know."[46]

Within the Marsh of Reeds there is both a Tribunal in a Broad Hall and a Great Tribunal. Judgment is not a final reckoning but a purification that enables the deceased to continue through the otherworld. Terrors are here portrayed as obstacles rather than eternal torments, though the fate of those who fail to overcome them is annihilation in the Great Void—the worst possible penalty following judgment. In one passage, the deceased instructs Osiris to undertake judgment of them, for the deceased has judged Osiris. As souls become Osiris in death, this is effectively self-judgment.[47]

Grains of monumental proportions grow in the Marsh of Reeds, such as barley six feet tall and emmer ten feet tall, "reaped by the horizon-dwellers in the presence of the Souls of the Easterners." They are aided by Horakhty (Horus of the Horizon), a divine calf, and the Morning Star. In the east of the Marsh is the Middle Gate through which Re appears. To the south is the Lake of Waterfowl and to the north are the Waters of Geese.[48]

The Marsh of Offerings is overseen by the scribes Double-Master and Name-Repeater. They record the gifts and food belonging to the deceased, offered during funerary rituals on Earth. The deceased becomes governor of the Marsh, and is referred to as "mistress in the Great Mansion" (including on the coffins of men). Within the Marsh are "towns, districts and waterways," which are depicted on a plan painted in the coffins. These places include Town of the Great Lady, Vegetable-Town, Town of Fair Offerings, Provision-Town, Milk-Town, Union-Town, Waterway of the Horns of the Mistress of Purity, and the "field-plots of the dwarfs," of which the deceased claims ownership. The Marsh has agricultural patterns similar to those on Earth, and there are spells allowing souls to avoid labor, and also to be able to have sex. All this shows that despite the more transcendent, divine, and rarified aspects, the afterlife was perceived in part as an idealized mirror image of Earth. Certain earthly locales are also mirrored in the afterlife, such as the Winding Canal being the celestial version of the Nile.[49]

The deceased is "cleansed in the Lakes of the Dwellers of the Netherworld among the blessed ones" and becomes a god. Isis will now reveal the knowledge of the actions of gods, and show how to reach Osiris and the divine offering table.[50]

The *Book of Two Ways*

Other than brief references to a Lake of Reeds, to the Marsh of Offerings, and to places of herbage and fields, the focus of the *Book of Two Ways* is on overcoming afterlife dangers. There's a long version and a short version, both of which begin at sunrise.

The long version starts with a spell for the deceased to navigate with Re to the sky and "to the stairway of the barque of Mercury." With Isis, Horus, and Seth in the bow, and Hu (the deification of the divine word), Sia, and Re in the stern, they traverse a "circle of fire."[51]

Now identified with Re, the deceased wards off snakes as they travel on the "paths of Rosetau," which are situated on the tops of high flint walls and are watched over by guardians. The paths are mazelike, "in confusion . . . each opposed to its fellow." Rosetau is a place in the center of the Duat in the "limit of the sky . . . on both water and on land."[52]

The "efflux of Osiris" is hidden in the darkness of Rosetau, encircled by fire. Rosetau itself is also described as "the corruption of Osiris"—that is, his decaying corpse. Reaching it was a goal for the deceased, for "He who sees the dead Osiris will never die." Knowing the paths there will make a soul divine, and the alternative is annihilation. Rosetau is also a place of rebirth, where the deceased will make the efflux of Osiris "raise itself" and bring the god back to life. This encounter with the corpse of Osiris brings about the enlightenment that enables immortality. Because the individual is identified with Osiris in death, the encounter is also with the deceased's own corpse. This enlightenment, brought about by souls of the dead witnessing the decomposition of their own body, is the realization that they are physically dead, yet spiritually still alive.[53] This is remarkably consistent with a very common feature of NDEs: the person realizes they're "dead" and yet paradoxically still conscious, only after seeing their own lifeless body during the out-of-body experience. In both the Egyptian text and in many contemporary NDEs, it is this revelation that enables the soul to proceed through the next stages of the experience.

On the north bank of the Winding Waterway are numerous towns surrounded by a million cubits of flame, with blasts of fire extending even further. The deceased asks the Protectress of the Blast to act as a guardian against a mysterious figure described as "him who would impose any kind of evil obstacle because of Him whose name is 'Secret-of-Wisdom.'" The riverside paths and bends are guarded by Great-Face "who repels the aggressors," the "foe who lives in the Fledgling-lake," and "He who is driven off with two faces in dung." At the lake of flame, the deceased is turned back by knife-wielders, for "no-one knows how to enter the fire." Further paths are guarded by "He whose face is covered," "Hippopotamus-Face, bellowing of power," "Dog-Face, whose shape is big," and "Snake-Face, lord of aggressors."[54]

Souls must also pass threatening beings who menace from below as they travel along the paths. These include Scowler, Oppressor, Monster, Trembler,

"He of the loud voice," and "He who is hot." A "gate of fire" and a "gate of darkness" are guarded by "the sad-voiced one" and by entities such as "She of the Knife" and "He who curses."[55]

At two further series of seven gates, the gatekeepers include "He who eats the droppings of his hinder parts," is made of various plants, and is armed with a throw stick; "He who glowers, the voluble one"; "He whose face is inverted, the many-shaped" who lives on those who lack the knowledge to pass; "He who lives on maggots" and on those who fail to reach the sky; and the "monster" Aikenty bellowing fire. Such monstrous figures are depicted in tombs, on coffins, and on late Middle Kingdom ivory wands. The latter served a protective function, particularly for children, suggesting that some of these netherworld entities were guardians of the deceased despite their demonic appearance and threatening aspect. Souls are also at risk of entering the Valley of Darkness and the Lake of Criminals, presumably places of punishment for the immoral and untruthful.[56]

The short version of the *Book of Two Ways* is specifically a "guide to the double doors of the horizon." Though it duplicates some material from the longer version, its contents are particularly esoteric. It describes how souls are guided by their own *ka*, having become "Lord of the secret things"—that is, Osiris. The deceased therefore has prior knowledge of the afterlife, which is consistent with the idea that the process is a return to the origin point or to the soul's true home.

Souls first arrive at a "gate with fire in front and hidden in the back, with a man in it who is bound." Nu guards the path against "he who has two faces," and an *akh* guards "the gate of the mansion of Many-faced." The royal ancestors, here called the Souls of Nekhen, attack the deceased's limbs with fire, though a path is opened by Hu, who "speaks in darkness."[57]

The path leads to "great fiery doors" which are guarded by Apep, "He whose mouth is open in darkness" and whose horn "gives darkness, pain and death." He provides protection from arrows shot by archers, though the deceased is now invisible and therefore a difficult target. In another passage, the deceased saves Re from Apep as he roars "on the great plain north of Stretching-the-bows." Among the many other unique and often cryptic perils the deceased must face are being attacked by "the great baboon who eats the gods," the mansion of the destroyer, and an invisible man a million cubits tall.[58]

The soul must then negotiate a high rampart guarded by snakes and flames, before finally reaching a "pure land" of green, fragrant herbs. A path leads to the Mansion of Incense where the deceased's flesh is on fire. At this stage, souls seem to enter a transcendent, omnipresent state. They become various elements, animals, grain, and deities, including Osiris, Re, Soped (a falcon war god), Atum, Thoth, Sobek, the serpent-deity Nehebkau "who takes away powers," Hathor, a scribe of Hathor, birds, Fire, Air, a child, and both male and female.[59]

Understanding the Egyptian Afterlife Experience

The multiple realms, transformations, and states of being found in these texts are sometimes viewed as contradictory, or containing "unresolved ambiguities." In attempting to resolve them, some Egyptologists have tried to impose dualistic categories on Egyptian afterlife conceptions. For example, William Murnane suggested that the solar afterlife with the sun-god Re was reserved for the king, while the Osirian afterlife and the Marsh of Reeds were for the populace.[60] As we've seen, however, the deceased is identified with Osiris and journeys to the Marsh of Reeds in the Pyramid Texts, which were primarily if not exclusively intended for royalty. In the Coffin Texts, which were *not* intended only for royalty, the deceased is also associated with both Re and Osiris. The solar and underworld aspects are clearly two different elements of a "single, coherent vision of the afterlife," as James P. Allen put it. This vision was essentially the process of regeneration brought about by the soul's journey to the netherworld and return through the sky.

Such is the esoteric nature of this complex literature that Leonard H. Lesko went so far as to question whether the Coffin Texts scribes knew what they were doing at all. Given the overall continuity of conceptions over 3,000 years, it's reasonable to assume that the Egyptians actually intended to write what they did. Notwithstanding the shifts in focus from the Pyramid Texts to the Coffin Texts as noted earlier, the texts do not actually reveal the ideological conflicts often claimed, and the same multiple afterlife goals can be found in each.

For similar reasons we can dismiss Lesko's alternate suggestion that Middle Kingdom Egyptians were ignorant of which afterlife fate was the most desirable and so had alternatives represented in their coffins.[61] Rather than assume that there's something "wrong" with the texts or with the Egyptians themselves, it's more likely that the difficulties in our understanding lie with scholarship—and perhaps some lurking ethnocentrisms therein. Specifically, the linear "either/or" mode of thinking characteristic of monotheistic religions often underlies interpretations of Egyptian religion, whether consciously or otherwise. But this kind of thinking is irrelevant when trying to understand polytheistic concepts of simultaneous opposite occurrences and cyclical unity. As the Latvian-German Egyptologist Erik Hornung stated, for the Egyptians, "the nature of a god becomes accessible through a 'multiplicity of approaches'; only when these are taken together can the whole be comprehended."[62]

Egyptian religious thought is typified by single concepts having multiple aspects. For example, Re, Khepri, Horus, Atum, Aten, Amun-Re, Osiris-Re, Re-Horakhty, and the soul of the deceased are all aspects of the sun—and beings of light. The *ba* and *ka* are microcosms of the complementary opposites of Re and Osiris, while the *akh* is analogous to the Osiris-Re union. Indeed, these soul elements are *one and the same* with the deities, not simply comparable to them. The texts can be more productively regarded as deliberate and lucid expressions of an afterlife system rooted in the concept of the reconciliation of dualities. This was meant to reveal the multivalence of the afterlife experience and the divine transcendence and omnipresence of the deceased.[63] Souls of the dead thus become *both* Re in the sky and Osiris in the netherworld—which itself is "paradoxically" located in the sky and under the earth, or an "undersky."

The afterlife as revealed in these texts was characterized by a cyclically renewing interaction of life with death.[64] Because the focus is more on the journey than on destinations, it's unclear whether the Marsh of Reeds was considered an intermediate state on the cosmic circuit, a goal beyond it, or a realm reserved for a particular segment of society. If the circuit itself *is* the ultimate state, one never reaches a final realm but instead spends half the time journeying through netherworld realms of darkness and danger and the other half journeying through celestial realms of light and abundance. Because the journey of the sun is eternal, it's unclear when or how any ultimate destination or state might be attained. Indeed, the idea of liberation from the cycle may be irrelevant.

On the other hand, the texts do depict the Marsh of Reeds and other locales as desirable goals and *dwelling* places. It's also difficult to imagine the point of the deceased being repeatedly judged on each cycle, with no subsequent effect on the journey's progress. Perhaps the most likely solution is that the deceased completed the cycle only once, was judged only once, and depending on the outcome of the judgment (and the ability to overcome dangers) was either annihilated or became divine in the Marsh of Reeds. The Duat would then be a "gestation" period prior to spiritual rebirth.[65]

At the same time, the multiple realms, states of being, transformations, and divinizations suggest an all-encompassing afterlife amounting to a transcendent state of universal totality of the deceased with the "Absolute" or "Ultimate Reality." The soul ascends in multiple forms to simultaneously dwell in the Marsh of Reeds and the Duat, to travel *with* Re and *as* Re on the sun's eternal cycle of rebirth, to dwell in the netherworld *with* Osiris and *as* Osiris, to exist in the firmament as a star, and so on. In other words, the deceased becomes another component of composite deities like Amun-Re and Osiris-Re. Just as Re-Osiris-Deceased simultaneously gestates in the womb of Nut, Re-Deceased journeys continually through the Duat and the Akhet, and Osiris-Deceased rules in the Duat.[66] This interpretation is actually supported by the seeming lack of a "logical" narrative progression in the texts. In many cases, the order of events and experiences is conjectural. In the

Pyramid Texts, for example, the deceased is instructed to sit on the throne of Osiris before ascent and undergoes the divinization of the body parts prior to passing through perils and judgment. The cyclical nature of the Egyptian afterlife could also account for this, though again a narrative sequence is elusive even in that light.

Dissenting from generations of Egyptologists, Mark Smith has argued that the ancient Egyptians did not believe that souls of the dead literally *become* Osiris or Re after death. He points to commentaries within the Pyramid Texts declaring that "whoever knows and recites that spell will be an intimate of the sun-god and join his following" and that "whoever worships Osiris and recites the spell for him will live forever." These statements clearly do *not* say that the deceased *is* or will *become* these deities, and Smith considers them to hold more weight and authority than the spells themselves. Indeed, they guide his interpretations to such an extent that he argues that only passages that agree with them are true descriptions of Egyptian beliefs. The spells, he argues, were not always reliable indicators of what Egyptians actually believed would happen after death; and the multiple references to divine unification with various deities only have validity as *ritual* texts. The deceased always remains separate from and subordinate to the deities. As Smith summarizes, "in the ritual moment, anyone could be Osiris, but in the world beyond the ritual there is only one god, with whom every deceased person hoped to enjoy the same relationship."

At the same time, the deceased was endowed with what Smith calls an "Osiris aspect," which resulted from the correct funerary rituals being performed and the dead becoming justified. This facilitated the deceased's rebirth in the otherworld as "a member of the community comprising the god's worshippers."[67]

While Smith makes an intriguing case in his remarkable work of scholarship, it's difficult to reconcile with what we read in so many passages of the texts, over and over again, throughout Egyptian history. Indeed, the references to the deceased actually *becoming* Osiris are so clear and so numerous that they seem emphatic. Furthermore, there is little to suggest that having an Osiris "aspect" and worshipping Osiris would preclude also becoming Osiris. Smith's use of rather monotheistic language seems uneasily applied to this esoteric polytheistic tradition, particularly when we consider the almost equal prominence of Re in these texts and the deceased being equated with him and many other gods. While it may be that these are also not literal divine transformations but ritual ones, and that the deceased merely takes on a temporary Re aspect, Horus aspect, Thoth aspect, and so on, that's not explicit in the texts, either. Smith's reading also echoes Murnane and Lesko in describing some of the descriptions as "contradictory" and showing "inconsistencies," which he believes are resolved by his interpretation. While his position does accept that the ancient authors meant what they wrote and wrote what they meant, there are other ways to resolve the multiplicity of experiences and transformations described in the texts.

In light of many other characteristics of Egyptian religion, the "divine union" interpretation is perhaps more compelling. Egyptian religion was quasi-pantheistic in that gods could be interassociated, both with each other and with concepts and elements—though each deity still had their own attributes and maintained their primary identities. The concept also applied to humans, who retained their individuality after death, despite divine transformation and unification. The fear of annihilation is essentially a fear of becoming undifferentiated, without selfhood. This means that while *total* unity isn't desirable, divinization and union with the divine are still the ultimate goals. This tension and dichotomy between unification and individuality signifies, once again, the reconciliation of dualities characteristic of Egyptian thought. The desire is not to transcend existence itself but to transcend the earthly state, becoming a spiritualized (that is, divinized *akh*) version of the present self. Because this imposes limits on "the propensity to extend and to change," as Hornung put it,[68] the divinity of *akhs* is not a true omnipresence, omnipotence, or transcendence in the strictest sense. The fact that the seemingly ever-changing bodiless spirit in the otherworld becomes multiple divine and transcendent identities, however, points at least to an effective omnipresence, omnipotence, and transcendence of the current reality. It should be noted that despite Smith's skepticism regarding the deceased's identification with Osiris, he does not dispute that souls of the dead become divine immortals.

None of this is to ignore the evidence that there are different after-life fates, depending on the individual. In addition to divinization and annihilation, some evidently have more servile roles—tending the fields or bringing water to the gods or to the deceased (divinized) individual addressed in the texts. There's no clear indication that such positions would be temporary or intermediate. Generally speaking, however, it seems that the choice of afterlife fates was between nonexistence (anni-hilation) and divine existence—returning "to the all-encompassing One from which we emerged at birth."[69] In the Middle Kingdom text, *The Man Who Was Weary of Life*, death is compared to recovery from illness, to understanding the unknown, and to a return home.[70]

In summary, despite some uncertainties of language and meaning, it's clear that multiple yet unified experiences are being described. In addition to encounters with and transformations into divine beings, the Egyptian afterlife included leaving the body in spiritual form, an otherworld journey that is considered a return to the "home" or origin state, an encounter with one's own corpse leading to the realization of spiritual immortality, enter-ing darkness and emerging into light via descent into the Duat and ascent into the Akhet, water crossings and ferrymen, interrogations with a stress on the knowledge of the deceased, meeting deceased relatives, judgment or self-judgment based on one's earthly moral conduct, a panoramic life review, obstacles, barriers and perils with the threat of annihilation, and a cyclical existence of rebirth and renewal. Although we have no narrative accounts of NDEs from the periods in question, on a thematic level, nearly all these elements have correlates in the phenomenon.

Excursus: Egyptian NDEs in Later Periods

It's worth taking a short detour here to look at some of the later evidence for NDEs in ancient Egypt. There are four relevant texts, from different eras, and occurring in a variety of contexts. While none can be considered documentary accounts, they offer compelling glimpses into how knowledge of NDEs might have been incorporated into stories about visits to the otherworld. Taken together, in fact, they seem to suggest that the phenomenon wove a thread through Egyptian afterlife beliefs through the ages.

Meryre the Magician

The tale of a magician named Meryre dates from sometime between the eighth and sixth centuries BCE, though quite possibly originated as far back as the thirteenth. It tells of how a fictitious pharaoh named Sisobek became ill and was given only seven days to live. The pharaoh summons Meryre to the palace to ask him how his life might be extended. Meryre explains that the only possibility is for another person to die in his place. After some coaxing and negotiating, Meryre himself agrees to die in place of the pharaoh. This gives the story both a return-from-death context as well as a shamanic one, for Meryre undertakes a deliberate journey to the netherworld. We're not given any details about how he accomplishes this, but because he's a magician, he embarks with the means of coming back to life: a statue of the goddess Hathor, which is supposed to magically enable him to return to Earth.

When he arrives in the netherworld, Meryre meets the real Hathor. He tells her that he's there in order to ask for an extension of life for the pharaoh. Hathor leads Meryre to Osiris, who questions him about how things are going on Earth under Sisobek's rule, if he's keeping the temples in good repair, and so on. When Meryre gives him a favorable report, Osiris grants the pharaoh an extension of life, and Sisobek returns to Earth to resume his rule. But poor Meryre is told he won't be able to return to life, and that he must stay in the netherworld forever.

One day, Hathor goes to Earth to celebrate one of her festivals and when she returns, she gives Meryre some bad news: Sisobek has betrayed him. He has married Meryre's wife, taken his house, and killed his son. The impressionable pharaoh had been influenced in this by Meryre's rivals—a group of fellow magicians who were jealous of him.

Hatching a plan, Meryre takes a lump of clay and makes a golem—a human-shaped zombie-like figure. He sends it to Earth with instructions to confront Sisobek with a demand that he burn all the magicians to death. The pharaoh does so, and the golem returns to the underworld with a bouquet of flowers for Meryre, who in turn gives them to Osiris. Under the mistaken impression that Meryre defied him and returned to Earth, and that the flowers were evidence of this, Osiris gets angry.

Unfortunately, the rest of the story is fragmentary, but it's likely that Meryre had brought the flowers to Osiris as a gesture of goodwill when asking for permission to return to Earth. In any event, he seems to have been successful in returning, for in an additional scene he is once again having a conversation with Sisobek.[71]

On the one hand, there's really not much about this narrative that reads like a genuine NDE. It's very clearly a *story*, with narrative structure and plotting tropes such as reversals of fortune, betrayals, and misunderstandings. And there was never any pharaoh named Sisobek.

On the other hand, there *were* a few historical figures named Meryre and the character in the story could have been based on one. If so, the story itself might possibly have been inspired by an actual NDE he could have had. Meryre does go to the netherworld by temporarily dying, he meets deities, has an evaluation of life on Earth (on the pharaoh's behalf, since he's his proxy), and ultimately returns to Earth. Unfortunately, we're missing the details about the journey to the otherworld and return—which in relation to NDEs are the most relevant parts of an afterlife text.

The Pharaoh Rhampsinitus, or Rameses II

In the fifth century BCE, the Greek historian Herodotus briefly discussed the otherworld journey of a pharaoh he called Rhampsinitus—a Greek form of "Rameses." Herodotus wrote that this king ruled before Cheops (Khufu), builder of the Great Pyramid at Giza. This would mean that Rhampsinitus was actually Sneferu who ruled sometime around 2600 BCE. It is believed by many scholars, however, that Rhampsinitus actually refers to Rameses II, who lived a good 800 years before Herodotus. Oral histories have remarkable longevity, however, especially when the events they relate are considered to be *important*—as this one appears to have been. It's possible, in any case, that Herodotus preserved a remnant of an otherwise lost or unrecorded account of an extraordinary afterlife experience by one of the most famous and prominent kings of Egypt.

The account unfortunately gives few details of the experience. The pharaoh descended "alive" to the underworld, but we don't know if Herodotus meant that the journey took place in physical form, or out-of-body, or even if there was a near-death context. Despite the Egyptian setting, he called the underworld "Hades" in keeping with Greek tradition. The only experience described there is Rhampsinitus playing dice with Demeter, the Greek underworld goddess, seen by Herodotus as the equivalent to Isis. The pharaoh lost some of the games and won others, and before he returned to Earth, Demeter gave him a golden scarf.

This event, according to Herodotus's sources, led to the foundation of "a festival based on Rhampsinitus' descent and subsequent return."[72] That the story of this king's journey to the underworld was not only remembered but still *celebrated* in a festival eight centuries after its alleged occurrence shows the significance it had for Egyptian religious thought. If Herodotus's account is to be trusted, this a rare example of a direct claim that an NDE-like experience led to the foundation of a new religious tradition.

The festival itself involved a ritual reenactment of Rhampsinitus's underworld journey and return: a priest was blindfolded with a scarf (probably symbolizing the one that the pharaoh brought back from the underworld), then led to the temple of Demeter-Isis by two wolves, who then escorted him back. These "wolves" were likely jackals, or rather priests dressed as the Egyptian jackal god Wepwawet, who helped the deceased as "Opener of the Way" on the afterlife journey. Being associated with the underworld, the temple would have been dark, perhaps even subterranean, symbolizing both the grave and the underworld. The priest's emergence, therefore, was a symbolic return from death, and a rebirth into a transformed, revitalized state.

This ritual described by Herodotus recalls the ancient Sed festival, dating back to the Old Kingdom, which itself may hint at a conceptual association between NDEs and Egyptian ritual and religion. The Sed festival was held in the thirtieth year of a pharaoh's reign, and its purpose was to renew his strength and revitalize his royal power. The ritual involved an enactment of a journey to the underworld, in which the pharaoh entered his own tomb where his funerary belongings had been placed. He's depicted in reliefs with green skin to indicate that he's dead, and also to associate him with Osiris and fertility. A god shows him the symbols of life, stability, and power, and he is then instructed to "wake up." When the pharaoh has "revived" from the ordeal, he's now associated with Horus rather than Osiris, and proceeds to his palace in this renewed, transformed, "reborn" state.[73]

Because Ramses II lived such a long time, and ruled for 67 years, his Sed festivals occurred multiple times in his life—as many as 14 over a period of less than 40 years. Each one would have involved a virtual journey to the otherworld and a return. This surely would have cemented his death-and-return afterlife story in the popular consciousness of the Egyptian people.

The High Priest of Ptah, Setna Khaemwese (Khaemwaset)

In fact, it seems that Ramses II was so deeply associated with afterlife visits that his son Khaemwaset became the subject of his own such story, involving another underworld journey which surely would have served to keep the family tradition alive. The sole surviving papyrus of the story dates to the middle of the first century CE, in the Roman period during the reign of Claudius. The story takes place, however, some 1,250 years earlier, though its true age and origins are unknown.

Khaemweset was a High Priest of Ptah at Memphis, and was known for his interest in ancient Egyptian history and monuments. He's sometimes called "the first Egyptologist." The story of his underworld descent combines Greek and Egyptian imagery and ideas. Although the text is incomplete and badly preserved, as well as being poorly written with grammatical errors, much can be gleaned from it.

It tells of how one day, Setna Khaemwese, as he's called here, happened to see the funeral of a rich man, his coffin being carried with great honors among wailing mourners. Nearby, the body of a poor man was being taken quietly to the graveyard on a reed mat, with no mourners or fanfare. Setna found this upsetting and commented that the rich man must be so much happier than the poor man.

In reaction to this comment, Setna's 11-year-old son, Si-Osire, decides to teach his father a lesson. He somehow takes Setna to see the seven halls of the underworld in succession. What happens in the first three is missing, but in the fourth we learn of two punishments. In the first, souls of the dead sit making ropes while donkeys keep gnawing on them as they do so. In the second, they try to climb up to reach food and water suspended above them while a pit is dug beneath them to reverse their progress. In the fifth hall a man is pleading and crying because his eye has been impaled.

The sixth hall is where reports are read out to the council of gods—probably judgments about new souls of the dead and their lives on Earth. In the seventh hall, Setna encounters Osiris sitting on his throne. The tribunal of gods sets up the balance for weighing souls, to "measure the faults against the good deeds." Anubis dictates the information to Thoth who keeps the records. Those who have more faults than good deeds will be annihilated; but those who have more good deeds will be taken by the tribunal of gods "to heaven with the noble spirits." Those whose good and bad deeds are equal will become servants to Sokar-Osiris.

Setna Khaemwese then notices a very rich, high-ranking soul close to Osiris. His son explains to him that this was the poor man whose funeral he saw on Earth. His good deeds were more numerous than his faults, so he was given this exalted status at the side of the Lord of the Dead. The rich man, however, whose funeral Setna had seen, was the one whose eye was impaled in the fifth hall, because his bad deeds outweighed his good.

The souls making rope were people who had worked too hard, day and night, only to have their earnings robbed behind their backs by their women. Those who had the pits continually dug from under their feet as they reached for food and water were people who had been prevented by the gods from discovering their own lives.

At the end of the tour, Setna and his son proceed back up to the necropolis at Memphis. Setna asks his son, "is the place by which we went down different from the place by which we came up?"—indicating his confusion. But Si-Osire doesn't reply, so how they got to the other-world and how they returned remains a mystery. In any case, Setna is left "earthshaken with wonder" at his afterlife experience. It "weighed upon him heavily," but he decided that that he was unable to share it with anyone.[74]

Although there's a lack of a temporary death or even illness, the story does feature some broad NDE themes, such as traveling through darkness, meeting deities, evaluation of earthly life, seeing other spirits of the dead known from Earth, and transformative effects after returning. While it could be that the "hellish" imagery reflects distressing NDEs, the account has a clear moralizing intent—to teach the reader that good behavior alone will ensure a positive afterlife, and that material wealth is irrelevant. The systematized afterlife with a bureaucratic structure of record keeping, weighing souls, a council, and judges goes back to the earliest Egyptian texts, and the description thus seems designed to reinforce existing beliefs.

As with Meryre, it's *possible* that the story of Setna's otherworld journey was inspired by some NDE in the remote past and then mythologized and elaborated. Given the fact that Setna was Ramses II's son, however, it seems more likely that it's simply a fictional sequel to the pharaoh's afterlife journey story. Drawing on the fame of his father, who repeated the netherworld journey many times through the Sed festival, a similar story about Setna would have been a popular way to teach some moral and religious lessons. The inclusion Setna's son Si-Osire means that at least three generations of the family had a journey to the afterlife and back.

A Magical Spell for Descending to the Underworld

One further text is worth noting, though it dates to almost the very end of ancient Egyptian culture—during the waning of the pagan Roman period, around the third or fourth century CE. Rather than being a literary text, it's a spell to enable the practitioner to undertake a visit to the otherworld through invocation rituals. Although of Egyptian origin, it was written in Greek and is an example of what scholars call the Greek Magical Papyri. What makes these texts particularly fascinating is that they were products of the multicultural cross-fertilization of the era, especially in the intertwined areas of religion and magic. This particular spell incorporates elements from Egyptian, Greek, Roman, and Hittite traditions—although given the fluidity of beliefs in ancient Mediterranean and Near Eastern polytheisms, these weren't really discrete culture-bound traditions to begin with.

The spell appears to have been intended for initiates of the Mystery cult of the Idaean Dactyls, a race of spirit-men or "mythical wizards and craftsmen" associated with healing magic and metal smithing. The cult's rituals involved enactments of journeys to the afterlife realm through a descent into an underground chamber—just as we've seen with Herodotus' account of Rhampsinitus, and the Sed festival of Ramses II. As this magical spell seems to suggest, however, the ritual led to a kind of shamanic trance journey experience as well, for it includes instructions on how to deal with threats from underworld demons and how to avoid punishment or even death during the experience. Although the spell is consistent with the millennia-long Egyptian afterlife textual traditions, rather than Osiris or another Egyptian deity, it associates the individual with a composite of the Mesopotamian and Greek underworld goddesses, Hecate-Ereshkigala.[75]

The spell was intended to be recited "late at night," suggesting that the process of journeying to the otherworld was similar to dream incubation, in which an individual would deliberately seek a divinely inspired dream for healing or other beneficial purposes. Indeed, the spell states that "what you wish" will be revealed during sleep. There is a risk, however, of being "led away to death," and the spell explains how to avoid such a fate. This reinforces that the intent of the spell is for one's consciousness or soul to visit the otherworld while still alive, but that visiting the realm of the dead comes with the inherent risk that one might not be able to return.

While all these texts involve people journeying to the other world and having various experiences there before returning, only that of Meryre has a clear near-death context: Rhampsinitus and Setna Khaemwese apparently visit the otherworld while still alive and possibly even in their bodies. The tales of Meryre and Setna are also obviously fictional. It's important to remember that they were written some 1,500–1,600 years after the Pyramid Texts, and were clearly impacted by centuries of existing Egyptian afterlife conceptions. At the same time, it's possible that they were originally based upon or inspired by actual NDEs. At minimum, these accounts, and that of Rhampsinitus, show *knowledge* of the NDE phenomenon, even if they're not based on actual cases. As a ritual text for Mystery cult initiates to travel to the underworld and back, the Greco-Egyptian magical spell may have likewise been grounded in knowledge of NDEs. Indeed, the shamanistic experiences it concerns were perhaps attempts to deliberately replicate NDEs without having to actually temporarily die, as has been found in other cultures in different parts of the world.[76] This dynamic will be returned to in Part III.

4

Mesopotamia
Otherworldly Descent
and Ascent

The Near-Death Experience
of a Sumerian King

The antecedents to the famous Babylonian *Epic of Gilgamesh* are a collection of Sumerian texts in which the hero king is known as Bilgames. It's believed that Bilgames was a real historical figure who ruled the city-state of Uruk around 2700 BCE. This means that the poem known as "The Death of Bilgames" may contain the world's earliest documented historical account of an NDE. It is obviously highly mythologized, though of course that does not mean that it wasn't based on an actual event.

The narrative describes Bilgames falling ill, "lying down, never to rise again." He's seized by Namtar, the footless and handless plague deity. Namtar was also minister to the queen of the underworld, Ereshkigala, who decrees the fates of the deceased (encountered in the underworld descent spell in the previous chapter).

Lying on his deathbed, Bilgames has a vision which is sent to him by Enki, the god of wisdom and of water, who gave civilization and culture to humans. Bilgames is instructed not to descend to the underworld "with heart knotted in anger," and that he should "let it be undone before Utu," the sun-god. In other Sumerian texts, Utu is described as the father of the underworld and as "the judge who searches out verdicts for the gods, with a lapis-lazuli beard, rising from the horizon into the holy heavens." After ascending on a chariot into the heavens, he then descended again into the horizon.[1]

Bilgames appears before the gods at their assembly to discuss his destiny. This group of divine underworld judges is called the Anuna. They are beings of light, for in Mesopotamian thought, deities were believed to be "surrounded by a blinding, awe-inspiring radiance." Because Bilgames is two-thirds god and one-third man, they must decide whether his fate is to be that of a divinity or that of a human. They review his career, his heroic exploits, his faithful perpetuation of religious customs and rituals, his foundation of temples, and his journey to find Ziusudra at the world's end. Ziusudra was the hero of the Sumerian flood myth, granted immortality by the gods, and Bilgames sought to obtain from him the secret of everlasting life.

Before his judgment, Bilgames attends a funerary banquet in the Great City where deceased priests and priestesses dwell. There he is greeted by his parents, grandparents, and siblings, along with kings, governors, and military commanders from Earth. They tell him not to despair, for he himself "will number among the Anuna gods."

Enki decrees that Bilgames must dwell in the netherworld but that he will be made a lesser god: a "governor" who will "pass judgment." The verdicts he renders will carry as much weight as those of Ningishzida, the god of snakes, the roots of trees, and the dawn; and of Dumuzid, the vegetation deity. Enlil, the father-deity and the husband of Ninlil, the goddess of destiny, tells Bilgames that he will be reunited with his family and with his friend and servant Enkidu. In other texts, Bilgames is referred to as "ruler" and even "king" of the netherworld, and as the little brother of Nergal, the scimitar-wielding underworld warrior-deity.[2]

Bilgames, Ningishzida, and Dumuzid evidently formed an underworld trinity and are also grouped together in a religious lament (songs expressing grief, often in mythological contexts).[3]

Although the gods vowed that after Ziusudra, humans would not be immortal, the fact that they make Bilgames a divine judge suggests that, by "immortal," they meant eternal life in the body on Earth as opposed to existence in spiritual form following physical death—or, as the text puts it, "in the form of a ghost, dead in the underworld."

An encounter with another being of light is then described: "The Dream God Sissig, son of Utu, shall provide light for him in the netherworld, the place of darkness." Bilgames then returns to his earthly body after a six-day absence. He arranges his tomb, equipping it with his entire harem and entourage—sacrificed so that they may accompany him to the underworld (a practice confirmed by excavations of the third-millennium-BCE royal cemetery at Ur). Bilgames also gathers gifts to take with him for the netherworld priests and deities.[4]

In addition to Bilgames' possibly historical NDE account, indirect references to near-death experiences in Mesopotamia can be found scattered among various ancient texts. For example, the underworld deity Nergal was said to have the power "to carry off and to bring back," meaning he could cause death but also bring about revival from death. There was also an Akkadian term for "one who makes the dead to live" (*muballit miti*). The myth of "Bilgames, Enkidu, and the Underworld" (discussed below) shows that the living can sometimes visit the otherworld. There are a number of further underworld journey myths as well as accounts of visionary dreams visits to a heavenly realm. As will be seen, at least on the general thematic level, all are evocative of NDEs to some degree.

Our main sources for Mesopotamian ideas about the afterlife are literary texts written in cuneiform script on clay tablets. Their content dates to at least 2000 BCE, though references to historical events and people suggest origins of up to 300 years earlier. The tablets themselves are mostly scribal copies dating to the eighteenth century BCE. Different versions show variations in language and story, and some parts of the texts are missing, so as with all ancient texts they come with a degree of uncertainty. But they were obviously a source of religious meaning and significance for the Sumerians, being concerned mainly with divinities, their actions, and worship. Most had cultic or royal ritual significance, and were used for religious, inaugural, or celebratory functions.[5]

Although Sumerian was the original language for most of the texts, a few were written in Akkadian. Even when Akkadian became the dominant language for daily use, however, Sumerian was still used for literature, carrying with it a priestly or sacred authority comparable to Egyptian hieroglyphs or Latin. Old Babylonian Akkadian literature is, in fact, dependent on Sumerian literature, while also incorporating Amorite traditions (a nomadic Semitic people who lived across much of the Ancient Near East). Culturally speaking, the distinction between Sumerian and Akkadian is fluid.[6] Ancient Mesopotamian scholars regard them as a single culture sharing two languages.[7]

Texts dealing with the afterlife that fall outside our date restrictions are mostly consistent with those discussed here, providing only additional details about the netherworld—particularly regarding deities and underworld gates. They'll be mentioned only to a limited extent, when they help illuminate the earlier literature.

The Further Otherworld Adventures of Bilgames

"Bilgames, Enkidu, and the Underworld"

The otherworld journey in this text take place before "The Death of Bilgames." It lacks a near-death context and has an even more mythical flavor, though still shows some general thematic similarities to NDEs.

It begins with Enki, who is sailing to the underworld. A storm causes his boat to knock down a tree, which Inana then replants. Inana was the principal Sumerian goddess, associated with love and war, and sister of the sun-god Utu (she was also the subject of her own afterlife journey myth, as we shall see later in this chapter).

Ten years later, Inana wishes to make furniture from the tree, though a "snake, thunderbird, and Demon-maiden" have nested in it. She first asks Utu for help, but he refuses. She then asks Bilgames, and he agrees. He removes the creatures from the tree, and cuts it into timber for Inana. He also makes two "playthings" from the wood—probably a ball and mallet—but he loses them when they fall into the underworld. Bilgames sits down at the entrance to the underworld—the "gates of Ganzer"—and cries.[8]

His servant, Enkidu, volunteers to go after the playthings. Bilgames warns Enkidu that he must not call attention to himself in the underworld by wearing clean clothes, fine ointments, or sandals; hurling throwsticks; shouting, kissing, or beating his wife; or insulting the spirits by holding a "cornel wood stick." This type of stick was used by Nergal to beat the newly arrived dead.[9] If Enkidu does any of these things, he risks being detained by underworld beings.

Meanwhile, in the underworld, Ninlil weeps disconsolately. She's naked, and her skin shines, her "fingernails she wields like a rake," and she pulls her hair out "like leeks." She's mourning for her son Ninazu, who is the earliest known underworld deity. Ninazu was associated with spring rain and ritual bathing, and was known for playing a musical instrument and singing sweetly.[10]

Enkidu has now embarked on his underworld journey and has done everything precisely as Bilgames had instructed him *not* to do. When Enkidu is captured, Bilgames seeks help from Enlil, telling him that Enkidu was not taken by the underworld deities Namtar, Asag, or Nergal, nor by "Nergal's pitiless sheriff," but by the underworld itself. The distinction here is likely that Enkidu did not die but descended willingly. Enlil refuses to help, and when Bilgames asks Nanna, the moon god, he also refuses.

Bilgames finally succeeds when Enki agrees to assist him in retrieving Enkidu. He instructs Utu to "open a hole in the underworld" and to bring Enkidu out "by means of [Utu's] phantom," apparently meaning the sun itself as opposed to Utu the sun-god. The sun then sets into the underworld and rises with Enkidu back to the Earth's surface.[11]

Upon Enkidu's return, Bilgames pleads with him to describe the underworld, though Enkidu warns him that it will make him weep. Bilgames persists, and Enkidu describes the dead as being like an "old garment the lice devour" and "a crack in the ground . . . filled with dust." He then explains how the afterlife fates of men are determined by the number of sons they have. The man with one son weeps because of the loss of his home, suggesting he's unhappy to be in the otherworld. The man with two sons has only bricks for a seat and eats only bread. The man with three drinks water from a skin on his saddle, while the man with four rejoices "like a man who has four donkeys." The man with five sons is allowed entry into the otherworld palace "like a fine scribe." The man with six has a joyous heart "like a man with ploughs in harness." The man with seven sons sits on a throne with the gods and hears proceedings and judgments.

In contrast, those with no heirs eat bread like bricks. Eunuchs sit uselessly in a corner, and childless women are considered as worthless as a broken or defective pot. They are cast aside and no one will have sex with them. Somewhat obscurely, young men who never undressed their wives weep over "a hand-worked rope," while women who never undressed their husbands weep over a reed mat.

Other fates depend on how the deceased died. Lepers twitch and are eaten by worms, or they eat "uprooted grass and roots for water," ostracized from the underworld city. A man who died in battle has his head cradled by his parents, while his wife weeps. Stillborn infants "play at a table of gold and silver, laden with honey and ghee." A man who died an early death lies "on the bed of the gods." A man who was burned to death rises to the sky: "his ghost was not there, his smoke went up to the heavens." Those who were eaten by lions lament the loss of their hand and foot. A man who drowned or who suffered from pellagra "twitches like an ox as the maggots consume him."

Disrespecting parents leads to constant thirst and only minute rations of water. If a man is cursed by his parents, he is "deprived of an heir, his ghost still roams." Blasphemers and cheaters of gods are denied water, while others are given only dirty water to drink. Those without funerary offerings eat crumbs and table scraps.[12]

The passage does much to refute the generally accepted scholarly notion that Mesopotamians believed in only a single gloomy afterlife state for everyone. It instead demonstrates a range of possible fates based on one's earthly behavior, social hierarchies, mode of death, and other circumstances. Certainly many will suffer in various ways, though some will rest, have good cheer, and dwell in a city with palaces where they may eat, drink, have sex, and dwell with the gods.

The Assyriologist Dina Katz argues that "Bilgames, Enkidu and the Underworld" is actually saying the opposite of what it appears to say: that the afterlife is really nothing but gloom. She bases her argument on the fact that when Enkidu is trying to help reconcile Bilgames to his mortality, he describes in graphic detail the fate of the corpse and its decomposition, saying that it will make Bilgames cry.[13] This argument, however, seems to conflate the fate of the corpse and the fate of the soul: while the corpse will inevitably rot, the soul has multiple possibilities, depending on individual circumstances, as Enkidu relates. Enkidu is thus helping Bilgames to accept his physical mortality by revealing to him the secret of spiritual immortality.

Gilgamesh's Journeys to Paradise

Although similar to the Sumerian texts, the Old Babylonian Version of the *Epic of Gilgamesh*, dating to around 1700 BCE, includes the hero's journey to the paradisiacal land of Dilmun (modern-day Bahrain). Gilgamesh travels there to seek Utnapishtim, the Babylonian version of Ziusudra. The name Utnapishtim means "he found life,"[14] and Gilgamesh hopes to learn from him the secret of immortality.

Although Utnapishtim resides in earthly Dilmun, the way there is portrayed as an otherworld journey. The land itself was seen as a "pristine" place where animals do not kill or steal food from humans; a place of silence, light, peace, fresh water, and fields abounding in grain; without disease, old age, or darkness.[15]

Gilgamesh first travels around mountains and along "the hidden road where the sun rises." The road is "hidden" because it leads beneath the earth at night, indicating that Gilgamesh actually travels through the underworld. The mountains reach to the heavens above and to the underworld below. The Sumerian word for "netherworld," *Kur*, also meant "mountains," and in a temple hymn, it is described as a "primeval place, deep mountain founded in an artful fashion, shrine, terrifying place lying in a pasture, a dread whose lofty ways none can fathom . . . your exterior is raised up . . . your interior is where the sun rises."[16] This suggests that the netherworld had associations not only with descent and darkness, but with also with ascent and light.

Gilgamesh asks Shamash, which is the Babylonian name for the sun-god, if the netherworld is a place of rest. He adds, "I have been asleep all these years [or perhaps, "I shall lie asleep down all the years"], but now let my eyes look on the sun so I am sated with light. The darkness is hidden, how much light is there? When may a dead man see the rays of the sun?"[17] Some scholars assume that these are rhetorical questions, intended to characterize the afterlife as a realm of sleep and darkness. However, Gilgamesh may genuinely be seeking answers, a notion supported by his curiosity about the afterlife in "Bilgames, Enkidu and the Underworld," and by his general preoccupation with discovering the secrets of immortality. That he addresses these questions to the sun-god before entering the mountain further demonstrates that he is indeed embarking on a solar-underworld journey.[18]

The ferryman, Sursunabu, then agrees to take Gilgamesh across the ocean to Utnapishtim. Gilgamesh first smashes the "Stone Ones," which impedes their crossing for they "must not touch the Waters of Death." This underworld river leads to the cosmic realm of the god Ea, the Babylonian equivalent of Enki. Gilgamesh cuts punting poles for the ferryman, but here the text breaks off.[19] We know from "The Death of Bilgames," however, that he succeeded in reaching Ziusudra in Dilmun.

In the Standard Version of the *Epic*, dating to some 500 years later,

Gilgamesh encounters an awe-inspiring, terrifying gate on the journey and is interrogated by the Scorpion People who guard the sun's gates at both horizons.[20] After entering the mountain, he outruns the sun and emerges before it into the bright light of a jeweled garden. This has been interpreted by the Finnish Assyriologist Simo Parpola as symbolizing the attainment of "ultimate wisdom," with the *Epic* as a whole being "a mystical path of spiritual growth culminating in the acquisition of superior esoteric knowledge." Benjamin Foster has also noted that a main theme of these texts is the acquisition of knowledge through netherworld experiences. Gilgamesh's transformation in Dilmun is symbolized when he is bathed and given new clothes.[21]

Utnapishtim reveals to Gilgamesh divine secrets and mysteries, particularly concerning the plant of rejuvenation. Gilgamesh finds the plant in the cosmic waters of the underworld, though later it is taken from him by a snake that sheds its skin as it slithers away, symbolic of rebirth.

It's important to clarify that while Bilgames failed in his quest for physical immortality in this life, he succeeded in gaining spiritual immortality in the otherworld. This is, in fact, the secret of the afterlife as revealed by Enkidu in "Bilgames, Enkidu, and the Underworld" as we have seen above. It also reflects the Prologue of the text, where it states that Gilgamesh "saw what was secret and revealed what was hidden."[22]

The Standard Version also features a descent of Enkidu into the underworld, though it contains no significant additions or contradictions to the other texts considered here. In fact, it mirrors parts of the much older Sumerian myth of "Inana's Descent to the Netherworld," which we turn to now.

Myths of Inana and Dumuzid

"Inana's Descent to the Netherworld"

Part of the function of this myth was to explain the circuit of Venus, with which Inana was associated, though it also embodies important teachings about the afterlife. It tells of how Inana wishes to conquer the underworld.

She dresses in fine clothes and adorns herself with jewelry and makeup, and by doing so she takes the seven *Me* with her. *Me* is both the concept of divine law and the power by which it's maintained. The seven *Me* are represented by each of Inana's adornments and items of clothing.

Before descending, Inana instructs her minister, Ninshubura, to perform mourning rituals for her. She also tells him to ask her father, Enlil, to protect her from being "killed in the underworld." If Enlil will not help, Ninshubura should try Nanna, then Enki (just as Bilgames did in "Bilgames, Enkidu and the Underworld").

Arriving at "the palace Ganzer" where her sister Ereshkigala dwells, Inana belligerently pushes on the gates and shouts for Neti, the gatekeeper: "I am all alone and I want to come in."

Neti asks, "Who are you?"

"I am Inana going to the east," replies Inana.

Neti asks why she wishes to go to the place from which no one returns, and Inana explains that she wishes to attend the funeral of her brother-in-law, Gudgalana. Neti goes to consult Ereshkigala, whose appearance is similar to that of Ninlil in "Bilgames, Enkidu and the Underworld"—naked, with long fingernails and hair like leeks.

In response to Inana's request, Ereshkigala slaps her thigh and bites her lip, and instructs Neti to bolt the seven gates of the underworld—but to let "each door of the palace Ganzer be opened separately." This will allow Inana into the palace, but she will not be able to escape the underworld as the gates lock behind her.

As Inana proceeds, at each gate an article of her clothing or other adornment is removed from her, including her lapis lazuli "measuring rod and measuring line" and her "garment of ladyship." Each time this happens, she asks, "What is this?" and each time Neti replies that Inana must not question "the rites of the underworld." She must be content that its "divine power has been fulfilled." Undressing the goddess of love also has a definite sexual and fertility element, associating the underworld with rebirth. Perhaps more importantly, however, since her garments represent the seven *Me*, she's being stripped of her divine power.

When Inana arrives, she removes Ereshkigala from her throne and sits upon it herself. This angers the seven Anuna judges, who shout at her, judge her, and find her guilty. As punishment they turn her into a corpse, which they hang on a hook.

After three days and nights, Ninshubura carries out the instructions Inana had left him. He asks Enlil and Nanna for help in rescuing her, but they refuse, answering that she should not have tried to usurp the powers of the underworld. "Whoever gets them must remain in the underworld," they explain, for "who, having got to that place, could then expect to come up again?"

Enki, however, does agree to help. From the dirt on his fingernails, he creates a *galatura* and a *kurngara*—cult singers and dancers in the earthly temple of Inana—and gives them the "life-giving plant" and the "life-giving waters." He instructs them to search the underworld palace like "flies" and "phantoms." They do so, and find Ereshkigala exhausted and disheveled "on account of her children." The *galatura* and *kurngara* win her favor by commiserating about her liver and heart, and she offers to grant them a wish. They insist that she swears upon it, which she does—but then offers them a river full of water and a field full of grain in lieu of granting their wish. The *galatura* and *kurngara* refuse both and ask instead for Inana's corpse.

Reluctantly, Ereshkigala gives them the corpse, and they revive Inana with the life-giving plant and water. Inana then prepares to ascend back to Earth, but she is stopped by the Anuna, who demand a substitute if she is to leave the underworld. Several armed demons surround her on all sides and escort her back to Earth to find one. The demons, called *galla*, don't eat or drink, make love, or have children, and are known for breaking families apart. They are nonhuman entities native to the netherworld. *Galla* was also the word for the earthly city officials responsible for the release of corpses to their families. Their underworld equivalents were characterized as agents of death, deputies, police, executioners, or even "bandits."[23]

These demons try to capture Ninshubura and other servants and worshippers who remained loyal to Inana, but she prevents them from doing so. Inana then sees Dumuzid, extravagantly dressed, sitting on a throne, and clearly not mourning for her. Angered by this, Inana commands the *galla* to take him to the underworld. Dumuzid prays to Utu to assist him in escaping by transforming his "hands to snake's hands" and his feet "to snake's feet." Utu obliges, and Dumuzid is saved.[24]

Filled with regret at her treatment of Dumuzid, Inana is told by a fly that she will find him in a pub. In order to lessen his time in the underworld, she decides that he and his sister, Geshtinana, will each spend six months of the year there. An incantation text relates that Geshtinana becomes an underworld scribe, keeping records on the lives and deaths of every person. She is sometimes associated with Ningishzida's wife Ninazimua, who is also an underworld scribe. Ninshubura becomes an underworld minister.[25]

According to the Assyriologist Thorkild Jacobsen, the story is actually a combination of three causally linked death-and-rebirth myths. Dumuzid is associated in a fertility context with the grain from which beer is made and in a descent context to beer being stored underground. "Geshtinana" means "the leafy grape vine"—a symbol of abundance and fertility. The connection between grain and grape here is that grain is harvested in the spring, then brewed and stored, while grapes are harvested in the autumn. This corresponds to the six alternating months each sibling spends in the underworld. The third linked myth is that of Enki, associated with spring waters, who causes the fertility goddess Inana's revival.[26]

Dumuzid and Geshtinana in the Netherworld

In the poem "Dumuzid and Geshtinana," demons encourage Inana to conquer the netherworld. To placate them, she instead gives them Dumuzid. They put his feet, hands, and neck in stocks, and "copper pins, nails and pokers were raised to his face." The demons sharpen their axes, make Dumuzid stand and sit, strip him naked, do "evil" to him, and cover "his face with his own garment." Dumuzid prays to Utu for help, and is transformed into part-snake and part-"soaring falcon," enabling him to escape and return to Geshtinana.

The poem "The Most Bitter Cry" tells of how Dumuzid falls into a river while being chased in the desert by "seven evil deputies of the netherworld." Near an apple tree on the riverbank, he's carried into the netherworld, a place where things simultaneously *are* and are *not*, with "cattle pens that are no cattle pens" and food and water that are not food and water. Although this is usually seen as the netherworld being a vague half-life, it could instead mean that seemingly physical objects are in immaterial form in the afterlife, or perhaps a reversal of the earthly order. In a lamentation text, an underworld messenger comes for a woman, "yet he has not come. He has eyes but he cannot see. He has a mouth but he cannot converse."[27]

"In the Desert by the Early Grass" is a collection of ritual laments to Dumuzid and gods associated with him. They include Ishtaran, with "bright visage," a snake god of borders and justice; Damu, a healing god, associated with spring tree sap; and Ninazu and Ningishzida, whom we have already met. Other netherworld beings include Alla, "master of the battle-net"; Ningishzida's assistant Dimpikug, and his deified harp Lugalshudi; Lusiranna, associated with clouds and rain; Niminur, meaning both "spider" and "frisky bull," who was the spouse of Nanshe, the fertility goddess associated with dreams; and Malaka, "king of warriors."[28]

The laments refer to Damu as "the dead anointed one," and describe how he is taken to the netherworld by demons—blindfolded, restrained, and forbidden to sleep. His mother wishes to follow, believing he will return "out of the spring grass." At the base of a mountain, she passes down the "road of no return to him who lies in blood and water, the sleeping lord, to the traces of kings, to the grange of the anointed ones, the dining hall of the linen-clad ones" (the latter being priests).[29]

As a disembodied spirit, Damu says he's "lying in" the winds, "in the lightnings and in tornadoes," and therefore his mother cannot follow. Because she is a living person, she would also be unable to consume the netherworld food and drink, even though Damu is able to.

Damu meets spirits of the dead on the road to the netherworld, though he's unaware that he himself is one of them. He encounters a lost ghost child, and the soul of a singer promises to stay with it, adding, "As for me, setting up a spirit harp in the wind, what matters it? I am one versed in understanding spirits, in dirges, what matters now my understanding?"

Damu has the ghosts take a message to his mother, asking her to rescue him by bribing the netherworld ranger. The ghosts are unable to make the living hear them, though Damu does somehow manage to communicate to his mother: "dig up my blood for me, the which you are to chop up." She is to then take the pieces to Damu's sister, a divine leech called Amashilama (who's also a sister of Ningishzida). Amashilama is to brew beer from the congealed blood, which Damu is to drink, thus incorporating his own body within his spirit-self in order to be restored to life.

Somehow, Damu only realizes that he's dead when he's told that his mother and sister are looking for him and preparing the blood-beer to revive him. He says he is not in the grass, which will grow for his mother again, nor in the waters, which will rise. His mother blesses him, addressing her blessing "toward the foundations of heaven, toward the foundations of earth."

Amashilama dies and joins Damu in the netherworld, remarking that his face has become "luxuriant" and "lush." She tells Damu, "the day that dawns for you, will also dawn for me; the day you see, I shall also see." This shows that there's daytime in the netherworld, inverse to the earthly day-night cycle.[30]

More Sumerian Afterlife Journey Myths

"Ningishzida's Journey to the Netherworld"

This myth tells of how Ningishzida became an underworld deity. As he lies dying, he's commanded to "arise" and board the ferry to the underworld. "Arise" may refer to the spirit rising from the body. Ningishzida protests that he is young and doesn't want to die.

His sister Amashilama (here described as a cow deity rather than a leech) laments as he is being taken away on the boat. She prays to go with him, and tries to follow. Ningishzida doesn't notice her at first, but a demon calls his attention to her. Ningishzida tries to discourage her, describing the underworld as a place where the river has no water, the fields have no grain, and the sheep have no wool; therefore one cannot eat, drink, or be clothed. He tells her, "I am a field threshed by my demon—you would scream at it. He has put manacles on my hands—you would scream at it. He has put a neck-stock on my neck—you would scream at it."

Amashilama attempts to bribe the demon with her jewelry, though she fails. Ningishzida now relents and commands the ferrymen to wait for her. He rejoices when she boards. There's a gap in the text here, though it seems that another deity intervenes and the siblings are saved. Ningishzida is made divine throne-bearer of the netherworld, complete with scepter, crown, and "holy robe of office." The demon is warned not to raise his hand against Ningishzida, who is now happy and joyful, eating food, drinking wine, bathing, and being welcomed by his throne and bed.[31]

Ningishzida is associated with Damu and various other underworld deities, though a temple hymn describes him as "the holy one of heaven," and "the prince who stretches out his pure hand." Elsewhere, he is characterized as a hero unequalled in heaven, a commander who carries out "the underworld's business," "foremost one, leader of the assembly, king endowed with awesomeness, sun of the masses." An incantation to Utu mentions one who is seized by Ningishzida, only then to be allowed to pass.[32]

"The Death of Ur-Namma"

This hymn describes the afterlife journey of the historical king Ur-Namma, who died around 2096 BCE. He undertakes a "desolate" journey to the underworld, here called Arali, traveling by donkey and chariot, laden with gifts of livestock and luxury goods for the "seven chief porters of the underworld" and the various gods in their palaces.

He's cheered upon his arrival and provided with a banquet. Food in the underworld is otherwise bitter and the water is brackish. A statement that "after seven days, ten days had passed" may indicate that time passes more quickly in the underworld.

Ur-Namma is given a house, a throne, and "all the soldiers who had been killed by weapons and all the men who had been found guilty." He becomes an underworld judge alongside his brother Bilgames. This presumably meant that they were symbolically brothers, because Bilgames would have ruled hundreds of years earlier.

Despite his privileged position, Ur-Namma mourns the loss of his earthly life, missing his family, and wishing he could complete projects he had begun on Earth.[33]

"Enlil and Ninlil"

A section of this creation myth tells of how "the fifty great gods and the seven gods who decide destinies" deem it to be "ritually impure" when Enlil and Ninlil have sex. They have Enlil arrested and taken to the underworld. Ninlil follows, pregnant with the moon-god Suen, another name for Nanna.

At the city gate, Enlil arranges to trade places with the gatekeeper. He does the same with the guardian of the "man-eating" river and with the ferryman, so he can impersonate them all when Ninlil arrives. Each time, he pretends to her that he doesn't know where Enlil is. Ninlil offers to have sex with each man as she proceeds, ignorant of the fact that they are all Enlil in disguise.

Enlil always consents, however, and each time they have sex, he impregnates her progressively with Nergal, Ninazu, and the god Enbilulu, "inspector of canals" (perhaps here relating to the waters of the underworld). The narrative thus explains the birth of at least two underworld deities, as well as the moon-god, in a context that associates the afterlife with sex, fertility, and celestial bodies. Elsewhere, Enlil is described as refreshing himself "in the deep underworld, the holy chamber."[34]

Etana and Other Heavenly Ascents

Etana is referred to on the Sumerian king list as ruler of the city-state Kish around 2900–2600 BCE, though it's uncertain if he was a real historical figure. His ascent to the heavenly realm is referred to in the king list and is also depicted on Akkadian cylinder seals from 2390–2249 BCE.[35]

In an elegy, the soul of a deceased person requests assistance from Etana along with various underworld gods, placing him in an afterlife context. The relevance of an *ascended* king to the underworld journey of the deceased isn't fully clear—but it could mean that the deceased joined Etana in the heavenly realm after a time in the underworld, or that Etana descended to the underworld after his ascent. Etana is in the underworld in the Standard Version of the *Epic of Gilgamesh* and is often listed among underworld gods in later incantations.[36]

The earliest accounts of Etana's ascent are found in Assyrian texts dating to 1500–600 BCE. They tell the story of Etana seeking the "plant of birth" from Ishtar, the Babylonian name for Inana. He experiences a visionary dream of the heavenly realm in which he travels through the gates of various gods before arriving at the house of Ishtar. When lions spring at him from beneath a throne, he awakens. He was also said to have been taken to heaven by an eagle. Echoing the myth of Gilgamesh, the plant of birth, as well as Etana wishing to "disclose concealed things," suggests rebirth and the attainment of knowledge in the spiritual realm.[37]

Another reference to ascent occurs in the Old Babylonian creation myth of Atrahasis, whose name translates as "Surpassing Wise." In it, the mother-goddess Mami, known in Sumer as Ninhursaga, contemplates escaping from Earth, the "abode of grief." She wonders, "Should I go up to heaven, I would take up my dwelling in a well-provisioned house."[38]

Inana, of course, also ascends, being the Morning Star, and the prominence of her descent myth makes her ascent relevant here. In a

Sumerian hymn she is described as ascending to heaven "like a warrior among youths and heroes."³⁹ This shows that heavenly ascent was a possibility for at least some segments of society.

Ascent is also mentioned in an elegy, with the prayer, "May Utu bring forth for you bright light from the netherworld . . . May Ninkura [the mountain goddess, daughter of Enki and Ninhursaga] stand by you, may she raise you high."⁴⁰ As we saw in "Bilgames, Enkidu and the Underworld," those who are burned to death ascend to heaven, and Enkidu is rescued from the underworld via the ascending sun. In "The Death of Bilgames," the hero's journey should also be considered an ascent since he reaches Dilmun ahead of the rising sun.

Other Afterlife Texts

A late-third-millennium "prayer for a dead person pleading to be admitted to the netherworld" expresses hope that the underworld palace will provide "clear water to me in the forest where *gur* birds live," and notes that a "great oven is lighted" there. The deceased hopes that the door leading to the otherworld will remain open and unbolted, for its crossbar to "be the Lama [protector deity] at my favorable side that shines brightly on my right shoulder," and for the gate to be "proud" of the deceased. With Inana in the lead and the soul's personal god in the rear, "May my gatekeeper bow down, so that I might raise my neck on high!"⁴¹

The translator Niek Veldhuis suggests that the text indicates that "the dead have to cross a fire in order to reach the netherworld." This is based on his identification of the palace as Ganzer, and the observation that *ganzer* is the same word for "flame." He further states that the "great oven" and the request for water attest to extreme heat, and that the forest is "inhospitable" and dangerous to cross.⁴² The text, however, may not have been intended to be so ominous. A palace in a forest full of birds is not necessarily a negative place. Birds were associated with souls of the dead at least by the first millennium, and it is conceivable that they have a similar symbolism here. The oven may be welcoming, associated with warmth, food, and home—particularly given that it is coupled with the reference to "clear water." Both the identification of the palace as Ganzer and the connection between *ganzer* and "flame" are not verified. In fact, the two words are actually spelled differently, and *ganzer* can also mean "darkness." Finally, it's doubtful that the deceased would be praying for admittance to the underworld if it were a strictly dangerous, objectionable place. Indeed, a proverb refers to the underworld as "the most honored place." An elegy wishes contentment for the deceased in the underworld, saying "may your spirit be pleased, may your heart be at rest," and may the gods provide "fresh food."[43]

In an inscription on an axe dedicated to Nergal, he is described as "full of furious might, an angry sea, inspiring fearsome terror . . . a dragon covered with gore, drinking the blood of living creatures." At the same time, Nergal has the power to "create life," to "determine destinies," to "render judgments," and "to carry off and to bring back"—a possible reference to bringing people back from death, as mentioned earlier. His "terrifying anger smites the wicked . . . single-handed crusher who tortures the disobedient, fearsome terror of the Land, giving just verdicts like the noble youth Utu."[44] The fact that Nergal's verdicts are "just" is a further indication that he is a complex deity and not simply a demonic torturer, and that there he bestows both positive and negative afterlife fates. The prayer, "may he provide me with clean water in the underworld after my death" shows that access to clean water is a possibility, and that thirst or drinking brackish water are not the only options. The same may be said for the wishes expressed for food and clean water in the afterlife in "Bilgames, Enkidu, and the Underworld," "The Death of Ur-Namma," and elsewhere.

Understanding the Mesopotamian Afterlife Experience

The widespread view that the Mesopotamian afterlife was universally gloomy, shadowy, negative, and not determined by a process of judgment has a long and prestigious pedigree. In the 1940s, Thorkild Jacobsen characterized Mesopotamian death beliefs "as an almost complete destruction of the personality." Over half a century later, Bottéro described it as "inevitable indefinite drowsiness," stating that the only basic, unwavering belief throughout Mesopotamian literature "is that death put an end to all that is positive, bright, noisy, joyous, active, comforting, and happy in our existence."[45]

The texts reviewed here tell a different story. Decades of adhering to this scholarly "received wisdom" has resulted in references to judgment and to more-positive afterlife descriptions being overlooked. The numerous afterlife judges, rejoicing, banquets, meeting deceased relatives, and becoming or dwelling among gods are either ignored or interpreted to conform with the preconceptions. Katz, for example, argues that because positive afterlife possibilities are described in "Bilgames, Enkidu and the Underworld," it "is not a reliable source" for our understanding of the afterlife conceptions of the period. Likewise, Jerrold S. Cooper sees the judgment-based afterlife in the text as heterodox, in contrast to the orthodox view of simple afterlife "gloom."[46]

It's more productive—and accurate—to view Mesopotamian afterlife conceptions not in terms of orthodox versus heterodox, but in terms of the multiplicity of beliefs and possible fates actually found throughout the texts (that is, not exclusively in "Bilgames, Enkidu and the Underworld").

The reasons for the prevailing views may be found in the history of the study of Mesopotamian religion, which is rooted in Old Testament theology. Because of historical, cultural, literary, and (in the case of Akkadian) linguistic connections, it seems that scholars have regarded Hebrew and Mesopotamian traditions as bearing more similarities than is actually evident from the existing sources. In other words, characterizations of the Mesopotamian afterlife have been influenced by the cultural traditions of scholars themselves, habitually viewing the evidence through a lens of presumed darkness and gloom, which has impacted the study of the subject to the present day. In the Hebrew Bible, everyone goes to the realm of the dead called Sheol, described only as a subterranean place of joyless silence and darkness, where souls exist without memory.[47] There is famously precious little on the afterlife in the Hebrew Bible—in contrast to Mesopotamia—and it contains nothing like the texts discussed here.

The claim that Mesopotamian afterlife beliefs did not include judgment and was morally neutral has been particularly overstated. In the 1960s, the comparative religion scholar S. G. F. Brandon, for example, went so far as to suggest that there is no judgment because there is nothing to be judged—the person disintegrates in an "irreparable shattering of the psycho-physical organism." As seen here, however, this was clearly not the case. There was indeed judgment, and the usual fate of the deceased was certainly not annihilation.[48]

Although Bottéro acknowledged that afterlife fates were actually determined by one's "conditions on earth," he also claimed that the otherworld was almost universally a realm of "despondency and torpor," where only a lucky few were marginally better off. He further wrote that judgment didn't involve any sort of logical process or decision at all, let alone one based upon morality, and that one's afterlife fate was a matter of "chance." Not only does this conflict with what we have actually seen in the ancient texts, there are deeper problems with these characterizations. For one thing, it's possible that a person's conditions and social status in life were determined by the gods according to their behavior. This would amount to a form of "premortem" judgment that has consequences in the afterlife. This was the case with Mesoamerican afterlife beliefs, as we shall see, which *also* featured judgment in the underworld. It may be *technically* correct that "there is no indication that it was believed that a just man would enjoy a better afterlife than his less virtuous neighbor," as Harriet Crawford put it,[49] but it may rather have been a case of what's right and proper—what upholds the principles of *Me*. "Bilgames, Enkidu and the Underworld" shows that it was deemed right and proper to have many sons, for example. While it's not necessarily virtuous or just, virtue and justice are, after all, culturally relative concepts. For Mesopotamians, it may have been "just" for the diseased to continue to suffer in the afterlife if the gods had decided that they "deserved" to be diseased on Earth in the first place. That is, they may have been judged premortem by the gods to suffer both on Earth and in the underworld.

Moreover, the texts *do* have references to "just verdicts" and the "wicked" being punished. The life review in "The Death of Bilgames" clearly demonstrates that Bilgames's good deeds and righteous behavior were evaluated by the gods in the process of deciding his afterlife fate. Again, whether heroic exploits, piety, and building temples to the gods can be called "just" is debatable, though these things certainly reflect the Mesopotamian ideal of royal character and virtue. Similarly, the soldiers and guilty men in "The Death of Ur-Namma" were seen as being in a different category from others, and received a correspondingly different afterlife fate.

Katz acknowledges that in "Bilgames, Enkidu and the Underworld" one's "previous conduct during life" was linked with afterlife judgment, though as mentioned earlier, she doesn't see the text as a true expression of Sumerian beliefs.[50] But the existence of so many otherworld judges throughout the texts reveals both that there were souls to be judged and that some of them must have been given better fates than others. The Anuna, Nergal, Bilgames, Utu, Ur-Namma, and even the man with seven sons in "Bilgames, Enkidu and the Underworld" are all underworld judges. In addition to these, the moon-god Nanna carries out judgment and decides "sublime verdicts" in the underworld, and Enki and his wife Ninki "determine fates" there. The deity Hendursaga was described as "accountant" and "chief constable of the dead people who are brought to the underworld." There are also numerous references to throne-bearers, sheriffs, gatekeepers, porters, scribes, ferrymen, and so on.[51] The existence of this complex bureaucratic afterlife infrastructure is obviously explicable only if there's a need to judge and process the souls of individuals who arrive in the underworld after death. It's inconceivable that judgment could be such a clear feature of the realm of the dead but that the dead themselves are not judged. Any speculation that the function of this infrastructure was to judge other gods, or earthly matters, or to settle internal underworld disputes is not sustainable in light of the afterlife contexts themselves. The contexts tell us exactly what these texts are about.

Even more evidence of afterlife judgment is found in the "Hymn to Nungal," a prison deity, daughter of Ereshkigala, and self-proclaimed underworld ruler. While it primarily concerns a prison, or "prison-temple," it uses the underworld as a metaphor to warn readers of possible parallel fates in this life and the next. This is most forceful with the idea of judgment, wherein the prison is described as "underworld, mountain where Utu rises. . . . House which chooses the righteous and the wicked. . . . The gods of heaven and earth bow down before its place where judgments are made." The metaphor is further strengthened by the reference to the underworld as a prison in the poem, "In the Desert by the Early Grass."[52] In an elegy, the deceased is informed that "Utu, the great lord of the netherworld, after turning the dark places to light, will judge your case." It continues, "May Nanna decree your fate on the day of sleep," followed by a prayer asking a goddess to show pity. In a "Prayer-letter to Enki," a man in the netherworld asks the god for pity, adding "After you will turn my dark place into light I shall sit in your gate of 'Guilt-Absolved' and sing your praise."[53]

Any remaining doubt that there was individual judgment based on earthly behavior is dispelled by this passage in which a youth prays to his god:

after you have made me know my sins, at the city's gate I would declare them, ones forgotten and ones visible. I will declare my sins before you. In the assembly may tears rain like drizzle. . . . May your holy heart have mercy and compassion for me. . . . May your heart, an awe-inspiring wave, be restored toward me.[54]

Judgment obviously implies that there were different afterlife fates determined by the outcome. If there was only one vaguely negative experience for everyone, judgment would be pointless. This is also supported by archaeological evidence of burial sites. They demonstrate that the degree of comfort one may expect in the afterlife is proportionate to the quality and quantity of one's grave goods, reflecting a belief in a diversity of possible fates.⁵⁵ Expressing *hope* for a positive afterlife indicates *belief* in one. Positive afterlife possibilities are described in "Bilgames, Enkidu and the Underworld," in "The Death of Ur-Namma," and in texts referencing ascent. The lapis lazuli mountain in "Inana's Descent to the Netherworld" suggests beauty and riches rather than gloom and despair. The underworld and especially its deities are often portrayed as radiant with light. A hymn to Nergal says that it has an "awesome radiance." In his capacity of underworld judge, Enki is described as a being of light, illuminating darkness and radiating beauty and joy. Lugalera, a shepherd aspect of Dumuzid, is described as emitting "a bright light" to the underworld princes as they bow before him.⁵⁶ The dream-god Sissig is also a being of light, as is his father Utu.

In contrast, there are actually only three references to netherworld darkness in the texts, and two of them also describe the darkness being illuminated by Utu or Sissig. In the Old Babylonian "Sunset Prayer," Utu is is the "judge of those above and below," emerging in the morning at the "level place"; that is, the horizon where judgment took place. Together with an elegy emphasizing his role as underworld judge, a connection is clear between divine light and the process of judgment, or "the judging of a dead individual with the bringing of light to the netherworld" as Wolfgang Heimpel put it. After judgment, the sun continues its progress back to the heavens, leaving the underworld once again in darkness—meaning that half the time it was actually illuminated.⁵⁷ The Old Testament theologian Klass Spronk argues that the Mesopotamian ideal was to become divine in the afterlife and dwell forever with the sun-god, though most were resigned to a gloomy fate. The exceptions of Ziusudra and Etana show that a beatific afterlife was at least a possibility, even if a remote one. Dilmun was also a paradisiacal place of creation and immortality.⁵⁸

As with some Egyptologists, rather than accepting that difficulties of interpretation lie with us, some Assyriologists believe that the problem lies with the very people whose myths and beliefs we are trying to interpret. Bottéro, for example, argued that Mesopotamian afterlife beliefs were based on dreams and that they are thus "contradictory, like everything else that comes out of the imagination alone." They were, he alleged, illogical, "confused," vague, and "full of inconsistencies and variable or contradictory elements." He even went so far as to claim that the Mesopotamians were incapable of thinking in abstract terms.[59] Once again, the texts themselves prove otherwise, being filled with symbolism and earthly concepts with otherworldly counterparts, including locales and bureaucratic systems. Indeed, the very concept of nonphysical existence in a nonearthly realm demonstrates abstract thinking.

To view these texts as inherently defective denies their status as sources of spiritual or religious meaning. The possibility of multiple or even simultaneous beliefs, or of theologies involving concepts such as omnipresence or transcendence (as evident in the poem "In the Desert by the Early Grass"), is rarely considered. Bottéro went so far as to write that "There was absolutely nothing 'mystical' about Mesopotamian religion." Not only is this merely a subjective opinion, it doesn't seem to be based on a balanced or nuanced consideration of the evidence. Bottéro's literal-minded interpretation of the stripping of Inana, for example, was simply "death takes everything away from us."[60] This can't possibly do justice to such a complex and elaborate text, and certainly doesn't encapsulate its full meaning.

John D. Evers has a more compelling interpretation of "Inana's Descent to the Netherworld." He sees it as being "about the fracturing of the fundamental life-death dichotomy," and its integration through the constant cycle of death and rebirth.[61] The fact that Inana and Ereshkigala are sisters could represent a similar reconciliation of opposites—of heaven and the underworld. In fact, dual roles and abilities are found throughout the texts. Inana is said to have the power "to turn a man into a woman and a woman into a man." Ninshubura is sometimes referred to as male and sometimes as female and is characterized as both heavenly and underworldly. Ningishzida is both throne-bearer of the underworld and "holy one in heaven." Etana and Gilgamesh are underworld officials despite their heavenly ascent. The cosmic waters of Ea, which border paradise, are one and the same as the underworld Waters of Death.

The concept of death-and-rebirth also fits this pattern. That the cycle takes place in afterlife contexts shows that it encompassed the human world as well as the divine world, and the natural and cosmological worlds. The death-and-rebirth of the deceased was thus associated with the cycles of nature and with the descent and ascent of Inana/Venus, Utu/sun, and Nanna/moon. If everything in nature and the cosmos dies and is reborn following a descent into the netherworld, surely people must as well.[62]

Transformation and transcendence are recurring themes in the texts. Damu is transformed, transcends his own death, and is reborn after consuming beer made of his own blood. Inana becomes a corpse that is then reanimated, Bilgames an underworld judge, Ningishzida a throne-bearer, and so on. Other kings, including Bilgames's father Lugalbanda, achieved divinization. Some who journey to the otherworld become judges following their own judgment, hinting at a semidivine or at least spiritualized state. Although Bilgames is only half divine, he nevertheless becomes one of the Anuna gods. A reference to Inana as "the most awesome lady among the Anuna gods" could hint at self-judgment, for the Anuna are the very gods who judge her.

This pattern may extend to humans, who are partly divine to begin with, according to the Old Babylonian Atrahasis creation myth. The myth explains that the spiritual element in humans is actually the flesh of a slaughtered god, and it's because of this spark of divinity that people survive after death in spiritual form. The Sumerian word for "soul," *gedim*, is often written identically to the word *utukku*, "supernatural being." Names of deceased individuals were sometimes written with the designation "god" (*ilu*) and in the script reserved for gods. While there's a distinction between individuals who became spirits and those who became gods, divinization was perhaps not quite as restricted as one might gather from the literary texts, and spiritualization may have been common. Some rulers' names were written with the designation for "star," which might indicate a further distinction, between divinization and a stellar afterlife.[63]

The historian of religions Jonathan Z. Smith cautions that because Gilgamesh isn't entirely human, we shouldn't extrapolate human experiences from his experiences. Katz, however, categorizes both Gilgamesh and

Etana as human, as opposed to Dumuzid and Inana, for example. Both were purportedly historical, born as humans, and of earthly existence. That Bilgames's fate is exceptional is clear when he's told in "The Death of Bilgames" that "Another king there will never be, whose destiny is the same as yours."[64]

It's surely significant, in any case, that the divinity of these figures is directly related to their experiences in afterlife realms. Furthermore, "The Death of Ur-Namma" along with some of the hymns and elegies doesn't concern the descents and ascents of gods, but rather the expected afterlife experiences of humans. Those experiences include traveling though darkness, trials and obstacles, arriving in a realm of light, meeting a divinity of light who assists in the process of judgment, encounters with deceased relatives, an ultimate fate based upon one's earthly experience, transformation, transcendence, and perhaps omnipresence and divinization. Heimpel has shown that the various references to "the doors, bolts, keys, gates and gateways of heaven refer to the points of entry to and exit from the invisible world below the horizons," that is, the underworld. This suggests intermediate states of multiple experiences, transitions, and realms.[65]

Because Bilgames, Ur-Namma, and Etana were all historical figures, the accounts of their afterlife journeys could have been grounded in actual NDEs. Ur-Namma does not come back to life, and Etana's experience doesn't have a near-death context—though he does awaken after his heavenly journey. Only Bilgames returns from a temporary death, and therefore his account is the only one that could strictly qualify—and indeed may be the world's earliest recorded example of an NDE. "The Death of Bilgames" is also the only early Mesopotamian text that *seems* very much like an NDE, in both its structure and themes.

5

India

Paths of Gods and Ancestors

Ancient Indian Otherworld Journeys

There's a continuous stream of NDE-like afterlife journey narratives throughout ancient Indian religious history. They served to teach readers about the secrets of the afterlife and the nature of the soul, suggesting that the accounts were accepted as truth (or were at least intended to be). These stories seem to form a tradition within a tradition, and it's worth exploring them separately before moving on to Vedic afterlife beliefs chronologically.

A Boy Follows His Father to Yama's Realm (*Rig Veda*)

Our first journey to the realm of the dead appears in the *Rig Veda*, the earliest Indian religious text, dating to around 1500–900 BCE, if not earlier. This brief story is found in a hymn to Yama, Lord of the Dead and the first mortal ever to die.

It concerns a boy who travels to Yama's realm, Yamaloka, in search of his father. It seems that his father was to be reborn in Yama's realm because he had a son and because he had carried out correct sacrifices on Earth. Though he went there by following "the track of the ancient ones"—the ancestors—to the "leafy tree where Yama holds symposium with the gods," the boy is afraid to go "along yonder evil way." Instead, he makes a chariot with his mind that "faces in all directions"—suggesting some kind of visionary, shamanic, or out-of-body journey.

The hymn actually concludes with the boy's arrival in the other-world, at "the seat of Yama, which is called the palace of the gods. Here is his pipe blown; here is he adorned with hymns."[1] There's no description of the boy's return, so it isn't strictly an NDE-type narrative, but it seems to be a prototype for those that followed.

Bhrgu and Varuna I (*Shatapatha Brahmana*)

This story dates to sometime around 700–900 BCE, making it either contemporary with the above, or perhaps 200 years later. It also involves a boy traveling to the realm of the dead, though in this case he's sent there by his father, the god Varuna. The boy, named Bhrgu, thinks that he knows more than Varuna. In response, Varuna sends him on a journey to gain knowledge in the four quarters, which apparently are regions of hell. In each of them, Bhrgu sees men dismembering and devouring one another, "sitting in silence," or crying loudly.

The northeast, the direction of heaven, is treated as a fifth region. When Bhrgu arrives there, he meets Yama, who has yellow eyes and black skin. He's holding a stick and standing between an ugly woman and a beautiful woman. Bhrgu is so frightened that "terror seized him, and he went home, and sat down." His return to Earth allows us to categorize this as an NDE myth.

Varuna then explains the symbolic meaning of what his son saw, including that the women symbolized faith and lack of faith, and Yama symbolized wrath. This indicates afterlife judgment, in which Yama is the judge and the two women dispense the judgment, depending on a soul's faith or nonfaith.[2]

Bhrgu and Varuna II (*Jaiminiya Brahmana*)

Of a similar date, this is an alternative version of Bhrgu's afterlife journey in which the boy's "lifebreaths" are taken away by Varuna, causing him to lose consciousness: "Having fainted he passed from this world. He arrived in yonder world."

Bhrgu travels through six realms, and at the sights he sees in each of them he exclaims, "Ah! Has this really happened? What is the meaning of this?" Each time he's told, "Ask your father Varuna. He will explain it to you."

In the first three realms, men are dismembered and devoured by other men. In the fourth realm, Faith and Nonfaith guard "a secret treasure." In the fifth world are "two streams flowing on an even level." The first is filled with blood and is guarded by Yama, again called Wrath and described as "a naked black man with a club." His nakedness may symbolize fertility, or rebirth in the natural or newborn state.[3]

The second stream is filled with ghee from which men made of gold fill their golden cups with "all desires." Gold was symbolic of immortality, so the golden men may represent the divinized or blessed deceased. It's not clear if this realm is above, below, or level with Earth. The fourth and fifth worlds contain both positive and negative elements, and may have been transitional or intermediate.

The sixth realm, which is for the worthiest, is filled with beautiful fragrances, music, and dancing, singing, semi-divine nymphs called Apsarasas.[4] There are five rivers there, "with blue lotuses and white lotuses, flowing with honey like water."

After touring these six realms, Bhrgu revives and tells his father what he had seen. Varuna explains to him in symbolic terms the meanings of his experience: that each punishment corresponds to a specific transgression of the Agnihotra fire-sacrifice ritual. Animals, rice, and barley that have been improperly sacrificed take on human form in the other world and will eat those who conducted the rituals in ignorance. The victims will cry out in agony. This shows that there's a risk of the earthly order being reversed in the otherworld, for the things that are eaten on Earth will now eat those who ate them. The sacrifices of those who conduct the ritual without faith will be sent to the woman Nonfaith.

Concerning the two streams, Varuna explains that the blood in the first one belongs to those who have shed the blood of Brahmins (members of the priestly caste). The stream of ghee is for those with "true knowledge," faith, and a history of proper ritual participation. The souls of people who understand all this will achieve the sixth realm of lotuses if they correctly performed the Agnihotra.[5]

Rjishvan and Vrsashusma (*Jaiminiya Brahmana*)

In this story, a man named Rjishvan died suddenly while performing a sacrifice. His young son, Vrsashusma, wanted to complete the sacrifice on behalf of his father, even though he was in mourning. But he, too, lost consciousness.

Vrsashusma "went to the world beyond, and in that world he came to his father." It was a beautiful realm, but not as beautiful as the one that awaited Vrsashusma, his father told him. When Vrsashusma asked why, his father explained that it was because the boy had carried out his vows of sacrifice better than he had. He told the boy, "Go back; you will complete the sacrifice. And whatever you desire, that desire will be fulfilled." The son returned to Earth and completed the sacrifice as instructed.[6]

Nachiketas and Yama (*Katha Upanishad*)

Our final narrative of a boy traveling to the otherworld is found in the *Katha Upanishad*, dating to perhaps the fifth century BCE. It begins with Nachiketas watching his father give away all his possessions. Puzzled by this, the boy asks, "Father, to whom will you give me?" Vajashravas ignores him so he asks again, and then again, at which point the father becomes so annoyed that he shouts, "I'll give you to Death!"—meaning, effectively, that he kills the boy.

Nachiketas goes to the otherworld, and he finds that Yama is away. The boy is left unattended without food for three days. When Yama finally arrives, he's abashed at his lapse in hospitality and grants Nachiketas three wishes.

The boy's first wish is for his father's kindness, and to be greeted by him joyfully when he returns to Earth (indicating that Nachiketas knows that his afterlife experience is temporary). Yama agrees, saying that Vajashravas's anger will be calmed, "seeing you released from the jaws of Death."

Nachiketas's second wish is for the mysteries of the fire-altar to be revealed, for it "leads to heaven." He also asks how "people who are in heaven enjoy the immortal state," but then seems to answer this himself, saying to Yama, "In the world of heaven there is no fear; there one has no fear of old age or you. Transcending both these—both hunger and thirst, beyond all sorrows, one rejoices in heaven."

Yama agrees to Nachiketas's wish to understand the Agnihotra, explaining that "the fire-altar that leads to heaven, to the attainment of an endless world . . . lies hidden, in the cave of the heart." Yama is so impressed with Nachiketas and his understanding of this wisdom that he gives the boy a "glittering disk of gold," which will help him attain a heavenly afterlife.[7] He explains:

uniting with the three, performing the triple rite, he crosses over birth and death. Perceiving the *brahman* [the Absolute, or Cosmic Principle] that is being born, as the god who is to be adored, recognizing this disk of gold to be that, he attains unending peace. . . . Piling the altar of Nachiketas, he shoves aside the fetters of death before him, passes beyond sorrow, and rejoices in heaven. This, Nachiketas, is your fire that leads to heaven, which you chose with your second wish. People will proclaim this your very own fire.[8]

For his third wish, Nachiketas seeks to understand the mysteries of the afterlife. He says to Yama, "There is this doubt about a man who is dead. 'He exists,' say some; others say, 'He exists not.' I want to know this."

Yama is reluctant to impart this wisdom to the boy, however, saying "it's hard to understand, it's a subtle doctrine. Make, Nachiketas, another wish. Do not press me! Release me from this."

Nachiketas persists, arguing that there is no one better than the Lord of Death to explain the secrets of the afterlife. Yama promises instead to give him a long life, riches, land, chariots, women, and even for all his desires to manifest at will—if only the boy will stop asking him about death.

But Nachiketas argues that such wealth is worthless after death and that people only live as long as Yama will allow. His wish remains to know only "what happens at that great transit" from this world to the next world.[9]

Eventually Yama reveals the importance of the word *Om*—a transcendent sound representing the divine and the cosmos:

> For this alone is the syllable that's *brahman*; for this alone is the syllable that's supreme! When, indeed, one knows this syllable, he obtains his every wish. . . . And when one knows this support, he rejoices in *brahman*'s world. The wise one—he is not born, he does not die; he has not come from anywhere; he has not become anyone. He is unborn and eternal, primeval and everlasting. And he is not killed, when the body is killed.[10]

Although the narrative doesn't describe Nachiketas's return to life, returning to Earth is included in his first wish, to which Yama agrees, giving the account an NDE context. That Nachiketas chooses knowledge for his other two wishes reinforces the connection between death and the attainment of wisdom. The story further explains the concept of *atman*, the inner unchanging self, in relation to the afterlife: it is immortal and continuous. Realization of this leads to "that final step, from which he is not reborn again," and only by discerning it can one "escape the jaws of death." A line with profound implications that we will explore later reads: "A certain wise man in search of immortality, turned his sight inward and saw the self within."[11]

Keshin Dārbhya (*Jaiminiya Upanishad Brahmana*)

Dating to sometime between the tenth and sixth century BCE, the *Jaiminiya Upanishad Brahmana* recounts the story of a boy named Keshin Dārbhya. Though it lacks an NDE journey, the text concerns events leading up to one—along with an encounter with a ghost and a quest for bringing about an out-of-body experience to the otherworld.

After his beloved uncle Uccaihshravas dies, Keshin is wandering through the woods in mourning. Suddenly, the ghost of Uccaihshravas appears to him. He tells Keshin that when he "found the guardian" of the otherworld, he was able to appear to the boy in order to "dispel his sadness" and to "teach him."

When the boy tries to embrace Uccaihshravas, he finds that he's immaterial, like "smoke or wind or space or the gleam of fire." Uccaihshravas explains to him that he achieved this bodiless state through a chant sung for him by a Brahmin: "by means of that disembodying chant he shook off my body. If someone who knows that chant sings it for you, he sends you to the same world that the gods live in." In fact, it's the same chant that enabled the sages and gods themselves to shake off their bodies.

Keshin goes in search of a Brahmin who knows the chant, and finally comes upon "a man who was lying on his funeral litter in a [cremation] burning-ground, engaged in a secret ritual. And this man's shadow had not left him." The man knows the correct chant, and sings it for Keshin, presumably allowing him to join his uncle in the next world.[12]

There are a number of other indications that NDEs were known in ancient India. Four hymns in the *Rig Veda* call upon the soul to return from the realm of the dead to the body of a dying person. The *Atharva Veda*, from around 900 BCE, contains magical-medical "charms to recover a dying man," which describe the soul as ascending from the underworld and returning to the body. Another is intended to retrieve the lifebreath from the underworld to return the person to life.[13] The *Jaiminiya Brahmana* mentions individuals who visited the realm of the dead and returned.[14]

The Afterlife Experience in the Vedas

Descriptions of afterlife experiences can be found in the Vedas, Brahmanas, and Upanishads, spanning a period of some 1,200 years. None of these texts focus primarily on the afterlife, though relevant material can be found within them. All have the status of *shruti*, meaning "that which is heard"—that is, by humans through divine revelation. They are fixed, sacred texts with no variation between editions. This is in contrast to the later religious texts such as the epics—the *Mahabharata* and *Ramayana*—and the Puranas, which are *smirti*—human thoughts and stories in response to *shruti*. Those post-Vedic texts show marked influences from Chinese Buddhism, resulting in far more detailed after-life descriptions that, as with the later Egyptian and Mesopotamian texts, mainly elaborated upon existing ideas.

The *Rig Veda*

The *Rig Veda* is a collection of over a thousand hymns, recited by priests during ritual sacrifices. Most of the hymns are concerned with life on Earth rather than with metaphysical speculation, though embedded within prayers for the gods to grant health, wealth, longevity, and children are descriptions of afterlife experiences. It's an incredibly complex work, described by the Romanian-French Indologist Charles Malamoud as "a staggering web of metaphors," the very obscurity of which "is a symbol of the mystery of the cosmic reality to which it refers." As such, it defies any single correct understanding. The translators Stephaine Jamison and Joel Brereton wrote that some of the passages were "composed to be enigmatic, to be never fully decipherable," and "seem deliberately and cleverly designed to mislead and confuse, and in that they have admirably succeeded."[15]

The most relevant passages—including the first Indian otherworld journey recounted earlier—are in the latest section, Mandala X. It also includes a "vision of heaven," found in a hymn to Soma, both a deity and an intoxicating ritual drink of immortality. The implication is that the vision was caused by drinking this powerful entheogen, and that Soma enabled the visionary to experience the other realm. Following the ritual preparation of the drink, the visionary asks Soma to make him immortal in the heavenly realm—the place "where the inexhaustible light is, in which world the sun is placed." It's "the immortal, imperishable world," ruled by the son of a sun-god named Vivasvant. This is a reference to Yama, the Lord of the Dead, though Vivasvant was also the father of Manu, the progenitor of the human race. A ladder reaches down from the "three-vaulted, three-heavened place of heaven," a place "where one can move following one's desire" (recalling the "chariot of the mind" in the otherworld journey story). It's a solar realm of "youthfully exuberant waters," "where there are worlds filled with light." Immortal souls there still have "desires and yearnings" though "the desires of desire are obtained." They gain "independence and satisfaction" in a state of "joys and delights, elations and exaltations." This vision is found again in the Upanishads, where it serves "to characterize the mystical realization of the self." [16]

A hymn describing the euphoric effects of soma proclaims, "we have drunk the soma; we have become immortal; we have gone to the light; we have found the gods." Soma enables one to see the light of heaven and to find the sun.[17] The soul was considered a microcosm of the sun—an inner light hidden in the heart, just as the sun hides under the earth. Both the sun and this inner light were symbolized by birds. In Vedic cosmology, the sun emerges from the stone of Varuna, the god of *Rita*, principle of moral and cosmic order. The Dutch Sanskrit scholar Henk Bodewitz equated the stone of Varuna with Yama's realm, suggesting that the deceased journeys with the sun through the netherworld on its way to the dawn, sailing on the primeval ocean. The celestial and subterranean realms are associated with each other in the father-son relationship of sun-god Vivasvant and netherworld-god Yama. Likewise, the visionary equates the face of Varuna with the face of Agni, the god of fire, light, and the sun.[18]

A cremation ritual hymn describes the soul of the dead ascending to the world of the ancestors on the smoke of their own funerary fire, to "lead at the will of the gods." This is followed by the blessing, "Let your eye go to the sun, your life-breath to the wind. Go to heaven and to earth as is fitting. Or go to the waters, if it has been fixed for you there [by fate]. Take roots in the plants with your limbs."

The German Sanskrit scholar Klaus Butzenberger interprets this passage as saying that the individual soul does not survive at all—that "the dead person is supposed to dissolve into the macrocosm." This seems to ignore prayers for the deceased to proceed "by his own powers" to the world of those who conducted proper rituals, to the ancestors, and to join the other souls ruled over by Yama.[19] Instead, the passage likely has the same meaning as a very similar one in the much later Upanishads (as will be seen). Here it prefigures the later doctrine of *atman* and *brahman*. The *atman* is the inner unchanging self, while *brahman* is the Absolute, or the transcendent universal reality. True spiritual enlightenment comes only with the full realization that *atman* = *brahman*; that is, that the individual is in essence nondifferent from and one with the divine. This is the actual "doctrine of correspondences" that Butzenberger intuited, for *atman* is the microcosm *brahman*. While the body parts may find new life in plants or in the waters, the soul goes to Yama's realm.

Another line subject to interpretation reads, "Clothing himself in life, let him go in pursuit of his remains: let him unite with his body." Since souls would not normally seek to unite with their own human remains burning in the cremation fire, the body the deceased is to "unite with" is likely a nonphysical subtle body in the otherworld, perhaps a revitalized duplicate of the earthly one. Alternatively, it could be a plea for the soul to return to the body before it's fully burned, enabling the person to return to life. The text actually includes a prayer to the fire-god, asking "Don't burn him through, Agni; don't scorch him; don't singe his skin, nor his body. When you will make him cooked to readiness . . . then impel him forth to the forefathers." We can also reject claims that it's the *physical* individual having afterlife experiences. Not only are there descriptions of the multiple components of the deceased having different fates, and to the body being cremated, there are numerous references to a surviving disembodied self as we've abundantly seen.[20]

Shamanic out-of-body journeys are also mentioned in the *Rig Veda*. In a hymn about long-haired ascetics known as *munis*, they drink some kind of poisonous substance that enables the experience. Though it's not named, the descriptions of the experience bear much similarity to those of soma. The drug, in any case, allows "the gods to enter" these shamanic individuals. One of them proclaims, "we have mounted the winds. You mortals see only our bodies," a clear reference to an OBE. They soar into the air looking down upon the earth, getting close to spiritual beings and becoming godlike.[21]

The heavenly realm of the ancestors is described as the place "where those of good action" dwell, having been placed there by Savitar, the god of the sun's power. Souls are led there by the psychopomp Pushan, another sun-god, who "knows all these regions through and through." Pushan is also mentioned in various hymns relating to visionary experiences. This "glowing one" guides the soul past afterlife dangers "along the least perilous" path, "granting well-being." Those who were generous in life gain immortality. They'll stand with the gods in the highest of heaven amidst streams flowing with ghee, and "rivers, embodiments of joy, milk-cows," and "suns in heaven." What the deceased has given will return in abundance. Those who were not generous, however, will experience "difficulty or outrage" and "the flames of pain."[22]

A funeral hymn explains to the soul of the dead:

Here is one light of yours, and far away is another one. Merge with the third light. At the merging of your body, be one cherished and dear to the gods at this highest means of begetting . . . in order to uphold the great gods, you should exchange your own light as if for the light in heaven.

The deceased is "the prizewinner with a winning spirit," going into the dawn and heaven, "well gone to the gods, well gone along your flight." The "mental force" of the deceased ancestors dwells among the gods, and the dead enveloped "those things that were in vibrant motion. They entered into their bodies again. With their powers they strode around the whole airy realm, measuring the ancient, unmeasurable domains."[23]

Another funeral hymn urges the soul of the newly dead to go and join the ancestors in the otherworld. The ancestors are described as "those for whom honey flows forth . . . who have gone to the sun because of their fervor, who have made their own fervor into greatness." Among them are "those who fight in prize-contests, who as champions abandon their bodies, or who confer a thousand priestly gifts," "ancients who were servers of truth," and "poets of a thousand devices who protect the sun."[24]

In another hymn, the recently deceased are told to "go forth along the ancient paths on which our ancient forefathers departed," and they will see Yama and Varuna. There appears to be more than one path, perhaps even a unique one for each individual, for souls go "along their own paths." The soul is then to "unite with the forefathers, unite with Yama, with what has been sacrificed and bestowed, in the highest distant heaven." The heavenly realm is filled with "well-being and freedom from disease" and is "a resting place anointed with waters through the days and nights" given to souls by Yama. It's a place of "exhilaration in joint revelry with Yama" and other gods, together with ancestors, poets, teachers, and priests of the past. This "pasture-land" will "not be taken away," perhaps suggesting that souls remain there eternally.

There are potential dangers on the journey, however, and malevolent beings are warned to keep away. They include two four-eyed dogs that guard the path, described as "broad-nosed, reddish-brown messengers of Yama, stealers of lives"—though they're also able to "grant a fortunate life again to us, to see the sun."[25] The soul is encouraged to "come home again" and "unite with your body in full luster," which could indicate coming back to life. The reference to "home," however, more likely means the spiritual home, and a return to the origin point and a spiritual body.

According to a hymn intended to bring a soul back to the body, other places to which the consciousness of the dead or dying can travel are "the four-cornered land far away," to heaven, Earth, the sea, the sun, dawn, "light-beams," plants, mountains, "to this whole moving world far away," "to the distant distances far away," and "to what has been and what will be." The deceased seems to have the power of omnipresence, becoming effectively divinized. Once-human ancestors have become gods, and the deceased creates stars, darkness, and light. They share Indra's chariot, and live on offerings made to them by the living. Those who have gone to the otherworld have avoided "the wolf," and now know "the truth." The ancestors can be both harmful and benevolent to the living, and indeed some remain "seated here in the earthly realm," or are "now among the clans of good community."[26]

A desire to go to the realm of Vishnu, the all-pervading solar deity, is also expressed, presumably as an afterlife destination. It's a place "where men seeking the gods find elation," "where there are ample-horned, unbridled cows," and a "wellspring of honey," which symbolizes a fountain of immortality. The realm is to be found in Vishnu's highest footstep, which refers the cosmic Three Strides he took from Earth to heaven.[27]

There are also references to punishments in subterranean hellish places, such as "falling into the pit" or being thrown there by gods—a fate for those who fail to perform proper rituals. A prayer to be free "from the shackle of Yama" suggests that he carried out punishments. Some who "fly away, never to return" are at risk of being eaten by ravening wolves, or they "lie in the lap of Dissolution" or Nirrti—a goddess of the earth, death, and destruction who represented the underworld. The underworld is located "below the three earths"—the same location as Naraka, the hellish realm in later texts.[28]

The distinctions between "the pit," the realms of Yama, heaven, and the ancestors aren't always clear. They may have been different regions of Yama's realm, for one text states: "There are three heavens: two are the laps of Savitar, one is the hero-vanquishing one in the world of Yama."[29] The fact that the land of the dead is in the heavens doesn't necessarily mean that it didn't have an underworld, for as we've seen in the Egyptian case, underworlds can be conceived of as being in the sky or undersky.

An account of the heavenly journey of the soul of a sacrificed horse should also be mentioned, considering that it was the same type of journey undertaken by the souls of dead humans. The visionary poet writes, "With my mind I recognized your lifebreath from afar, a bird flying below heaven." Horses become "dashing youths," are identified with the sun-god and with Yama, and meet their kin in heaven. They are treated with rubdowns, given refreshments and fine halters, assemble in formation with other "heavenly chargers," and run on "dustless paths easy to travel."[30]

The *Atharva Veda*

The *Atharva Veda* is a more popular text than the *Rig Veda*, written for a wider section of society than just the priesthood. Dating to around 1200–900 BCE, it may actually reflect even earlier beliefs. The afterlife descriptions build upon those in the *Rig Veda*, particularly with details about the heavenly realm, or Svargaloka.

A passage intended to revive a dying man confirms again that NDEs were known to the ancient authors. The spirit is advised that he should "not heed the departed who lead one to the distance" and should instead ascend to the light (presumably in this case, the light of Earth in contrast to the darkness of the afterlife realm). The soul is in danger of lightning and fire from heaven. Yama's dogs, Shyama and Shabala, might be encountered on the path of the Fathers—that is, the ancestors. A prayer for the soul to "stay safe" from the dogs reinforces their threatening aspect. Another path is described as "murky" and "dread-filled," and the soul is warned against descending into its "lowest darkness." Those who do, risk death at the hands of "a fiend with snapping jaws," "the tongue of the demon," "wild-haired women," "dismal howlers," flesh-eating ghosts or demons, "the brood of sin," and Malignity and Destruction themselves.[31]

Within the abyss is "the house infernal" where Decay, witches, and "evil ghosts dwell." Souls of the immoral "sit in a stream flowing with blood, devouring hair" or are given to "the serpent." There are prayers against being "tied with a rope" in Yamaloka, and against "devourers in the abyss" who "thrive in darkness." Sinners might also go to the pit, a cave, darkness, an abyss, and so on. Those who mistreat Brahmins will not go to Pitrloka, the realm of the ancestors.[32]

More fortunate souls of the dead ascend to the peak of the Third Firmament, either on rays of light passing the "great darkness" or by being carried by Maruts, the storm-gods. Thirty-three deities act as psychopomps, leading the deceased to the "supreme heaven" where husbands, wives, and sons also dwell. The spirit of a goat sacrificed on Earth on behalf of the deceased "smites away the darkness," precedes the souls, and announces them to the Fathers.[33]

In contrast to the *Rig Veda*, there are separate afterlife realms and intermediate states. Yamaloka, where "the cow grants all desires," is distinct from both the heavenly realm of Svargaloka, and from Naraka where sinners go. Paravátas are realms reserved for moral transgressors, and one proceeds to them after encountering Yama. Paraloka is yet another afterlife term, meaning "far away land."[34]

Svargaloka is a land of lotus ponds, lakes of ghee, "banks of honey, streams of milk and water and curds, and draughts of wine, free-flowing like water." The deceased are reunited with family members and they experience eternal "goodness," enjoying the company of Apsarasas and reveling "with the soma-drinking Gandharvas," or heavenly musicians. They ride celestial chariots, and fly with wings "all across the skies." The roads, the buildings, and the ship of the gods are all made of gold. A mysterious passage states that "after sixty autumns" one "may seek unto the treasure-keepers," suggesting that there's a realm beyond even Svargaloka.[35]

The *Krishna Yajur Veda*

Also dating to around 1200–900 BCE, the *Krishna Yajur Veda* is a collection of ritual instruction texts made up of verses and commentary. It contains only a few relevant passages, revealing the various afterlife fates of those who do and do not properly conduct rituals. This could be either following correct procedure or possessing accurate knowledge as to the meanings of the rituals.

Those who fail to burn the plant offerings after placing them on the altar to Yama will be bound and dragged by the neck by those plants in the afterlife. The one who knows "the seer, the hearer, the reciter, sacrificer is united in the yonder world with what he has sacrificed and bestowed." "Knowing" here includes knowledge that the seer is Agni; the hearer is Vayu, the elemental god of air and life; and the reciter is Aditya, another sun-god. Another rather mysterious line states that the one who "piles up the fire with itself and with a body; he becomes his body in the yonder world." This not only stresses the importance of cremation, it again seems to indicate that souls have spiritual bodies in the afterlife. Sacrificed cows go to the souls of the dead who conducted the proper rituals, with which they "milk" the fire.[36]

There are references to prospering in the otherworld, to becoming "rich in cattle," and to ensuring that one is "possessed of a head." The otherworld is filled with light.[37]

The Afterlife Experience in the Brahmanas

The Brahmanas, dating to roughly 900–700 BCE, explain the meanings and functions of Vedic rituals. The afterlife they portray is largely consistent with the earlier texts, though with further elaborations and clarifications.

The *Shatapatha Brahmana*

This is the text that featured the first version of Bhrgu's journey to the otherworld. It also describes how souls are judged by being weighed in a balance. The dead traverse two fires: the good will pass easily and proceed to Pitrloka or to the sun, and the wicked are burned. There is another danger of a reversal of the earthly order, for "whatever food a man consumes in this world . . . consumes him in yonder world." To reach the heavenly regions, the deceased must wrest them "from his hateful enemy," risking attack from Asuras and Rakshas—demons, evil spirits, and enemies of the gods. The Asuras have a heavenly golden castle and magical powers, but they're unable to speak intelligibly.[38]

Svargaloka is located "at the back of the sky," reached by ascending "the golden light." The sun's rays embody immortality, and Death itself is personified as "that person in the yonder orb," associating it with light and renewal. A ship that sails to Svargaloka is composed of elements of the Agnihotra ritual: its sides are the flames, and its steersman is the milk-offerer. Pitrloka lies southeast in Yamaloka and is associated with a pit, showing that it was not exclusively a heavenly realm. The ruler of the ancestors is Aditi, goddess of infinity.[39]

The stars in the sky are the lights of righteous men in Svargaloka, and the rays of the sun are their souls. They're also said to be gods. The sun itself is the "final goal," causing one "to die again and again in yonder world," a reference to its cyclical journey. "The cloudy ocean . . . is the yonder world"—perhaps the Milky Way. Those who led especially pious lives are reborn as golden gods who become Agni, not requiring food, and "complete with offspring and a mate."[40]

Death occurs in all three worlds, showing that afterlife realms are not eternal, but intermediate phases of death and rebirth. The ignorant and evil "come to life when they die again and they become food time after time," an apparent early reference to reincarnation.[41]

The *Jaiminiya Brahmana*

The *Jaiminiya Brahmana* is more of a folkloristic and mythological work. In addition to the NDE myths summarized at the beginning of this chapter, it describes how the lifebreath of the dead ascends to Svargaloka and reports to the gods on their good and evil deeds. The souls announce themselves to the doorkeepers, who are personifications of the seasons, asking to be led to "immortality." The doorkeepers take the souls to the Sun, who asks "Who art thou?" If the dead give their regular names, the Sun replies that although the *atman* originated in the Sun, it will remain with the *atman*. At this point, the seasons run at the deceased "from all sides" and "grasp him by his feet and drag him away. Night and Day take possession of his world." The deceased's reply should have demonstrated knowledge that the *atman* is one and the same as the Sun (apparently synonymous here with *brahman*). This would cause a merging with the sun, and the formation of a "second self."[42]

The deceased might also be met by one of the seasons, descending on a ray of light, wielding a hammer, and asking, "Who art thou, man?" Those who have *some* spiritual knowledge may refuse to reveal their names, and are then struck with the hammer. Their merits split into three parts, which dissipate in the air, go to the seasons, or accompany the soul to Svargaloka. The merits of others will return to Earth with them, apparently in another incarnation, continuing the cycle of "repeated dying."[43]

When the souls of deceased "mystics" "shake off the body," they travel from their cremation smoke into the night, then to the day, to the "half-month of the waning moon to the half-month of the waxing moon," and then to the month where "both the body and the life-spirit come together." When asked their identity by the hammer-wielding season, their reply must show an understanding of reincarnation, and knowledge of the identification of King Soma with semen and of the self as his offspring. The seasons then give King Soma to the deceased and lead them to immortality, "through the twelve- or thirteenfold father, through this mother, through this faith, through this food, through this truth. Day is my father, night my mother. I am truth." Those who possess this knowledge are no longer humans, but gods.

Admitted to Svargaloka, the deceased is greeted by "fathers and grandfathers, swift as thought." They ask what the deceased has brought them, and the reply should be: "Whatever good I have done, that is yours." The ancestors therefore benefit from the good deeds of the newly dead, while the evil deeds go to the deceased's enemies. Souls will then proceed "to coexistence in one world with the one that burns here" (the Sun). Svargaloka is a place beyond time where a soul "resurges" in a spiritual "resurrection," and where "coming into existence is realized in fact."[44]

The Afterlife Experience in the Upanishads

The Upanishads represent the culmination of Vedic philosophy and date to 700–300 BCE. To some degree, they can be compared to "books of the dead" in that part of their function was to guide readers through a spiritual evolution that is realized in death. They differ from the rest of the Vedas, being concerned more with philosophy than ritual. Although they were written in different regions over a period of at least 500 years, the Upanishads show an overall consistency. It is, nevertheless, "futile to try to discover a single doctrine or philosophy" in them, as the translator Patrick Olivelle put it.[45]

The *Katha Upanishad*—the source of Nachiketas's NDE myth—explains that the "person" is higher than intellect, the soul, the self, and the unmanifest: "Higher than the person there's nothing at all. That is the goal, that's the highest state." The person is described as a being of light—"resembling a smokeless flame." In the form of a goose, the deceased "dwells in the light" as a god in the sky. The person "lies awake within those who sleep; That alone is the Pure! That is *brahman*! That alone is called the Immortal! On it all the worlds rest; Beyond it no one can ever pass." Those who do not have this knowledge, and who view reality as "diverse," will experience death after death. Some are reincarnated, while "others pass into a stationary thing." On various states of being, the text summarizes: "As in a mirror, so in the body; As in a dream, so in the father's world; As in water a thing becomes somewhat visible, so in the Gandharva world; Somewhat as in shadows and light, so in *brahman*'s world."[46]

The *Mundaka Upanishad* tells us that those with knowledge of *brahman* travel through "the sun's door to where that immortal Person is, that immutable self." Thought is the creative and active force, so that any "purified" person may obtain any world, fulfil any desire, by the power of the mind alone.[47]

The *Chandogya Upanishad* describes a series mystical afterlife states. After souls leave the body they ascend to "the highest light," then emerge in their "own true appearance." Beyond human emotions, this "highest person" wanders the realm of light, "laughing, playing and enjoying himself with women, carriages, or relatives, without remembering the appendage that is the body." This transformation is described as passing "from the dark into the multicolored" and back again. Now free of evil, the deceased says, "I, the perfected self, cast off the body, the imperfect, and attain the world of *brahman*."[48]

Afterlife fates depend even more upon spiritual enlightenment, though the idea was already found in the *Krishna Yajur Veda* with its emphasis on understanding ritual meanings, and in the *Jaiminiya Brahmana* with knowing the nature of *atman*. The possibility of reincarnation is also more prominent, and so is the goal of *moksha*— liberation from the cycle of rebirth. The path of the Fathers leads to Pitrloka, now described as an intermediate realm prior to rebirth. For the spiritually enlightened, the sun is a doorway, reached by ascending on rays of light accompanied by the universal sound, *Om*: "No sooner does he think of it than he reaches the sun." For the unenlightened, the sun is a barrier.

The path of the gods leads to Svargaloka, and is colored white, blue, orange, green and red. It's traveled by "the knower of *brahman*, the doer of good, the man of light." Elaborating on the *Jaiminiya Brahmana*, enlightened souls travel this path, passing successively from the cremation fire "into the day," "the fortnight of the waxing moon," "into the six months when the sun moves north" toward Svargaloka, then "into the year," the sun, the moon, and lightning. There the deceased is met by a "a person consisting of mind" and is led "to the worlds of *brahman*" from which there is no return. The third heaven is no longer the realm of Yama, but the world of Brahma, the creator deity. It has two oceans, a Soma tree, a lake with intoxicating waters, a citadel, a golden palace, and five doorkeepers in the court of *brahman*.[49]

According to the *Kausitaki Upanishad*, souls of the dead travel to the moon, which is "the door to the heavenly world." The moon asks, "Who are you?" and the answer determines the fate of the deceased. Those who give their real names show an attachment to their identity, and they are sent in the rains to be reborn in a new earthly incarnation. Those who answer, "I am the season! Who am I? I am you!" demonstrate a realization of the identification of *atman* with *brahman*. They are allowed to pass and achieve *moksha*.[50]

These liberated souls then follow the path of gods to "the world of fire," then the worlds of wind, Varuna, Indra, Prajapati (the primordial father god), and ultimately *brahman*. At Lake Ara, the deceased must cross "with the mind," and the ignorant and unenlightened drown. The lake is made of the enemies of liberation, such as wrath and desire. Souls then encounter "the watchmen Muhurta," which are actually deified brief units of time. Fleeing from them, the deceased reaches Vijara, the river of immortality, which must also be crossed with the mind. The river purifies both good and bad deeds, which will fall to Earth upon loved and unloved relatives, respectively. This purification results in a divine omnipresence in which the deceased has a life review, and "looks down and observes the days and nights, the good and bad deeds, and all the pairs of opposites."[51]

Various gods and demigods are then encountered, including Manasi and Cakshushi, the deifications of Mind and Vision, symbolizing the beautiful and ugly sides of the soul. They bring flowers to the deceased, encouraged by Brahma, who tells them, "Run to him with my glory! He has already arrived at the river Vijara! He will never grow old!" Five hundred Apsarasas appear, bearing fruits, ointments, garlands, clothing, and perfumes. "Decked with the ornaments of *brahman*," the deceased "who has the knowledge of *brahman* goes on to *brahman*."[52]

The deceased now begins to take on attributes of Brahma: first his fragrance at Ilya, the tree of refreshment; then his flavor at the plaza Salajya, resplendent with rivers, lakes, and gardens where heroes dwell; and finally his radiance and glory at the palace Aparajita. Indra and Prajapati are doorkeepers at the palace hall, and they flee as the now divinized soul of the dead arrives at the throne of reason, deified as Vicaksana. The various parts of the throne are identified with various divinities, spiritual ideals, and Soma-ritual chants. Upon the throne sits *brahman*, and the one who recognizes this also sits upon the throne.[53]

When *brahman* asks souls of the dead, "Who are you?" they should answer: "I am the season! I am the offspring of the season. I was born from the womb of space as the semen for the wife, as the radiance of the year, as the *atman* of every being! You are the self of every being. I am who you are." When *brahman* asks again, "Who are you?" the deceased should reply, "The real," which is described as "the full extent of the whole world. And you are this whole world." *Brahman* then asks the means by which the deceased grasps *brahman*'s names, odors, breath, sounds, and so on, and the answers must correctly correspond to each: "with my mind," "with my sense of smell," and so on. Finally, *brahman* says "I see that you have truly attained my world. It is yours!" Liberation is not described, for of course it is indescribable, though the deceased is identified with Yama, Prajapati, and life and death themselves.[54]

The *Brhadaranyaka Upanishad* tells us that leaving the body at death is to leave evil behind. The vital energies, senses, and body of the deceased dissipate among the cremation fire, the air, the sun, the moon, the four quarters, the earth, space, and waters. The spirit goes to the wind, then through subsequent holes in the air, sun, and moon to "a world where there are no extremes of heat and cold," to live "for years without end." Yama is identified as the sun, and as the son of Prajapati.[55]

The "complete freedom" found in Svargaloka is attained "by means of the mind, by means of the moon." The self is the "inner controller, the immortal," with power over the elements and over the "intermediate region." Souls that will be reborn remain in the lunar world for "as long as there is a residue" (presumably of merit). They then return by the same path on which they arrived, passing from space into wind and then into a thundercloud to be rained upon the earth in a new incarnation. The good will have a positive rebirth, though the unenlightened and impious are reborn as beasts.[56]

According to the *Prashna Upanishad,* souls who remain attached to earthly possessions, concerns, and desires, proceed "to that very place to which his mind and character cling" before being reborn. Those who focus on ritual offerings take the path of the Fathers to the moon, which is *substance* (perhaps referring to physical rebirth). "Those who seek the self by means of austerity, chastity, faith, knowledge" take the path of the gods to the sun, "the lifebreath, where they gain immortality and are free from fear."[57]

The unenlightened but pious ascend on their cremation smoke to the moon, referred to here as King Soma. "Reaching the moon they become food. There the gods feed on them." The deceased instructs the moon to continue its cycle, commanding, "Increase! Decrease!"[58]

Interestingly, hellish realms and negative fates play little role in the Upanishads. "People who worship ignorance" go to "joyless" regions characterized by "blind darkness." The darkness is even worse for those "who delight in learning" and, paradoxically, "those who are not learned or wise." In the later Upanishads, the ignorant and those who take their own lives go to dark "Demonic" realms. Dwellers in Yamaloka are referred to as being "in a state of great fear," indicating a more negative conception than in earlier texts.[59]

Understanding the Indian Afterlife Experience

Notwithstanding the different emphases in the various texts, in general the Vedic afterlife includes ascent and descent to celestial and subterranean realms by various means; existence in a nonphysical form as light or "the mind"; dissolution into component parts that go to different places; encounters with deities and deceased relatives; barriers, obstacles, and perils; judgment of earthly behavior followed by subsequent reward or punishment; a world created by the mind alone; and identification of the deceased with various deities, celestial bodies, seasons, natural phenomena, and transcendent concepts.

The continuity of tradition is evident in the series of otherworld journey stories spanning many hundreds of years, in which a father sends his son to the otherworld to gain knowledge and wisdom.[60] Whether they were all variations on the same root story and share a common origin (as the two versions of the Bhrgu's story obviously do), or whether they're unique accounts with different origins is impossible to say. It's also impossible to say if they were based on actual historical events—though it seems clear that they reveal a longstanding awareness of NDEs as a valued source of knowledge, important in the creation and development of afterlife beliefs.

The main evolution from the *Rig Veda* and *Shatapatha Brahmana* to the Upanishads is a stress on enlightenment and wisdom over correct ritual behavior and generosity. Rather than piety or good deeds, the realization of the nature of *atman* and the knowledge of immortality admits one to Svargaloka. This doesn't mean that it ceased to be an ethical or morally based system, for the immoral and unethical would not become enlightened to begin with.

The cyclical solar afterlife of the *Rig Veda* begins to fade in the Brahmanas. Fear of an underworld abyss and "primordial chaos" also gives way to a more positive longing for unity of the self with the infinite, evolving into the idea of *brahman*. The focus is less on reaching the realm of the gods and the sun, and more on the realization that the self is already a microcosm of the divine. The fear of nonexistence is reconciled by the introduction of the concept of *moksha* as the ultimate goal. Rather than fearing annihilation, one could hope for liberation from rebirth into a unified state of divine transcendence.

In addition to the prospect of annihilation, there are also many threats, perils, demons, and a variety of negative afterlife possibilities—particularly in the earlier texts. The character and function of Yamaloka changed over time: in the *Rig Veda* it was a goal, but in the Upanishads it became a negative intermediate state for the unenlightened and immoral prior to a low rebirth. A heavenly realm was retained as a temporary reward for meritorious behavior, prior to a high rebirth.

Notwithstanding these observations, it's important not to overemphasize the idea of "stages of development," for most of these concepts were coexistent throughout the texts. Other than the introduction of reward through enlightenment as opposed to correct ritual behavior, and punishment through rebirth as opposed to annihilation, it's less a matter of development than of refocus. In a more general sense, some form of religious knowledge was required to gain a positive afterlife. Alongside references to the world of the immortals in the *Rig Veda*, there also seem to be early indications of a belief in reincarnation, as the inevitable conclusion to a temporary stay in a heavenly realm (at least for those who escaped annihilation). The length of the stay was determined by a person's ritual conduct on Earth. Reincarnation is more clearly alluded to at least as early as the *Shatapatha Brahmana*, and grows increasingly important. The *atman* will continue to try to achieve *moksha* in subsequent incarnations.

As with Egyptian religion, Western scholars often attempt to divide the Vedic afterlife into a binary heaven-and-hell system that seems never to have been entirely relevant. Bodewitz characterized it as a threefold division—Naraka for sinners, Yamaloka for the majority of the populace, and Svargaloka for the lucky few. Even this, however, seems to be an oversimplification. While there were indeed different realms and different experiences based on the soul's level of piety, knowledge, moral behavior, and so on, it's not clear that these worlds were specifically reserved for these particular classes of individuals.[61]

Butzenberger particularly oversystematizes the Vedic afterlife, attempting to chart chronologically the development of key themes in texts. But the texts themselves are of uncertain dates to begin with, and also demonstrate a multiplicity of beliefs from the very beginning. His attempt to reconcile the various elements that seem to him contradictory led him to conclude that the most "common and popular" conception was in fact a combination of various apparently conflicting elements. While this probably gets us closer to the truth, at the same time (recalling some scholars of Mesopotamian religion), Butzenberger portrays the *Rig Veda* afterlife as a vague, Hades-like shadowy existence, which is clearly not borne out by the texts.[62]

Butzenberger also shares with certain scholars of Egypt and Mesopotamia an assumption that whatever we don't understand in the texts is the fault of the ancient authors rather than of modern scholars. Commenting on the issue of which element of the soul goes to Pitrloka and which to the gods, he wrote, "Accounting for the fact that we are not concerned with refined philosophical systems, we may assume that the problem was not thought out carefully." There's no basis for such an assumption, for ancient India or any past society. While the problems with understanding are most likely our own, as noted in the introduction they're aggravated by the ancient authors' deliberate obfuscations, occult meanings, and ritual or metaphorical associations now lost to us. As Jamison and Brereton wrote, despite esoteric obscurities of the *Rig Veda*, "interpreters of the text have been able to make progress by the simple assumption that the hymns do make sense and that the poets did know exactly what they were doing."[63]

Accepting what the texts tell us, without assuming they were contradictory, vague, or internally confused, the afterlife was a series of intermediate states and experiences. The *Rig Veda* described a cyclical solar journey, the "six broad places," and numerous physical and nonphysical realms. In the *Shatapatha Brahmana* the deceased rises "from the darkness, the world of the Fathers," then goes "to the light, the sun," and to all three realms. In the *Atharva Veda*, souls go from Earth to Yamaloka to hell; and a series of "intermediate regions" are described in the various Upanishads. Heavenly and hellish realms are merely phases of reward and punishment on the journey to rebirth or liberation, which is beyond description.[64]

Transcendence and cosmic unity are also recurring themes, expressed as the reconciliation or integration of opposites of deities and their realms. In the *Jaiminiya Brahmana*, for example, two words for "heaven," Paraloka and Asáuloká, actually refer to *underworlds*, perhaps even hells (again recalling the Egyptian "undersky"). The Fathers, Yama, and Varuna are all associated with both the upper and lower realms in the early literature. It was only later that Yama became the fearsome underworld lord he remains today. Bodewitz speculated that Yama actually began as a "dark" god and that his character changed in the later portions of the *Rig Veda* "as a consequence of the discovery of heaven for human beings." He then reverted to his original character following the Upanishads. It seems more likely, however, that Yama originally had two aspects that were integrated or reconciled in death. As Jamison and Brereton wrote, Yama embodies "the absolute disjunction between and the ultimate complementarity and unity of the mortal and the immortal, life and death, men and gods . . . heaven and earth." He is equated with the sun in the *Brhadaranyaka Upanishad*; and in one of the earliest Upanishads, the *Jaiminiya Upanishad Brahmana*, the sun becomes Yama in the underworld when it sets, then becomes Soma, then king of the Fathers before entering the dreams of humans.[65]

Enlightened and worthy souls are microcosmic counterparts to the divine and all the simultaneous multiplicity and universality it entails. The various transformations and integrations involved in this divine-human association are manifested in the afterlife experience. "The One" is an all-encompassing immortal principle in the *Rig Veda*—the culmination of the deities, the elements, the celestial bodies, and the *atman*. Equating the One with the *atman* prefigures the Upanishadic equation of *atman* with *brahman*, of microcosm with macrocosm. "God" is not the Other, but the One, the Self.[66]

In conclusion, there are four different types of indicators that ancient Indians were not only aware of NDEs, but that their afterlife beliefs were likely informed by them. First is the series of afterlife journey narratives in which a boy travels to the other world. Second are the texts designed to restore life to a dead or dying person and bring them back from the realm of Yama. Third are the visions of the otherworld in shamanic contexts, resulting from ingesting soma. Fourth are the instructions regarding the journey to the otherworld and the conditions there, which often recall NDEs in thematic ways: a series of experiences involving OBEs, darkness, light, deceased relatives, spirit beings, evaluation of one's earthly life, and ineffable transcendent feelings. Taken in combination, knowledge about the otherworld journey seems likely to have come from return-from-death and shamanic-type experiences. The stories of a boy going to the otherworld seem to be retellings of NDEs, highly mythologized to teach spiritual lessons. It's important to note that each of these categories of evidence can be found in India's first religious text, the *Rig Veda*, which contains its earliest descriptions of the afterlife.

6

China

From the Yellow Springs to Mount Kunlun

Ancient Chinese Near-Death Experiences

The world's first unambiguous documented near-death experiences come from ancient China. Rather than appearing in religious or mythological texts, as with the Sumerian "Death of Bilgames" or the Indian afterlife NDE-type legends, these accounts were recorded as history.

The surviving copies of them are all far later than the events they record. Whether the accounts were based on earlier models, oral traditions, or were simply invented is impossible to say. They claim, in any case, to be official reports of factual occurrences, and their authors made a point of emphasizing that they were duly recorded and filed with government offices. We'll review these ancient NDEs before looking at ancient Chinese afterlife beliefs, and how the experiences and beliefs might relate to each other.

Muh of Ts'in and Kien-tsze

The earliest Chinese account actually involves three interassociated NDEs that occurred some 150 years apart. This unique and somewhat complex narrative is found in *Records of the Grand Historian* (or *Shiji*), a sweeping chronicle of ancient China. The work was begun in the late second century BCE by the astrologer and historian Sima Tan and completed by his son Sima Qian in around 91 BCE. The NDEs it contains, however, date to hundreds of years earlier.

Kien-tsze, a ruler in Chao principality, had an NDE in 498 BCE. Embedded in the account of his experience is a brief description of the NDE of the ruler Muh of Ts'in, around 150 years earlier. Both focus on the prophetic information given to the experiencers by the Emperor of Heaven, though Kien-tsze's contains more details about the otherworld—as well as featuring an encounter with the soul of a child who happened to be having an NDE at the same time.

The report tells of how Kien-tsze was so ill that he was unable to recognize those around him. A doctor was called and noticed that despite his grave condition, Kien-tsze still had a pulse. He remarked that this should not be too surprising because long ago, the ruler Muh of Ts'in "was in a similar state; he awoke on the seventh day," and reported, "I went to the residence of the Emperor [of Heaven], and greatly enjoyed myself. I have been absent so long because I had to learn something there."

Muh of Ts'in claimed that the Emperor of Heaven informed him that the state of Ts'in would undergo political turmoil for five reigns. A "usurper" would then take over, only to die early, and would then be succeeded by his son. At this time, "no distinction will be made between the two sexes" and it will be an era of "debauchery and lewdness." A number of years later, the prophecies were fulfilled.

The doctor explained that Kien-tsze's disease was the same kind as Muh of Ts'in's, and that they should expect him to die and return within three days. The doctor was right, and when Kien-tsze revived from his near-death state, he told of his otherworldly experience:

I went to the residence of the Emperor, where I much enjoyed myself.
With the host of *shen* [deities or spirits] I wandered about in the all-
ruling heaven. The music in nine tunes, resounding far and wide with
accompaniment of ten thousand dances, was other music than that of
the three dynasties; its tunes moved my heart.

The account then takes a surreal turn. A bear appeared and tried
to attack Kien-tsze, but he killed it when instructed to do so by the
Emperor of Heaven. The same thing happened again with a spotted
bear. In admiration, the Emperor then gave Kien-tsze two baskets,
"each containing a set of things," and assigned a dog to Kien-tsze's
bravest son on Earth. He then prophesied that the realm of Ts'in
would fall into decline and end after seven reigns. The local ruling family would be defeated by another, who would be unable
to rule.

Before returning to his body, Kien-tsze noticed a child standing at
the Emperor's side. Years later, this would lead to a validation of the
reality of his NDE. One day a mysterious man in the street would
not move out of his way. Kien-tsze recognized him from somewhere,
and the man not only explained their previous acquaintance, but also
interpreted the signs in Kien-tsze's NDE. He explained that he was,
in fact, the child who had stood by the Emperor. He also confirmed
the episode with the bears and recounted the Emperor's predictions.
He explained that the bears symbolized two ministers who Kien-tsze
was supposed to assassinate and that bears were actually the ministers'
ancestors. The baskets represented Kien-tsze's sons politically subduing
two regions, and the dog represented the land of Kien-tsze's ancestors
that he would soon reclaim.

All of the predictions came true, and by validating the information Kien-tsze had been given in the otherworld, the ancient Chinese
historians affirmed their belief in the genuineness of NDEs. The reader
is assured that each part of the account was correctly documented, and
the records were deposited in the government archives.[1]

Dan

An official record found in a tomb relates the NDE of a man named Dan in 297 BCE. After injuring another man by stabbing him, Dan killed himself, but he returned to life a full three years later. His revival was arranged by his patron, Xi Wu, who advocated on his behalf with Gongsun Qiang, an underworld official called the Scribe of the Director of the Life Mandate. Xi Wu convinced him that Dan's death was premature, and the authorities of the underworld decided that he should be returned to life.

Gongsun Qiang, an actual figure from Chinese history, sent his white dog to Dan's tomb to dig him out. Dogs may have been seen as psychopomps as well as guardian figures. A white dog is depicted on a later tomb door, and dog sacrifices are found in burials as far back as the Shang period (1600-1046 BCE), probably intended to cause the dog's spirit to accompany the deceased on the afterlife journey. Another cultural symbol in the account is the recurrence of the number three—perhaps because in Chinese numerology it sounds like the words for "to part ways" and "to live." Dan was buried after three days, he stayed dead for three years, and he stood on his tomb for three days before reentering society.

During his time in the underworld, Dan learned about the kinds of offerings the dead prefer and that people are not to spit when performing sacrifices at tombs. His NDE also had physical effects, for he couldn't hear for four years or eat "human food." His body had scars from his self-inflicted wounds, "and his four limbs were useless."[2]

Unnamed Woman

A text called the *Five Agents Treatise* mentions a woman's NDE from the year 1 CE. She died and was placed in a coffin but revived after six days. She reported having seen her deceased father-in-law, who told her that it was not yet her time to die.[3]

Du Xie

The near-death experience of Du Xie, a governor of the Jiaozhou region, occurred in the second century CE, according to a text of some 200 years later, *Biographies of the Deities and Immortals* (*Shenxian Zhuan*). After temporarily dying due to accidentally ingesting poison, Du Xie was revived by a Daoist master named Dong Feng and told of his experience.

"When I died, it was suddenly as if I had entered a dream," he said. He described how twelve men dressed in black came for him and put him in a cart. They led him through "a great red gate" to a prison cell with a narrow door. Then they put him inside and buried it.

He soon heard voices above, saying "Taiyi [the deity of Grand Unity] has sent a messenger to summon Du Xie!" Some men dug up the prison cell and pulled Du Xie out. There were "three men on a horse-cart with a red canopy" there to meet him. He was commanded to get into the cart, and when they reached the gate again, he revived.[4]

Li O

The collection *In Search of Spirits*, or *Researches into the Supernatural* (*Soushen Ji*), contains a number of narratives about marvels, ghosts, dreams, and souls. It was compiled from various sources around 350 CE by the Chinese historian Gan Bao, for the purpose of proving that "the way of spirits is not an illusion." Gan Bao was motivated to embark on the work after seeing his own brother return to life after several days of apparent death, and hearing about his NDE.

The collection includes an account of the NDE of a woman named Li O, who "died of an illness" in the year 199 CE. It is, in fact, a rare example of a shared NDE—involving a second experiencer named Li Hei.

Fourteen days after her burial, Li O's grave was disturbed by a neighbor, Ts'ai Chung, hoping to rob it of anything valuable. As he hacked into the coffin with an axe, he heard a voice saying, "Ts'ai Chung, watch out for my head!" The robber fled in terror, but word spread that Li O was alive. After her son went to the grave and rescued her, the Grand Administrator of the province summoned her to tell him about her experience.

She explained that while in the otherworld, she was told that the Arbiter of Life had made a mistake in bringing her there, and so she was sent back. As she turned to leave through the "western gates," she saw her deceased cousin, Liu Po-wen. Li O explained to him that she'd been wrongly brought there and had been sent home, but that she didn't know the way. She asked Po-wen if he could find someone to take her back. She was also worried about how she would get out of the tomb after reentering her body, because she'd already been dead and buried for over 10 days.

Po-wen went to ask advice of the chancellor of the Bureau of Households, explaining the situation to him. The Chancellor told him that a man named Li Hei was also being sent back to Earth following an error, and suggested that he could take Li O with him. The Chancellor would also instruct Li O's neighbor, the would-be grave robber Ts'ai Chung, to go and free her.

Before she left, Po-wen gave her a letter to take to his son on Earth. When Li Hei and Li O successfully returned to life, the Grand Administrator of their district took an interest in the case and wanted to verify it. First, he decided to be lenient in the grave-robbing case against Ts'ai Chung. Though the offense normally called for the death penalty, it was reasoned that "Although Ts'ai Chung did indeed break into the grave, he was made to do so by ghosts and spirits. He couldn't have helped it, even if he hadn't wanted to break in."

The Grand Administrator also wanted to confirm the shared-NDE element of Li O's story, so he tracked down Li Hei and questioned him, finding that his account collaborated that of Li O.

The letter that Po-wen gave to Li O to give to his son back on Earth was also investigated. The son, T'o, "recognized the paper as having been among the writing materials in a box buried at the time of Po-wen's death." Nobody could decipher the script of the letter, however, so the famous necromancer Fei Ch'ang-fang was called in to read it. In the letter, Po-wen informed T'o that he would be accompanying "the Lord of the Underworld on a tour of inspection" at a particular watercourse and that T'o should be there on a specified day and time.

T'o did as instructed, and his deceased father Po-wen did indeed appear. After visiting for some time, Po-wen prophesied that a great sickness would come in the spring, and he gave T'o a special "medicine ball" to protect him from it. The prediction came true, and T'o was spared. The account concludes: "When Fei Ch'ang-fang inspected the medicine ball, he said, 'This is the brain of Fan-hsiang, the god who protects against pestilence.'"⁵

Ancient Chinese literary works also reveal knowledge of NDEs. These include Daoist poems intended to call the soul back to the body from dangerous afterlife realms. In one example from the second century BCE, a spirit trying to reach the otherworld is forced to return to his body when his progress is halted by a celestial waterway.⁶ There are also many examples of return-from-death accounts from the third century BCE onwards. Although they sometimes lack descriptions of any disembodied adventures the people may have had, they nevertheless show a keen cultural interest in the phenomenon of coming back to life. In just a single source, the *Extensive Records of the Taiping Era* (*Taiping guangji*), there are 127 such accounts spanning over a thousand years. Unfortunately, this and many other Chinese sources have not been translated, though it's almost certain that there are further NDE accounts waiting to be discovered in them. There are also many NDE accounts known from medieval China that fall outside our time period.⁷

Descriptions of afterlife journeys are found in various pre-Buddhist traditions, including ancestor-based local religions, Confucianism, Daoism, and poems that don't correspond neatly to any of these streams. These traditions often mixed elements from others, so that it's difficult to distinguish the origins of a particular shared belief. Generally speaking, Daoism focused more on spiritual and philosophical matters, while Confucianism was largely concerned with social and ethical issues. This is somewhat of an oversimplification, though, beause Confucian ideas about the afterlife might reflect earlier ancestor-based traditions.⁸

Despite their name, much of the "Confucian" Classics actually predate Confucius by at least a thousand years and were products of a long evolution. They mostly concern earthly propriety, ritual, and moral behavior. Confucius himself saw little point in metaphysical speculations about life after death when we know so little about this life. This explains why, for example, the third-century philosopher Xunzi did not once mention afterlife conceptions in his discussion of funerary rites and the nature of god and heaven. While Confucian texts such as the *Book of Documents* (*Shujing*) reveal beliefs in ancestors surviving bodily death, their postmortem experiences and the realms they inhabit are scarcely discussed.[9] Nevertheless, relevant material can be found scattered among the *Classic of Poetry* (*Shijing*), the *Book of Rites* (*Li ji*), and other works.

The early Daoist poetical and literary works such as the *Zhuangzi* and the *Book of the Prince of Huainan* (*Huainanzi*), as well as the unclassifiable *Songs of the South* (*Chu ci*) are of a more overtly metaphysical character, often rooted in shamanism. Finally, there are funerary documents of the Han period (221 BCE–220 CE), which were intended to guide souls of the dead to the otherworld. They reveal further information about afterlife experiences.

As with the other civilizations we've considered so far, there have been a number of unfounded scholarly assumptions about the Chinese afterlife. According to the historian Ying-shih, "the Chinese conception of the afterlife did not become fully developed until the Han period." Similarly, the British historian Joseph Needham wrote that in the Shang period, people had "very little idea" of any possible afterlife state. Such assertions are arguments from silence, based solely on the limited surviving textual evidence. As we'll shortly see, evidence from Shang oracle bones suggests very early afterlife beliefs consistent with those of later times.[10]

The move toward Buddhism began between the first and third centuries CE, roughly corresponding with the end of the Han period. As with other ancient texts, however, the dating of the Chinese sources is notoriously difficult. Parts of the *Taipingjing* (*Scriptures of the Great Peace*), for example, may date to the second century CE, though most scholars believe it has Buddhist influence. At the same time, it's impossible to determine the degree of such influence, because as we've seen, similarities alone don't indicate influence from one culture to another. For these reasons, while we'll focus on the era before the first century CE, we'll also look at some texts through the end of the Han period in 220 CE.

The Afterlife Experience in Oracle Bones and Confucian Classics

The earliest Chinese references to the afterlife appear on oracle bones from over 3,000 years ago, during the Shang period. The bones were used in a form of divination, which involved inscribing questions on them, applying a heated metal rod to create cracks in the surface, and then "reading" the patterns made by the cracks. Although the information about the afterlife they provide is limited, it attests to very early beliefs that are consistent with later ones. The inscriptions mention that the souls of kings ascend to a heavenly realm where they join the "Lord-on-High." The world of the ancestors appears to be the same as that of the gods. Shang documents also refer to feeding the ancestors with offerings, revealing a concern with proper nourishment in the afterlife.[11]

The *Classic of Poetry*

It's not until at least 300 years later that we find more detailed descriptions, during a time of religious syncretism after the Zhou dynasty conquered the Shang in 1046 BCE.

The *Shijing*, or *Classic of Poetry*, dating to the eleventh through eighth centuries BCE, describes spirits of the dead as "very bright, very glorious." The soul of King Wen, founder of the Zhou dynasty, "shines in heaven" in a "glittering light." Having attained divine or semi-divine immortality, he "ascends and descends; on God's left hand, on His right." Heaven is the home state to which souls return, for it "gives birth to the multitudes of the people." It's a place of joy "where we shall have our place," "where no sad songs are sung," and where the Milky Way is a flowing river. "Heaven" was synonymous with Tien, or god, the unifying force of order in the universe, though it also had even clearer afterlife connections: Tien could also refer to the collectivity of ancestor rulers living in heaven or to "the destination of the ashes of cremated sacrificial victims."

The fates of souls were determined by an evaluation of their earthly life. Heaven is "that happy kingdom where we shall get our due," but slanderers are thrown "to Him of the north," Yo Pei, the ruler of the realm of the dead. If he refuses to accept them, they're thrown to the Lord of Heaven, Shangdi. Both of these deities, however, were associated with both heaven and the underworld. Yo Pei was an astral deity—specifically the polar star—indicating that he was a being of light. In early times, Shangdi was also an underworld fertility deity associated with dogs— themselves seen as psychopomps.[12]

The *Zuo Zhuan* and Other Historical Works

Two historical works also mention the afterlife. The *Book of Documents,* or *Shujing* (sixth century BCE) refers to ancestors being "kings in heaven," which is located "in the eastern sea," though is also said to be in the west.[13] The *Chunqiu*, or *Spring and Autumn Annals* (721–481 BCE) states that Shangdi "pacified the good and humane ones in death, but he suppressed the inhuman ones."[14]

By 389 BCE, more detailed descriptions begin to emerge—including two brief accounts of extraordinary experiences of the afterlife found in the *Zuo Zhuan*, a collection of commentaries on the *Chunqiu*. The first mentions the Duke Yin, who hoped to find his deceased mother by digging a tunnel to the underworld realm of the dead, called the Yellow Springs. Yellow was considered to be the color of the soil, and the most common term used to describe the place was *you*, which can mean hidden, deep, profound, moon, night, dark, far away, and blood. While these associations have led modern scholars to view the Yellow Springs as a shadowy, indistinct underworld, it's actually described as a place where "joy and concord will be found." Indeed, springs are often associated with life, regeneration, and immortality, for they're continually refreshed and renewed. It's significant that the realm isn't called Yellow Swamp or Yellow Pit, for although it is a realm of darkness, it's also a realm of rebirth.

The second account tells of a spirit from heaven who visited a man in a dream, which shows that had have the ability to move between heavenly and earthly realms.[15]

The text also describes the deceased as having two souls. As they grow spiritually strong after death, they become brighter and more ethereal until they become fully spiritualized, disembodied intelligence.[16]

The *Book of Rites* and *Ten Wings*

The *Book of Rites* (*Li ji*) of the fifth century BCE is concerned with ritual procedures and Confucian history and philosophy. It explains the concept of dual souls, called the *hun* and the *po*. After death, the *hun*, the intelligent and spiritual soul, returns to the heavens from which it came; while the *po*, "the animal soul," returns to the underworld with the body. These realms are also referred to as "the bright region" and "the dark region." This duality of souls reflects "the Yin-Yang antithesis of two fundamental forces in the universe." Yin-Yang can be defined as the "complimentary forces [which] permeate all aspects of the spiritual, natural, and animal worlds, accounting for growth and decay." When the two elements of the soul return to their origin points at death, it brings about a reconciliation of these dual forces.

The word *po* is related to the word for "bright light," which originally referred to the light of the moon—which was itself associated with the cycle of death and rebirth because of its waxing and waning. These radiant souls going to "the dark region" is paralleled by Yo Pei and Shangdi having both underworld and heavenly associations. The dead are transformed in the otherworld, possessing "abundant and rich" powers that make them silent and invisible. "They enter into all things and nothing is without them."[17]

After ascending to heaven, the *hun* "is displayed on high in a condition of glorious brightness." Although these souls are "greatly virtuous," there are no morally divided realms of reward and punishment. Both the *hun* in the upper realm and the *po* in the lower attain a state of divine transcendence. This conflicts with the writings of the philosopher Mozi (479–438 BCE). He developed a rival philosophy to Confucianism called Mohism, stating that heaven is the highest level, spiritual beings live on the middle level, and humans on Earth are on the lowest level.[18]

In the *Ten Wings* (*Shi Yi*), a commentary on the *Book of Changes* (*Yi Jing*) (third century BCE), the cycle of life and death is compared to those of nature: "the characteristics and conditions of spiritual beings are similar to those of Heaven and Earth."[19]

Early Daoist Texts

Laozi

Two works attributed to the philosopher Laozi (c. fifth century BCE), contain a few details about the afterlife. According to the *Dao de jing*, all human problems are due to being in a physical body, implying a worry-free afterlife in a spiritualized state. The *Wenzi* explains that death results in "no changes in the self." The "higher soul" is made of "heavenly energy," the lower of "earthly energy," and "each abides in its abode." In the upper realm, "there is a continuity with universal oneness, and the vitality of universal oneness connects with heaven." Death is considered to be the spirit returning home.[20]

The *Zhuangzi*

This mystical and philosophical work by Master Zhuang, one of the founders of Daoism, dates to around 319 BCE. It shows faith in the Creator regarding the afterlife: "Where could he send me that would not be all right? I will go off to sleep peacefully, and then with a start I will wake up."

After casting off the body, souls experience "turning and revolving, ending and beginning again, unaware of where they start or finish . . . they wander free and easy in the service of inaction." Once they arrive in the heavenly realm, they can "wander in the mists, roam the infinite, and forget life forever and forever," then join the Creator "to wander in the single breath of heaven and earth." A soul's emotions survive the body, and dying is compared to awakening from a dream.[21]

The Perfect Man becomes "godlike," riding the clouds over the sun and the moon and wandering beyond the seas. "Even life and death have no effect upon him." He mounts "the regularity of Heaven and Earth, riding the changes of the elemental forces to wander infinity," and "is without self." The loss of the self is a merging with the Absolute: "I expel my intellectual faculties, leave my substance, get rid of knowledge and become identical with the Great Universality." Advanced spirits can "enter into the mother of breath," ascend to the "cloudy heavens," dwell in the Dark Palace, or become stars in the Milky Way. The spirit of The Nameless Man rides "the Light-and-Lissome Bird out beyond the six directions, wandering in the village of Not-even-Anything and living in the Broad-and-Borderless field."[22]

Similar abilities are attributed to a shamanic holy man, who "sucks the wind, drinks the dew" and "rides a flying dragon." It's not always clear whether the descriptions of out-of-body experiences have an afterlife or shamanic context, however. The word for "shaman," *xian*, also means "the power to ascend," a "spirit who dwells in the upper reaches of mountains," and "one who lives for a long time" or who is immortal. It might also refer to a spirit of the dead ascending from the body on its own cremation smoke. In any case, the shamanic spiritual realms and states appear to be one and the same as the afterlife—a notion supported by encounters with other souls, and the shared concepts of oneness and transcendence.[23]

The afterlife realm also has a distinct earthly character, with geographical features such as mountains and subterranean waters. In fact, it's not always clear if a place described is an actual earthly realm, a mythical earthly realm, or a metaphysical realm envisioned as an idealization of

Earth—though the distinction might be conceptually irrelevant. While some realms may be earthly, they're accessible only to the spirit, and only via the spiritual modes of travel of ascent or descent. This makes them effectively mythical to the nonspiritualized person. There was also a belief that ghosts could haunt earthly locales, reinforcing the distinction between spirit-earthly and genuinely Earth.[24]

The *Huainanzi*

Dating to around 122 BCE, the *Huainanzi* is a collection of essays on metaphysics, philosophy, religion, and other subjects. It states that the soul "undergoes a series of transformations without end, dying and coming to renewed life," though its subsequent fate depends on a number of factors determined in the four heavenly palaces, "which oversee recompenses and punishments." Ordinary people will have conflict and lack of peace. Those who die prematurely become ghosts on Earth. The Sage-man "penetrates the three fountains below"—the Yellow Springs—and "seeks the nine entrances into heaven above." The mind "penetrates into the depths of creation. This is the sage's movement of spirit." The True-man "moves in the regions of the completely immaterial and travels the deserts of anni-hilation." Riding a mythical long-haired, winged animal called the Fei Lien and following the immortal genie Tun Yü, the soul travels to "extra-mundane regions and rests in a spiritual house. He has the ten suns for his candle, the wind and rain for his servants, the thunder-lord is his minister." The genie Kua Fu is his messenger, the female genii Mifei and Chihnu are his allies, and he is not constrained by heaven and Earth.[25]

Reminiscent of the *Zhuangzi*, when the body has returned to Earth and the spirit has returned to heaven, "the 'I' is dissolved." The spirit asks, "how can I exist?" and is described as "a living part of the whole universe," which "is placed in an environment of great clarity." Spiritual knowledge is also a factor, for "He who is aware of the joys of a former existence will not be alarmed by death. . . . To pass from non-existence to a state of existence; to pass from existence to a state of non-existence is a continuous round without end or beginning."[26]

Songs of the South and Other Poetry

The poems in *Songs of the South* (*Chu ci*) are culturally distinct from their northern counterparts in the *Shijing* (which we looked at earlier in this chapter). Their unorthodox, cosmic, and fantastical character is highlighted in verses about love affairs between shamans and deities, while references to some of the more usual afterlife themes such as the Yellow Springs are rare. In addition to their colorful imagery and profuse detail, they are also quite repetitive, so only the general substance of a few of these poems can be conveyed here.

"On Encountering Trouble" ("Li Sao")

This mid-fourth-century BCE poem describes a spiritual ascent on a phoenix-shaped chariot pulled by jade dragons. The soul reaches the "fairy precincts" of the Hanging Gardens, a paradise on a terrace of Mount Kunlun. Dragons that carry souls drink from the Pool of Heaven and are tethered to the heavenly Fu-sang tree that grows in the east, an axis mundi that connects Heaven, Earth, and the Yellow Springs. The sun ascends this tree when it rises, and the ten suns roost in it at night. The tree is also sacred to the underworld deity the Queen Mother of the West, who enables the maintenance of cosmic order so that immortality and the cycles of rebirth can continue.[27]

From this paradise, the soul stops the sun from setting, then strikes it with a branch broken from the Ruo tree, which is the source of the red light of the sunset. Accompanied by the Wind God, the Bird of Heaven, the Thunder God, and the charioteers of the sun and the moon, the soul is welcomed by whirlwinds, clouds, and rainbows.[28]

Arriving at the gate of Heaven, the spirit in the poem asks the porter to let him through, but the porter eyes him with suspicion. Presumably he's allowed to pass, for he then crosses White Water, which flows through Mount Kunlun, and arrives at the House of Spring, a celestial locale presided over by the Green Dragon. Desiring to woo the river goddess, Fu Fei, he commands Feng Long the Thunder God to find her.

Other locales visited include Qiongshi mountain and the realm of Lord Y the Mighty Archer. The soul reaches Mount Kunlun via a long, winding road that passes through the Ford of Heaven, a constellation that leads beyond "the world's western end." Phoenixes accompany him to the Desert of Moving Sands and the Banks of the Red Water, where water-dragons make a bridge for him to cross. He's assisted in the crossing by the God of the West—perhaps the counterpart to the Queen Mother of the West. Further difficulties are encountered on a subsequent long journey until the spirit is joined by a thousand chariots of jade, drawn by dragons with "cloud-embroidered banners." Amid music and dancing, they pass the celestial Mount Buzhou in the west of Mount Kunlun, presumably continuing their wanderings.[29]

"Summons of the Soul" ("Zhao hun")

As its title indicates, this mid-third-century BCE poem concerns bringing a soul back to its body. There's a stress on the perils the soul might encounter, such as eastern "giants a thousand fathoms tall" that hunt souls, who are then consumed by the fierce heat of the ten suns. In the south are poisonous snakes that devour souls, and people with "tattooed faces and blackened teeth" who "sacrifice the flesh of men and pound their bones for meat paste." In the west, souls face the eternal punishment of the "moving sands," which stretch for a hundred leagues in a land of burning, empty desert filled with "red ants as huge as elephants and wasps as big as gourds." At Thunder's Chasm, souls are "dashed in pieces." In the north are walls of ice and a hundred leagues of snowdrifts.

The gates of heaven are protected by a number of guards, including tigers and leopards ready to tear apart "mortal men," a "man with nine heads that can pull up nine thousand trees," and "slant-eyed jackal-wolves," pacing, restless and sleepless, ready to drop humans into an abyss. In the Land of Darkness lies Yo Pei, with nine coils, a horned tiger's head with three eyes, a bull's body, a hunched back, and bloody thumbs. He's also referred to as Lord of Heaven, further associating these two opposite deities.[30]

"Far-Off Journey" ("Yuan You") and "Seven Remonstrances" ("Qi Jian")

In "Far-Off Journey" from around the second century BCE, the immortal ancestors, or Pure Ones, "lived on in a star." "In the ether's transformations they rose upwards; with godlike swiftness," and attained "oneness." Ascending on the south wind, "their bright spirit forms dart across the sky."

Seeking a similar experience, the poem's narrator undertakes a shamanic NDE-type soul journey to the Land of Immortality, among green-feathered ancestors on the Hill of Cinnabar, a mineral believed to have life-giving properties. With a face like radiant jade, he bathes in the Gulf of Brightness, dries himself on the coast of heaven, drinks "the subtle liqueur of the Flying Spring," and ascends on a cloud higher than the highest heaven. Passing through the gate of heaven, the Thunder God acts as a psychopomp, leading the poet to the Palace of Mystery, through the Bright Walls, and into the Court of Heaven in the House of God. This is only an intermediate phase, however, for the soul continues onward, riding a chariot with banners of clouds and rainbows, and visiting an abyss in the Eastern Sea into which the ocean drains.

Accompanied by horses and 10,000 chariots, he journeys to other divine realms through the constellations of the four directions. The wind god is now his psychopomp, and they are joined by phoenixes as they cross the eastern heaven and the celestial regions. The soul meets Ru Shou, an axe-wielding tiger-human spirit, then drifts "on the moving waves of fleeting mist" to meet Xuan Wua, a turtle guardian of the Palace of Winter who has a snake wrapped around his middle. With the gods in his retinue, he travels the endless road to "the height of heaven."[31]

The poet's "inner being" is suffused with "boundless satisfaction," a "reckless sense of freedom," "contentment," and a reluctance to return to life—a common feeling among many NDE'rs. After a moment of doubt, and nostalgia for his earthly life, the spirit heads straight for the sun (the Fiery God) and "into the emptiness . . . beyond the world's end." The sun's attendant, Zhu Rong, warns him to "turn back," but the spirit instead makes the Xiang river goddesses "play on their zithers." The Sea God dances with the River God, and goddesses dance with "water monsters" encircled by the "woman-rainbow." The music swells "into infinity" as the spirit proceeds to yet more divine realms, enlisting the creator god Qian Lei as guide. Traveling "the lightning's fissure, the Great Abyss," and "transcending Inaction," he arrives at Purity, then finally enters "the neighborhood of the Great Beginning."[32]

A contemporary poem, "Seven Remonstrances," shows less optimistic feelings about the afterlife. The soul passes through the "gates of the House of Darkness hidden in caverns under the rocky cliff-face," which are inhabited by water-serpents and dragon-spirits. "Deep below the surface," the poet says, "my unhoused spirit drifted disconsolate. . . . If only I could be sure that my acts had been faultless I could still be happy, even in my dissolution."[33]

Nine Songs, Nine Laments, and Nine Regrets

The *Nine Songs* were compiled around the second century BCE, though some of the content is far older. One song mentions the Greater Master of Fate (Da si ming), who greets the spirit in the heavens. In earlier times, this shamanic underworld god was a heavenly and stellar deity. The god of Fate, "the bestower of life and death," is also associated with the spiritual journey, indicating afterlife judgment. When the shaman-poet ascends to bathe with Fate "in the Pool of Heaven, he says, "You only, Fragrant One, are worthy to be judge over men."[34]

The Lord of the East is a solar deity associated with shamans. One song describes the shaman ascending from the east on horseback, before descending on a "gloomy night journey back to the east," meaning that he joins the sun-god on his journey through the sky and underworld.[35] In another song, the shaman joins the River Earl to wander the nine rivers in a water chariot. Surviving whirlpools and waves, they ascend Mount Kunlun to the god's palace, built of shells, pearls, and fish and dragon scales. They ride a white turtle, chase fish, and wander in the islets before returning east.[36]

In "Nine Laments" ("Jiu tan"), dating to around 77 BCE, the spirit describes the blinding brightness of Mount Kunlun's Hanging Gardens. He becomes vaporous and formless, "mounting the void, treading the dark sky" before entering "the House of God shaking his wings." He races the wind and rain, and "wanders without end."[37] In "Nine Regrets" ("Jiu hua"), the soul radiates brightness and floats over Weak Water to visit the Lord of Heaven. Arriving there, he remarks that his "mind is illuminated with understanding: Here in this place I shall find self-knowledge."[38]

Popular Songs

Around 200 BCE, the governmental Bureau of Music began collecting songs from across China, some of which had afterlife-related themes. One involves a shamanic trance visit to the realm of the immortals, called Mount Tsung Kao. The mountain has five peaks with golden turrets, jewels of many colors, unicorns, antelope, chimeras, various birds, and magical mushrooms—probably hallucinogenic ones that enable the shamanic journey.

At the gates of Jade Hall, the spirit of the shaman is questioned, "What do you seek?" He replies, "I wish to follow the holy way, to seek only long life."

He is told to "gather the sacred herb from the tip of Illusion Tree," which will be processed by a white hare and a tortoise and will make the spirit divine.

Another song mentions the afterlife realm of Mount Hao Li, ruled by the King of Ghosts. It's also called Burial Village, and is "teeming" with "souls and spirits, none wise, none fool."[40]

Yet another song states that those who are good attain "the way of holy immortals" at death. They're met by the psychopomp Red Pine "four or five leagues away from Heaven," and he takes the reigns (presumably of a chariot) and steers them the rest of the way. They visit the Royal Father and Mother—perhaps Shangdi and the Queen Mother of the West—and live on Mount Tai, north of Mount Hao Li.[41]

The *Classic of Mountains* and Seas (*Shanhaijing*)

This is a largely mythological geography of China and other realms—including the afterlife. A section dating to the third century BCE tells us that the Queen Mother of the West lives on Mount Jade, while Mount Kunlun is "the Great God's City Here Below." It's ruled by a nine-tailed tiger-human deity, Land My, who "presides over the Nine Parts of the Sky and the Great God's Park for the Seasons." A ram-like animal with four horns called "earth-cricket" devours humans, and a large bee-like bird called "awe-source" kills with its sting. Various magical-medicinal plants can be found there, such as a pear-like fruit that keeps people from drowning when they consume it.[42]

A section from the late first century BCE describes the plateau of Mount Kunlun, "the dwelling place of the hundred deities," as being 800 leagues square and 80,000 feet high. There are nine wells on each face of the mountain, each with jade railings and gates guarded by nine-headed tiger-like animals. One of them stands atop the mountain, surrounded by magical trees and beings, including the Divine-Wind Bird, Wonderbirds adorned with snakes, and the self-devouring but self-regenerating Shihjou, which "looks like a lump of liver." There are also alligators, apes, snakes, and leopards.[43]

The corpse of the murdered human-headed snake god, Ya Yü, is encircled by a group of shamans—"custodians of the secret of preserving life." Ya Yü holds "the never die drug to ward off decay." There are also references to twelve corpses of humans who were transformed into gods, or into composite human-animal beings, following a heroic death. The idea of life being found within death was related to the concept of "immortality gained through shamanic techniques."[44]

Funerary Documents

Han funerary documents of the mid-second-century BCE depict an afterlife bureaucracy that mirrors the government system of China at the time. Purported to originate with the heavenly deity, the documents were intended to introduce the deceased into the underworld community. Written on bamboo, they record grave goods and titles of officials such as Lord of the Underworld, Assistant Magistrate of the Underworld, and Assistant of the Dead.

Some of the texts reveal anxieties about the efficiency of these officials, appealing to them to make sure that they've taken the right person, and at the right time. Others are ordinances decreeing that souls will not be punished for wrong behavior and will not have to pay taxes and fines to the underworld demons. There are even references to the deceased receiving rental income. One document refers to the soul as "heavenly light." In another, the deceased takes a 3,000-mile journey to the "Heavenly Emperor and Sacred Teacher," and encounters dangers such as the soul-eating demon of the South Mountain.[45]

Inscriptions on bronze mirrors from around 100 BCE–150 CE were also meant to help integrate souls of the newly dead into the afterlife. While generally consistent with the Daoist poetry, over time their focus shifted from the energies of Yin and Yang, to the inhabitants of the afterlife realm, and then to the Queen Mother of the West."[46] These developments overlapped with changes to afterlife beliefs that appeared under Emperor Wu, emphasizing immortality through ascent to heaven *before* death. This was enabled by the *xian*, both a state of being and an element of the soul. Because the *xian* and the *hun* belonged to different categories of being, a separate realm for the *xian* was required. The afterlife was therefore restructured, and the *hun* were relocated to Mount Tai, ruled by the Lord of the Mountain who lived on the nearby hill of Liangfu. The title "Lord" was a bureaucratic designation, for he actually ranked lower than the earthly emperor. He was assisted in governing the dead by lesser officials in a system that mirrored that of the Han government.

The peak of Mount Tai, however, became the exclusive preserve of *xian*, so that the *hun* were left with only Liangfu hill. Mount Tai became symbolic of immortality, while Liangfu grew to symbolize death. Finally, there was a third realm for *po* souls, an underworld that was also called Po, or the "court of ghosts."[47]

Understanding the Chinese Afterlife Experience

Although there were changes over time, the earliest Chinese afterlife references on the Shang oracle bones have basic elements that remained consistent through most of the texts: ascent to a heavenly realm, meeting deceased relatives, and divinization or dwelling with the gods in a godlike state. The nature of the oracle bones precluded more detailed descriptions, which first appear with the more substantial Classics. They added beings of light, judgment and morally determined fates, the afterlife being a return "home" to our place of origin, the concept of spiritual progression and intermediate states, afterlife realms that were interassociated with both underworld and heavenly realms and deities, dual souls, universal oneness, and divine omnipresence.

For the most part, those elements were also thematically present in the Daoist texts and other poetry, though they also featured a wealth of detailed descriptions of various realms and entities that don't correspond to anything in the Classics. In many cases they're unique and idiosyncratic. This may be partly due to their shamanic origins. They also show a greater focus on metaphysical concepts, such as the transcendence of the self and merging with the divine. Other differences from the Classics include afterlife realms that are idealized mirror images of Earth and quasi-earthly mythical locales, a proliferation of mythical beings, river crossings and other obstacles or barriers, more emphasis on solar, lunar, and celestial associations, and rebirth. The funerary documents supplement rather than contradict the other material, while emphasizing afterlife bureaucracy that mirrored earthly bureaucracy.

Attempting to untangle the reasons for the differences over time leads to more speculation than certainty. Some would have been due to cultural differences between varying regional traditions, and others to literary elaboration and descriptions simply growing more detailed. Still others were due to deliberate new developments in conceptions over time, such as the displacement of *hun* souls to accommodate the *xian*. At the same time, the absence of any element of the afterlife experience in the earlier texts doesn't mean that it didn't exist in the minds of the people. These works weren't comprehensive theological treatises about the afterlife, and indeed in some of the sources—such as those concerned with divination or with earthly matters—the afterlife material is almost incidental. It's interesting to note that despite cultural peculiarities, the afterlife conceptions of the northern and southern poetry do not differ significantly. This could reflect their shamanic contexts, meaning that similar types of experience were leading to the creation of similar types of afterlife literature (idiosyncrasies notwithstanding).

Judgment isn't an obvious feature until the later texts and is never particularly stressed, though hints do appear as far back as the *Classic of Poetry*, the *Spring and Autumn Annals*, and *Huainanzi*. In all of these, judgment is passed by heaven or the heavenly deity. In *Songs of the South*, it's a matter for the Lesser Master of Fate, though self-judgment is also hinted at when the soul says, "If only I could be sure that my acts had been faultless I could still be happy, even in my dissolution."[48]

Punishment is evident from descriptions of the abyss in *Songs of the South*, the deceased being thrown to deities in the *Classic of Poetry*, and the many colorful perils detailed in the poetry. Although judgment takes place in the underworld when it concerns the living,[49] in these early pre-Buddhist times it appears that for the dead, there is no morally based distinction between the upper and lower realms. In general, heavens aren't in direct opposition to underworlds—on the contrary, they're associated with each other, as are their gods.

The differences between some of the various afterlife states are also unclear. We don't always know which individuals go where and on what basis, or even whether the heavenly realms and the state of universal oneness are one and the same. The divine omnipresence in the *Book of Rites* and elsewhere may hold the answer, for if souls of the dead become gods, they are capable of multiple transcendental experiences, separately or at once. Indeed, the afterlife is characterized as eternal cosmic wandering in the *Zhuangzi* and later.

However, multiple experiences and intermediate states don't explain key differences between texts, such as the introduction of the *xian* concept. It seems clear that there was never a single, all-pervasive conception of the afterlife experience, but rather variations on a number of themes held by different groups of people, or even individuals.[50] Nevertheless, a core of *thematic* similarities occur across all the traditions reviewed here. They're found in the supposedly historical accounts of NDEs reviewed at the beginning of this chapter, as well as in all the other classes of evidence we have discussed. This suggests a deep connection between NDEs, shamanic experiences, and afterlife beliefs throughout ancient Chinese history.

Excursus: The NDE of Princess Miaoshan

Though it belongs firmly to the Buddhist era, it's worth mentioning the legendary NDE of Miaoshan, the youngest daughter of King Zhuang. Though said to have occurred around 700 BCE, according to Chinese tradition, it originated with the visionary and medium Daoxuan in 596–667 CE. The earliest surviving version with the NDE episode, however, is much later, dating to around 1300.

Though Miaoshan was a devout Buddhist dedicated to religious discipline, her father believed she should marry. Miaoshan was distressed and disgusted at the thought of being forced into marriage when in her heart she desired to become a nun. After performing a number of miracles with the aid of the dragon spirit—causing vegetables to grow in abundance and a fresh spring to appear—her father accused Miaoshan of sorcery and sentenced her to death.

Just as she was about to be beheaded, however, the executioner's sword broke in half and a tiger appeared. It rescued Misohan, running away with her into the forest.

Miaoshan had lost consciousness—whether from being struck by the sword before it broke or from being mauled by the tiger is unclear. But during this state, she had a vision that two boys dressed in black took her on a tour of the underworld. There she met King Yan, the Chinese equivalent of the Indian Yama, who treated her with kindness and respect. Miaoshan also saw sinners being punished in a variety of ways, including dismemberment, immolation, and being ground to a pulp. She recited Buddhist sutras on their behalf, delivering them from their punishments.

An eighteenth-century version of the story is more explicit about the near-death theme: according to the modern translator, in that version Miaoshan "voluntarily accepts death by strangulation, and it is her dead body that the tiger bears into the Forest of Corpses. Her tour of hell and later revival take her more clearly across the frontiers of life and death."[51]

Following her NDE, Miaoshan became known as Guanyin—one of the most famous and important *Bodhisattvas* in East Asian Buddhisms. While there's little evidence to suggest a genuine 700 BCE date to the text—especially considering that it would be nearly 150 years before the Buddha's birth!—it's possible that there really was a woman named Miaoshan who had an NDE and that it was preserved in oral tradition and adapted to the story of Guanyin. Even if entirely fictitious, however, it was clearly written with knowledge of the phenomenon, and is another testament to the power of NDEs to shape not only afterlife beliefs, but religions themselves.

7

Mesoamerica
Places of the Fleshless

Two Nahua Near-Death Experiences

A Mexica Princess of Tlateloclo

A remarkable NDE was preserved by the Spanish Franciscan missionary and ethnographer Bernardino de Sahagún in his collection of indigenous oral narratives known as *Primeros Memoriales*, or *First Memoranda*. Beginning in 1547, Sahagún interviewed native elders—primarily priests and nobles—and faithfully recorded what they said in the original Nahuatl language. The results are genuine indigenous primary texts, otherwise unknown. This NDE was recounted to Sahagún by the Mexica people as a factual occurrence. It involves the daughter-in-law of a known historical figure, Moquihuix, a ruler of the Tlateloclo city-state from 1460–1473. The genuine historical background supports the notion that the account was at least grounded in an actual NDE, rather than being purely a myth.

The woman, named Quetzalpetlatl, fell ill after being "half-killed" by Moquihuix. The elder members of her family were going to cremate her, but others protested, saying, "She must not be cremated; we must just bury her." The text carefully emphasizes that "she had indeed died," explaining how her corpse had been prepared, her grave dug deeply, the earth packed down, and the grave covered with stones.

After four days, "a sickly, deformed youth" appeared to Quetzalpetlatl and said, "And you, first-born, Quetzalpetlatl, you have suffered. Come on! Sing!"

Quetzalpetlatl sang: "The jewel on the shield is with me: the jewel on the shield is with me. Let us die for only a day. Let us die."

The youth then guided her "to the land of the dead," across grassy plains, past lizards, stones, and women who were weaving. The boy instructed Quetzalpetlatl not to call to the women, "then he took her to Tlalocan"—the paradisiacal land of the dead and of the rain god Tlaloc—"where there were frogs as in the springtime." At the end of the road, surrounded by mist, were the souls of those who had died from drowning or from being struck by lightning. There Quetzalpetlatl met her nephew who had drowned, though again she was instructed not to call out to him—instead he would call to her.

"Here you come" was all her nephew said when they met.

The guide then took her to meet the god Tlaloc, here described as old and toothless, with his face blackened by liquid rubber.

Tlaloc asked the youth how he arrived there, who was the woman accompanying him, and if she had come to stay there forever.

"No," the youth replied, "she has come only to observe, and she has come only to see you."

Tlaloc turned to Quetzalpetlatl and told her to look at his priests "dancing for you on earth. Look at them, for they live here."

He then showed her the souls of "sons of noblemen" who died young. Among them was her own stepson who had died as a small child. Tlaloc told her that her that the boy, characterized as a hummingbird, would be reborn on Earth to grow up and become educated.

Quetzalpetlatl's guide then asked Tlaloc to bestow favor upon her, and Tlaloc gave her "a small coffer" and "a blue-green gourd vessel." The vessel was filled with a curative substance, and Tlaloc instructed Quetzalpetlatl to take it back with her to Earth "to remedy all who are in misery."

Before returning, however, Quetzalpetlatl was shown the place where the spirits of leaders and rulers lived, a grassy, windy plain without houses. She met some of them, including the famous Aztec emperor, Motecuhzoma I, who had died a few years earlier.

Unfortunately, the next page of the manuscript is missing, so we don't know the details of Quetzalpetlatl returning to her body, how she came out of her grave, or how she told her people of her experiences in the otherworld. While the narrative is obviously deeply culturally embedded, it nevertheless includes the familiar NDE elements of otherworld journey, a guide, a spiritual being, deceased relatives, multiple regions or states of being, an idealized version of Earth, and a return characterized by a positive transformation—here in the form of having the ability to heal the sick on Earth.[1]

An Aztec Woman of Tenochtitlan

A second pre-Columbian NDE from the neighboring city-state of Tenochtitlan, modern Mexico City, was also recorded by Sahagún. It dates to the reign of Motecuhzoma II, the ninth ruler of Tenochtitlan from 1502 to 1520. The experiencer is described in the text as "a woman of quality." She died of an illness and was buried, with stones piled on her grave. After four days, "she came to life at night," frightening all those who were present. Her grave "burst open," and the stones that were covering it scattered.

The woman, "after she had returned to life," went to tell Motecuhzoma what she had experienced. She told him that the reason she came back to life was to inform him that not only would his reign end, but that the city of Mexico would be subjugated and occupied by "they who come." Following this apparent prophecy of the Spanish conquest, the "woman who had died lived another twenty-one years."

It has been suggested that this account is the same as the previous one, revealing the missing "finale" of Quetzalpetlatl's NDE. Despite some similarities, however, this seems unlikely. There's a gap of 30 to 50 years between the two accounts, they take place in rival city-states, they are both found in Sahagún's reports, and their details are very different. The two accounts, in any case, firmly demonstrate that NDEs were known in preconquest Mesoamerica.[2]

For other possible evidence of knowledge of NDEs, we must again turn to the spheres of ritual and religion. There are two types of written sources for Mesoamerican afterlife conceptions. The most important here are the indigenous works written before the Spanish conquest in 1521 CE. Though they were *recorded* after the conquest—in indigenous languages using the Latin alphabet—they were partly transcribed from earlier hieroglyphic texts and partly dictations of preconquest oral literature. While the Spanish recorded them mainly as an aid to converting the populace to Christianity, from the indigenous perspective, their participation was a subversive attempt to preserve the ancient traditions from the Spanish efforts to eradicate them. These texts include the Maya *Popol Vuh* and the *Books of Chilam Balam*; and the Aztec *Legend of the Suns*, *Annals of Cuauhtitlan*, and *Cantares Mexicanos* (*Mexican Songs*).

Secondary are reports written by the Spanish conquistadores. Because such material is often compromised by Christianizing interpretations of local beliefs, and by dismissive, superior attitudes, they must be used with caution. An important exception is Sahagún's unusually reliable ethnography *General History of the Things of New Spain*.

Maya

The *Popol Vuh*

The *Popol Vuh*, or *The Light that Came from Beyond the Sea*, is an important work of revelation, divination, and myth. Though not written down until around 1554–1558 CE, it survived in oral form for at least a thousand years—originating perhaps even as early as 300 BCE. One section concerns the underworld journey of the Hero Twins—1-Hunahpu, a fertility god, and his brother 7-Hunahpu (the number one signifies creation, and seven signifies ending or finality). Despite being reached by descent, the underworld realm of Xibalba is described as "a world beyond the visible sky."[3]

One day while playing a ball game, the Twins annoy the Lords of Xibalba below by making too much noise. These underworld deities were called 1-Death and 7-Death, described as being "black and white," eager for conflict, "not really divine," "ancient evil," "makers of enemies," "inciters to wrongs and violence," and "masters of stupidity, and perplexity." They're accompanied by two staff bearers, Bone Scepter and Skull Scepter. Lesser underworld deities include Scab Stripper, Blood Gatherer, and Demons of Pus, Jaundice, Filth, and Woe, whose punishment techniques reflect their names. Another, called Packstrap, causes sudden death by inducing his victim to vomit blood.[4]

The Twins tell their mother that although they're going to the underworld, they "are not dying." They are taken on the journey by the messengers Shooting Owl, One-Legged Owl, and Skull Owl—a head with wings. Descending on the path to Xibalba, they pass the intersection of Rustling Canyon and Gurgling Canyon, then cross over Scorpion Rapids—literally rapids filled with scorpions, equated with the constellation Scorpius. They then cross Blood River and Pus River before arriving at a crossroads of four different-colored paths: red, white, yellow, and black.[5]

They take the black path, which leads to the "council place" of Xibalba. When they arrive, however, instead of meeting a council of gods, they find wooden manikins of them. The gods laugh at the Twins' dismay, then bid them to sit. But the only seat is a "burning-hot rock," and the gods laugh again when the Twins are burned.[6]

1-Hunahpu and 7-Hunahpu are then sent to the Dark House, a pitch black room devoid of light. A messenger brings them each a torch and a cigar that must be returned intact the next day—despite the fact that they've already been lit. The Twins also endure Jaguar House, Bat House, Razor House, and Rattling House, which is "heavy with cold," wind, and hail. These are only "the first tests of Xibalba."[7]

Having automatically failed the cigar-and-torch test, however, the Twins are sacrificed—though not before somehow, at some indeterminate point, becoming one person. Their head is placed in the fork of a melon tree, causing it to bear fruit and to transform into a melon. Blood Moon, the virgin daughter of Blood Gatherer, attempts to pick the head-melon, but it spits at her. In doing so, it imparts the knowledge it learned from the deities Newborn Thunderbolt, Sudden Thunderbolt, and Hurricane. The Thunderbolt deities carry "lightning-striking axes" and are associated with fertility, the underworld, and the rain god Chac. The knowledge they give to the Twins is that in death, "one does not disappear, but goes on being fulfilled . . . you will not die."[8]

Blood Moon then relays this knowledge to the Twins' mother on Earth, telling her that they "are alive, they are not dead. They have merely made a way for the light to show itself."

In addition to transmitting the revelation of life after death, the saliva of the Twins' head-melon has also made Blood Moon pregnant. She gives birth to another set of Twins, Hunahpu and Xblanque. Their birth encompasses a number of miraculous events, for they are divine twins born of father twins who became one in death, and a virgin mother who is goddess of the moon and the underworld.[9]

When Hunahpu and Xblanque are grown, they, too, are summoned to the underworld. To some extent, their journey duplicates that of their fathers, though with some differences. There is the added menace of large black hawks called "throng birds," and the yellow path has been replaced by a green one. This is notable because a prayer in the *Popol Vuh* tells the deceased to keep to the Green Road. In Maya iconography, green is the color of the axis mundi—the line through the center of the Earth than connects it with the upper and lower worlds. It's through this axis that the sacred Yaxche tree grows—the "first tree of the world," symbolic of life and fertility.[10]

Before proceeding further, Hunahpu plucks a hair "from his own shin" and it becomes a mosquito. He sends it to spy on the Lords of Xibalba and to determine if they're real or manikins by attempting to suck their blood. The first two prove to be made of wood, though the third and fourth are actually 1-Death and 7-Death. As each Lord is bitten by the mosquito, he is named by the one ranking below him (the Demons of Filth and Woe have been replaced by Bloody Teeth and Bloody Claws). The Twins now know the names of all the Lords of Xibalba, and this knowledge gives them some sort of advantage or new abilities. They're not fooled into sitting on the hot rock, and they outwit the Lords in the cigar-and-torch test by substituting macaw feathers for the torch's flame and fireflies for the cigar's ember.[11]

The Lords of Xibalba then challenge the Twins to a ball game played with a skull, "clattering and twisting all over the floor of the court." A sacrificial knife—the White Dagger—emerges from the skull, and the Twins accuse the Lords of trying to kill them. They resume play with the Twins' ball, but the Lords still win the game. As a prize they want one bowl of red flower petals, one of white, one of yellow, and one of whole flowers. Apparently unable to provide them, the Twins are then sent to Razor House where knives fly toward them, but they succeed in immobilizing them by saying, "This is yours; the flesh of all the animals"—apparently propitiating the knives with meat offerings. They then send ants to steal flowers from the Lords' own garden, and are thus able to outwit them once again by presenting them with the flowers they'd demanded.[12]

To the astonishment of 1-Death and 7-Death, the Twins survive not only Razor House, but also Cold House (apparently the same as Rattling House) and Jaguar House. In a new torment, the Midst of the Fire, the Twins are not burned, "just toasted, just simmered, so they were well when it dawned." In Bat House, however, Hunahpu is decapitated by a "snatch-bat"—"monstrous beasts" who eat the moon, "their snouts like knives, the instruments of death." Hunahpu's head rolls onto the ball court and the Lords rejoice at their victory.[13]

Xblanque now asks "all the animals" to bring their food. The coati, a racoon-like animal, brings a squash, which becomes "a simulated head for Hunahpu." Eyes are carved into it, and "brains came from the thinker, from the sky," from "the Heart of the Sky, Hurricane . . . who came down into Bat House." In the *Book of Chilam Balam of Chumayel* (see below), the brains of the sky are made of copal, a resinous incense. With his new brains, Hunahpu is made whole at dawn, and despite his squash-head he looks and speaks the same.[14]

Another game is played with the Lords of Xibalba, this time with Hunahpu's actual head. The Twins succeed in retrieving the head during play and restoring to Hunahpu. They then plant the squash-head, though somehow also substitute it for the head on the playing field. They win the game, but the "head" breaks open, spilling its seeds onto the court.

The Lords realize they have again been outwitted, and they burn both Hunahpu and Xblanque to death in an oven—but not before the Twins have made special arrangements for the treatment of their charred bones. They instruct two seers, Xulu and Pacam, to convince the Lords to grind the bones to powder once they are dead and put them into the river. When this is done, the ashes sink to the bottom. After five days "they become handsome boys; they looked just the same as before when they reappeared."[15]

This resurrection gives the Twins divine and transformative powers. They appear to the lesser underworld deities as catfish and perform ritual animal dances dressed as vagabonds. In addition to doing tricks such as swallowing swords and walking on stilts, they perform "many miracles," such as setting fire to a house and then restoring it. To the intense admiration of the gods, they sacrifice themselves and are resurrected yet again. The Twins are then taken on a path, with further "troubles" and "torments," to 1-Death and 7-Death so that they, too, might witness such wonders.

When they arrive, 1-Death and 7-Death ask Hunahpu and Xblanque their identities, their origins, their tribe, and their home. The boys reply, "we've never known."[16] This may suggest a further step in their spiritual transformation involving loss of ego or a state of transcendence in which identity and relations to earthly social labels like "tribe" are irrelevant. On the other hand, it may simply be an attempt to conceal their identity.

The Twins now perform a number of miracles for the Lords: sacrificing their dog and then reanimating it, setting fire to their house with flames that do not burn, and removing the heart from a human sacrifice victim, then resuscitating him. Finally, Xblanque sacrifices his brother Hunahpu. He ties him spread-eagle, decapitates him, and cuts his heart out, which is then "smothered in a leaf." He then brings him back to life, making this the fourth time Hunahpu has died and been resurrected in the underworld (twice by beheading).[17]

The Lords are so delighted with the spectacle that they ask the Twins to sacrifice *them*. The Twins oblige, killing both 1-Death and 7-Death—but they do not resurrect them.

Hunahpu and Xblanque accomplish their defeat of the Lords "only through wonders, only through self-transformation." The remaining underworld gods perform the heart sacrifice on the dead Lords, "for the purpose of destroying them."[18]

The Twins then reveal their identities to these other deities of Xibalba and tell them that they will be the next to die. They explain that they intend to "clear the road of the torments and troubles of our fathers." The gods weep and admit they were wrong to harm the Twins' fathers, 1-Hunahpu and 7-Hunahpu, and they tell the boys that they will find them buried beneath the underworld ball court.

The Twins show mercy, but only on the condition that the deities no longer live on human sacrifices. The origin of morally determined afterlife punishment is explained here, for the exception is that the gods may consume "worthless" beings, such as "the guilty" and "the violent"—though they are also permitted to eat "the wretched, the afflicted."

The Twins resurrect their father(s)—now referred to collectively as 7-Hunahpu—and put him back together again. When they ask him to name the parts of his face, he can only remember the eyes, nose, and mouth. The Twins depart, assuring him that he "will be prayed to" and remembered by future generations.

Hunahpu and Xblanque then ascend "here into the middle of the light" and go "straight on into the sky, and the sun belongs to one and the moon belongs to the other." They are joined by the 400 boys, perhaps the Pleiades star cluster, where they become "the sky's own stars."[19]

To this day, the Maya see the sun and Venus as Xblanque and Hunahpu, respectively. Elsewhere in the *Popol Vuh*, the gods send the Twins to vanquish 7-Macaw, the usurper and impersonator of the sun, the light, and the moon. This makes them protectors of the *true* sun, which through their underworld journey of renewal and their celestial ascent and transformation is associated with the afterlife. In an eleventh- or twelfth-century work on astronomy and medicine known as the Dresden Codex, the Twins, as well as the Earth-moon-childbirth goddess Ixchel, are associated with Venus. Represented as a skull, Venus itself is related to rebirth and renewal, and is referred to as the "sun-carrier." The Maya calendar associates both the Twins and 1-Death and 7-Death with Venus. The translator of the *Popol Vuh*, Dennis Tedlock, has suggested that the five perilous houses and the five manifestations of severed heads in the *Popol Vuh* might have paralleled the five phases of Venus.[20]

The sixteenth-century Poqomam Maya considered Xblanque to be a psychopomp. The name "Xblanque" is etymologically connected to the root for "sun" and a word that means both "jaguar" and "hidden." As a god of corn and fertility, 1-Hunahpu's death and resurrection reflects the agricultural cycle. Both the melon and the squash are symbols of agriculture and are prominent in the text—specifically in their association with our underworld heroes. When the Twins were burned in the oven, the corn they had planted in their mother's garden "grew again."[21]

Taken together, the Twins are associated with the sun, fertility and rebirth, the ancient Olmec Jaguar death-god, the circuit of Venus through the underworld and the sky, and the moon-goddess Ixchel. They achieve a state of divine omnipresence and totality involving various celestial bodies, divinities of both sexes, and the earthly cycles of nature in an ultimate union, brought about by death, an underworld journey, ascent, and spiritual transformation and rebirth.

Account of the Things of Yucatán
(Relación de las Cosas de Yucatán)

The afterlife described in this 1566 report by the Spanish bishop Diego de Landa diverges from other Maya texts, but interestingly, it's consistent with contemporary Aztec beliefs. The morally good, military heroes, women who die in childbirth, and those who die sudden, violent deaths go to paradise. Those who take their own lives also go to paradise, after being fetched by the suicide goddess Ixtab who wears a noose around her neck. Souls rest beneath the Yaxche tree, never have to work, and have plenty of food and drink.

Everyone else goes to Metnal, ruled by the god Hunhau. It's a place of grief and despair, filled with devils and torments of extreme fatigue, cold, and hunger.[22] The book is unfortunately incomplete, and also shows de Landa's Catholic biases, so may not be an entirely reliable source.

The *Book of Chilam Balam of Chumayel*

Despite being compiled in the late seventeenth and early eighteenth centuries, the *Book of Chilam Balam of Chumayel* contains little Christian influence aside from occasional token references to Christ and Jerusalem. Chilam Balam was a Maya prophet, and the text mostly concerns prophesies and oracles.

It explains that heaven consists of 13 levels and the underworld of nine, each with its own god. The number nine is also associated with rebirth in the book's creation myth, likely in reference to the human gestation period. Each set of otherworld deities is simultaneously one deity: the heavenly Oxlahun-ti-ku and the underworld Bolon-ti-ku. The realms of life and death are interassociated when Oxlahun-ti-ku adopts the guise of Bolon-ti-ku. He sits on a flower with a piece of wood in one hand, a tree in the other, blindfolded and full of sin. In a reversal of the earthly order, his food and drink cry out.

Four ancestral afterlife spirits or deities called Pauahtuns are associated with the cardinal points and the four winds and rains. They are colored red, white, black, and yellow—the same as the roads to Xibalba in the first descent myth of the *Popol Vuh*.[23]

Aztec and Other Nahua Peoples

The *Legend of the Suns*

The mythological work *Legend of the Suns* was recorded in 1558, and has been described as "one of the purest sources of Aztec myth." An afterlife journey is included in a creation myth in which the feathered serpent sky deity, Quetzalcoatl, goes to the "the emerald realm," the underworld of Mictlan. His intention is to obtain human bones from the Lord and Lady of the Dead, Mictlantecuhtli and Mictlancihuatl, in order to start a new race of humans.

As in the *Popol Vuh*, the underworld deities play tricks on him. When Quetzalcoatl outwits them, they tell him to go ahead and take the bones—but they instruct the spirits of the dead in the underworld to tell him that he must *not* take them. Quetzalcoatl outwits them again, calling out that he's leaving the "precious bones" behind, even as he takes them and ascends away.[24]

When the Lord and Lady of the Dead realize this, they send spirits of the dead to dig a trapping pit. Quetzalcoatl falls in, loses consciousness and drops the bones. When he revives, he sees that quails have been pecking at the bones and have "ruined" them.

Quetzalcoatl nevertheless takes the bones to the paradise of Tamoanchan, where they're powdered in a jade bowl by Quilaztli the "Serpent Woman." Quetzalcoatl bleeds onto the powder through a wound in his penis, creating the new race through self-sacrifice. A male child grows from the mixture on the fourth day and a female on the eighth.

Six gods then do penance, though their names are actually epithets of Quetzalcoatl himself, suggesting the attainment of divine unity. His underworld journey has resulted in a higher state of divinity as a creator god who brought forth life from human remains in the realm of the dead. He also becomes a fertility deity, bringing maize to the new race; and gains transformative powers, changing himself into an ant.[25]

In another relevant myth, the divinized planet Venus, Ce Acatl, buries his father the sun as he's setting in the west. To ensure that he'll be reborn at dawn, Ce Acatl fights off the stars. He then reaches Tlapallan, the "Red Place" at the morning horizon, where he dies and is cremated. He's then reborn as the Morning Star, in an eternal cycle of transformation and renewal. As the god of the Morning Star, Quetzalcoatl was also associated with Venus. His brother, Xolotl, was the Evening Star and guide for the deceased in the afterlife. Souls of the dead were also associated with Venus, suggesting divine union with both Quetzalcoatl and Xolotl as they ascend and descend. The fact that Venus was considered to be a fragment of the sun could mean that the ultimate goal is to reunite with the sun and return it to its unified state.[26]

The *Annals of Cuauhtitlan*

This Aztec mythical-historical work was first written down in 1570. One section describes the death and divine transformation of a Toltec ruler named Ce Acatl Topiltzin Quetzalcoatl, who lived from 817–895 CE. Though a historical figure, the ancient texts often associated him with the deity Quetzalcoatl.

The myth tells of how Topiltzin Quetzalcoatl loved his people, and therefore refused to perform human sacrifices. Instead, he sacrificed snakes, birds, and butterflies. This frustrates the sorcerers, and they start to ridicule him in hopes of driving him away. When that fails, they decide that the best thing to do is to "give him a way to see his flesh."

One of the sorcerers, Tezcatlipoca, goes to him and says, "I've come to show you your flesh."

Confused, Topiltzin Quetzalcoatl replies, "What is this 'flesh' of mine? Let me see it."

The sorcerer takes out a mirror, shows it to Topiltzin Quetzalcoatl, and says, "Know yourself, see yourself."

Looking into the mirror in horror, Topiltzin Quetzalcoatl sees his own corpse-like reflection with sunken eyes and a swollen, "monstrous" face.

More sorcerers arrive, and they succeed in getting Topiltzin Quetzalcoatl drunk with his sister Quetzalpetlatl, so that they neglect their morning rituals and sacrifices. In shame, the king decides to "go away" and has a stone sarcophagus made.

He's placed in the sarcophagus but after four days he suddenly arises. He tells his servants to gather all his valuables and hide them at the spring where he bathes. He wanders for a time, feeling disappointed everywhere he goes. Even when he arrives at the place he'd been seeking, he feels only sadness.

Finally, he goes to the ocean. After putting on his turquoise mask and other ceremonial attire, "he set himself on fire and cremated himself." His ashes ascend in the form of "precious birds," and his people "knew he had gone to the sky, had entered the sky."

According to a legend among the old people of the time,

when he died he disappeared for four days. They said he went to the dead land then. And he spent four more days making darts for himself. So it was after eight days that the morning star came out, which they said was Quetzalcoatl. It was then that he became lord.[27]

It's not clear whether Topiltzin Quetzalcoatl was already dead when Tezcatlipoca showed him his corpse-like reflection—or if it was merely an illusion accomplished by sorcery. It may be that lying in the sarcophagus for four days was meant to indicate that he was dead at *that* point, though alternatively, perhaps he was simply hoping to lie down and die of shame following his drunken episode. A literal reading may be the most likely interpretation: that he did not die at all until his own self-cremation. For that reason, as interesting and compelling as the narrative is, we should hesitate to consider it a historical NDE despite the historicity of Topiltzin Quetzalcoatl. In any case, there is at least one death and rebirth in the story, and it's the encounter with his own "corpse" that ultimately leads Topiltzin Quetzalcoatl to being reborn into a transformed, divinized state of being.

History of the Mexica (Histoyre du Mechique)

In this 1547 French translation of a lost indigenous text, Quetzalcoatl is referred to as Yohualtecuhtli. He was both the Evening Star and the sun at night, as well as a Tzitzimitl—a deified soul of a warrior who has become a star. These spirits of the dead were guardians of the sun and moon, and associated with different gods. Like Tlaloc and his priests, they're described as dwarfs of ambiguous gender, with long, wild hair. Like Cihuacoatl, a goddess of death and fertility, a contemporary illustration depicts a Tzitzimitl as a skeletal figure with a sacrificial knife for a tongue, wearing a shell-bordered skirt decorated with human organs and limbs, and a phallic snake between the legs. The association with both stars and the underworld, birth and death, and male and female, suggests a being that combines and reconciles opposite principles.[28]

History of the Things of New Spain and
Primeros Memoriales

As described at the beginning of this chapter, Sahagún's ethnography of Nahua peoples, *Primeros Memoriales*, is unique for its time. These primary Nahuatl texts dictated by Sahagún's sources were used as the raw material for his finished book *History of the Things of New Spain*. The texts are especially valuable because they reflect everyday belief, as opposed to official or priestly texts.

They emphasize how a person's status and achievements determine their afterlife fate. Members of the royalty become immortal and divine. "Some became a sun, others the moon, and still others planets." After this transformation, it was as if they had "awakened from a dream in which they had lived."[29]

Those who are sacrificed or killed in battle are taken by the goddess Teoyaominqui to the House of the Sun, "a place like a vast open space" with an abundance of mesquite groves, cacti, and maguey, a plant used to make the intoxicating drink *pulque*. They live a life of wealth, pleasure, and happiness. When the sun appears each day they rejoice, though only those whose shields were pierced in battle may look upon its radiance. In an apparent reference to reincarnation, these souls will "once again blossom on earth." After four years in the House of the Sun, they become birds or butterflies and live off the nectar of flowers.[30]

Women who die in childbirth also go to the House of the Sun. They enter the horizon and escort the sun to the Micteca, the dwellers of Mictlan. They carry it in a litter made of the feathers of the tropical, colorful quetzal bird, and when they enter the underworld, the dead arise. The souls of babies and young children also live in the House of the Sun, in happiness, peace, and contentment, without fear, awaiting "the good of heart." They're cared for by "the older sister of the gods," Chicomecoatl, who helps to settle them "beyond." Alternatively, children and babies go to Xochatlalpan, the Place of the Abundance of the Water of Flowers, where they are nursed by a tree with udders.[31]

Those who drown, who are struck by lightning, or die of certain illnesses go to Tlalocan and to Tlaloc's "house of the quetzal plumes." The god wears a feathered crown and jade necklace, his skin is "bluish green," and his face is spotted with soot. It's "eternal spring" in Tlalocan, where "never is there withering, forever there is sprouting." There are riches and abundance, including plentiful maize, squash, chilies, amaranth, and other local produce. Tlaloc is assisted by *tlaloques*, who are like fire priests and offering priests, "with long, disordered hair." Spirits of the dead are "submerged" in Tlalocan, despite the land of the dead being "above us, in the heavens."[32]

As long as they are free from "vice" and "filth," the morally good and the prematurely dead become "as precious green stones, as precious turquoises," and they dwell in the realm of Tonacatecutli, "Lord of Our Flesh." Tonacatecutli is a title of both the rain god and the supreme Dual God, Ometeuctli, or Bone Lord. His realm is filled with gardens, trees, and flowers full of nectar for souls to feed upon beneath the sacred tree.[33]

All other souls go north to Mictlan, arriving after a journey that takes four years and passes through the nine places of the underworld, which are simultaneously one place. There is a "complete disappearance" of the person, though since there are various further experiences, rather than annihilation this seems to mean that there will be no return to Earth.

A small yellow dog leads souls across nine rivers. Dogs of any other color will refuse. White dogs will claim "I have just washed myself," and black dogs will claim "I have just stained myself black." People could command the souls of their dogs to wait for them "at the edge of the water in the ninth underworld" to ensure that the dogs would be there to carry them across.[34]

Perils on the journey to Mictlan include a blue lizard, "the road which the serpent watches," eight deserts and eight hills, the "place of the obsidian-bladed winds," and being annihilated "where the mountains come together." Trees, sand, and cacti swirl in the air, blown by the wind. A person's diet on Earth determines their diet in the underworld: those who eat tamales must eat foul-smelling underworld equivalents stuffed with beetles; those who eat black bean stew must eat hearts. Indeed, "everything that is not eaten here on Earth is eaten there in Mictlan," including "poisonous herbs" and "prickly poppies," demonstrating fear of a reversal of the earthly order. Those who wasted grain on Earth will have their eyes torn out.[35]

Mictlan is sometimes referred to as Ximoayan, "Place of the Fleshless"—an epithet also used for Tlalocan. Whether this indicates a bodiless, spiritualized state or existence in skeletal form isn't clear. Bones play a prominent role in creation, as seen in the Quetzalcoatl myth above. As well as the transfigured Tzitzimitl souls, various deities are depicted in skeletal form, including Mictlantecuhtli and Mictlancihuatl, Omiteuctli, Quetzalcoatl, and the death and fertility goddess Cihuacoatl.[36]

Another name for Mictlantecuhtli is "Tzontemoc the One Who is Descending." He is "our mother, our father", but also "unsatiated, thirsting there for us, panting." He and his consort Mictlancihuatl eat severed limbs and beetles and drink pus from a skull. When souls of the dead finally meet Mictlantecuhtli, he gives them all their funerary offerings:

pipes, incense, wooden figurines, clothes, fabrics, and so on. After four years, the soul proceeds "to the nine places of the dead, where lay a broad river."[37]

A prayer to go to the otherworld asks that souls are reunited with their deceased relatives there: "may he know his great-grandfathers, his progenitors, who have gone to the land of the dead, who have gone to assemble there." The afterlife in general is described as "our ultimate home," where the wind people and the flower people reside. The deceased also go to nourish the sun, suggesting that souls are actually its food.[38]

In a myth reminiscent of that of Ce Acatl Topiltzin Quetzalcoatl, the deity Quetzalcoatl realizes his own death when he looks into a mirror. He builds a bridge to cross a river and reaches the Water of the Serpent, where sorcerers challenge and interrogate him regarding where he's going and why. He explains that he's been summoned by the sun to Tlapallan. Before allowing him to pass, the sorcerers make Quetzalcoatl give up his worldly goods. Continuing on the journey, he's accompanied by an entourage of dwarfs and hunchbacks, though they all die of cold when it snows as they pass between mountains. Quetzalcoatl finally reaches Tlalocan, where he shoots an arrow through the World Tree, and passes through the hole it makes, symbolic of rebirth. It leads north, where "he built a house underground . . . called Mictlan," meaning effectively that the creation of the realm of the dead resulted from his rebirth. As Quetzalcoatl originated first in Tlalocan, "the place from which the sun arose," and second from Mictlampa, the wind from the land of the dead, he's also returning to his places of origin.[39]

Mexica and Aztec Poetry and Songs

The "Twenty Sacred Hymns" found in *Primeros Memoriales* are believed to have been composed hundreds of years before the Spanish conquest. The "Song of Tlaloc" mentions "arising" in the otherworld after being dead for four years. It also emphasizes the association between afterlife transformation and creation: "In the place of the fleshless, the house of quetzal feathers, is the transformation; it is the act of the Propagator of Men."[40]

Preconquest songs were also recorded in *Cantares Mexicanos* (*Songs of Mexico*) during the second half of the sixteenth century. They're unique for the uncertainty and doubt they express regarding the afterlife, revealing tension between the personal perspectives of the poets and the more orthodox conceptions of Tlalocan and Mictlan. A song dating to the mid-fifteenth century refers to an afterlife realm called Quenonamican, "Where-In-Some-Way-One-Lives." The author questions whether, like Earth, it's a "region of the fleeting moment," if there are flowers and songs, and if happiness and friendship are possible. Another asks, "Where is the source of light, since that which gives life hides itself?" and "How many can truthfully say that truth is or is not there?" The land of the dead is called "the place of our downfall," and the authors question whether they will see their mothers and fathers there. They wonder how to find the God of Duality, if his home is "in the place of the fleshless" or in "the innermost heaven." Elsewhere the poet wonders about reincarnation—if one will return as mist, as a dove, as an ear of corn.[41]

Other songs are more optimistic: "We only came to be born, indeed our home is beyond, where all are shorn, where life is infinite, where things never end." The true Reality is in the afterlife, a place of happiness and the "abode of life" where one never dies. Another song mentions a vision of family members in the land of the dead.[42]

The deceased are "sky-dwellers" clothed in flowers, in the paradise of Tamoanchan. It's the "land of spirit becoming," the "eternal shore," "house of dawn," "house of colors," "land of fire," "origin," "our coming-out place," "hummingbird mountain," and "cavern house of flowers." The World Tree is there, "the tree of flowers," with roots in Tlalocan, the place of death and rebirth. Its "branches of light and fire" are the House of the Sun, where souls in the form of birds rest. It's "the singing place," "the life-giver's home," and it alone is the place of happiness. Birds take souls of the dead to a valley filled with flowers in a "sunstruck mistbow," and they themselves become singing birds and "a swan of green places." Finally, "he who has died, he becomes a god."[43]

A city of "dwellers-among-the-nine" is in the western horizon, where the sun journeys nightly into a realm plagued by rattlesnakes. There are nine fields of the underworld, as well as caverns, a house of jade, and Plume Town, which is inhabited by a deity called Cave Dweller.[44] Mictlan is "where we're all destroyed," and is the home of Smoker, "the Arbiter, Father Keeper of the Waters." Souls there are "in precious snares, they're weeping at the sacred shore."[45]

The Afterlife in Other Nahua Texts

Various other sources give further details about the rather complex metaphysics of the Nahua afterlife. In literature collected by the Spanish Franciscan missionary Andres del Olmos in the 1530s, Ometeuctli is also known as Huitzilopochtli, a sun-god often depicted as a mummy-bundle. Huitzilopochtli was the son of Tonacatecutli and Tonacacihuatl, and his brothers were Quetzalcoatl and red-and-black Tezcatlipoca—manifestations of the androgynous, omnipresent, one-footed god of discord, chaos, and darkness. Huitzilopochtli assisted Quetzalcoatl in recreating human life from the bones of the ancestors. He was also associated with Mictlantecuhtli. The reason he's fleshless is because he sacrifices his own health for that of his worshippers.[46]

The sun-god is further interassociated with the afterlife in annals dealing with the period 1168–1355 (though written much later). In a migration myth, Huitzilopochtli is transformed into the sun-god while inside his mummy bundle. Along with the other skeletal deities, he radiates *tonalli*—the sun's heat and light and the animating life force found in blood, as well as a component of the soul that originated in Mictlan. Bones and creation are also etymologically associated, for "bone marrow" in Nahua is related to the word for "semen." Mictlantecuhtli was associated with bones and blood in the context of death, but he also used his power to make bones and blood strong in newly created life. He and Mictlancihuatl, the quintessential Lord and Lady of the Dead, were associated with childbirth. This recalls similar ideas about deities among the Maya, for 1-Hunahpu's first wife before Blood Moon was Bone Woman, a maize deity associated with creation.[47]

Tlalocan was also said to be located on the moon. The celestial realm has thirteen levels and the underworld has nine. The Lord and Lady of Duality, Ometeuctli and Omecihuatl, dwell at the uppermost level, also called Place of Bones, or Omeyocan. Ometeuctli is described as "He who dwells in waters the color of the bluebird, he who dwells in the clouds. The old god, he who inhabits the shadows of the land of the dead, the lord of fire and of time."[48]

In the 1570s, the Spanish Dominican missionary Diego Durán was highly criticized by his missionary peers for his efforts at preserving the "heathen" Aztec culture. He was fluent in Nahuatl and his work *History of the Indies of New Spain* contains direct quotes from indigenous Aztec sources. They told him that the otherworld is:

the place where you will find your parents, relatives, and lords, your forefathers, where, like a small bird that soars, you have gone to enjoy the Lord of Creation. . . . resting in the shadow of the gloomy mead-ows of the nine mouths of death, and in the sun's house of resplen-dent light, where your ancestors are.[49]

Understanding the Mesoamerican Afterlife Experience

Various attempts have been made to understand the diverse and some-times enigmatic Mesoamerica afterlife beliefs. The Mexican historian Alfredo López Austin suggested that they might be explained by the belief that the soul is composed of different components, and that one goes to the sky while another goes to the underworld. However, for the modern Nahua, the same component (the *teyolia*) goes to Mictlan, Tlalocan, the House of the Sun, and/or becomes a bird or butterfly. The other two do not appear to be conscious: the *ihiyotl* is the shadow or the negative residue of one's personality, which dissipates as a foul gas at death, while the fate of the *tonalli*, the solar animating force, isn't specified. The *teyolia*, it seems, is the sole component that retains consciousness and the capacity for continuing experience after death.[50]

More intriguing, even if ultimately speculative, is López Austin's alternative suggestion that references to reincarnation indicate a process of "recycling." The soul undergoes "a purification" through intermediate states to remove the sins and impurities acquired on Earth. It's then returned "to its original state" as a "totally cleansed and depersonalized force" before being reincarnated.[51]

Whatever the case, a series of intermediate states or experiences is evident. The various transformations of souls of the dead, and their associations with multiple interconnected gods, emphasize that there were multiple experiences, including transcendence. In addition to becoming divinized, the dead become melons, birds, butterflies, jaguars, the sun, Venus, and stars. The death and rebirth of the deceased is particularly associated with the cycles of Venus in both Maya and Nahua texts. The rebirth of the human race, of Quetzalcoatl, and of the deceased who go to Mictlan correspond to the four days Venus takes to pass through the underworld and the eight days it takes to return.[52] At the same time, there's also an association between the dead and the sun.

Another recurring theme is that the reconciliation of opposites leads to ultimate divine union and omnipresence. Among many examples are the interassociation of heavenly realms and deities with their underworld counterparts, and of death with creation and rebirth. There are also differing conceptions of the same realms. Xibalba and Mictlan are places of both positive and negative experiences, though Mictlan is generally less desirable than Tlalocan or Tamoanchan (and is wholly negative in *Cantares Mexicanos*).

There has also been some debate regarding judgment and morally determined afterlife fates in Mesoamerica. It is true that the process of judgment is not generally explicit in these texts, though this is certainly one function of the Council of Xibalba in the *Popol Vuh*. Although the Twins are tested not for their virtue but for their knowledge and ingenuity, an afterlife based on judgment of some kind is clear. Unambiguous morally determined fates are found in the Nahua accounts recorded by Sahagún and in the Maya accounts recorded by de Landa. It is also implied in all the material by the very presence of underworld threats and demons, which presumably are survivable only by those of sufficient moral, social, intellectual, or religious worth. The Aztec confessed their sins before they died, indicating fear of afterlife retribution based on earthly behavior.[53]

Alongside the more metaphysical and esoteric ideas, there were also dedicated realms for certain classes of people and types of deaths. Evidence in de Landa, Sahagún, and other texts suggests that judgment was *premortem*—meaning that a person's afterlife fate was determined by their earthly social position. The same held true for certain earthly achievements: because it's right, good, and heroic to be a warrior, to bear children, and so on, these actions lead to a favorable afterlife. Mode of death is similarly decided by the gods based upon a person's moral behavior, purity, and valor—ensuring that everyone gets the afterlife they deserve.[54] The "pure" who die in battle or who are sacrificed are pure because they did so. Conversely, the good of heart are struck by lightning to ensure they'll go to Tlalocan. In *Relación de las Cosas de Yucatán*, those who die by suicide go to paradise because taking one's own life was seen as honorable.

Despite the cultural differences between the various Maya and Nahua peoples, overall the Mesoamerican texts reveal numerous common afterlife motifs: the association of the circuit of the sun and Venus with the ascent and descent of the spirit; fertility and agricultural rebirth parallels, and life emerging from realms of the dead; out-of-body journeys to otherworlds; encounters with human remains bringing about transformation and rebirth; meeting deceased relatives, ancestors, and divinities who radiate light; interrogation and perils, and the reliance on knowledge or wisdom to survive them; divinization, omnipresence, and multiple transcendent, transformational experiences. Many of these have obvious parallels in NDEs.

Excursus: Revisiting Quetzalpetlatl's NDE

In later years, the two NDEs discussed at the beginning of this chapter were conflated and reworked by Spanish missionaries as Catholic propaganda. Apparently working from Sahagún, in 1615 the Franciscan missionary Juan de Torquemada published his own version of the story in his *Monarquía Indiana* (*Indian Monarchy*). The woman is recast as a sister of Motecuhzoma II and is renamed Papan. No longer met by "a sickly, deformed youth," a shining winged angel in a white robe with a cross on his head appears to her. He takes her on an otherworld journey that's far more consistent with medieval European examples of the genre than with anything culturally Aztec. The prophecy learned from her very Christian experience was not the fall of Mexico but that she would become a leader in the baptism of her people.

Still later, in 1780, Papan became Papantzin under the pen of Francisco Javier Clavijero, whose version was sanctioned as historical truth by the Vatican itself. The protagonist was now a "perfect model of Christian virtues" who brought back from her NDE "the news of the true God, creator of heaven and earth"—and became the first indigenous person in Tlateloclo to be baptized. Stripped of any Aztec religious elements, the story was actually used to legitimize the conquest itself. According to a cleric writing against an indigenous uprising in 1811, the conquest was justified by the words of "the miraculously resurrected Princess Papantzin."

These adaptations of what was originally an indigenous account attest to the potential political and cultural force of such experiences— a dynamic also found most notably in Native American NDEs. This increasingly mythologized and conceptually altered story has been retold in various forms, and for competing purposes, in Mexico and abroad ever since, in religious literature, books of legends, folklore, fiction, paintings, poetry, and song.[55]

PART III

The Interface of Experience and Belief

Comparing Otherworld Journeys

The summaries at the end of each of the preceding five chapters highlight the main similarities between NDEs and afterlife beliefs in each civilization. These include the soul leaving the body and existing in nonphysical or quasi-physical form, darkness and light, journeys to other realms seen as a return to the origin point or the true spiritual home, meeting deceased relatives, evaluation of one's earthly conduct and an afterlife fate determined by the outcome, encounters with deities and other beings associated with light, obstacles or barriers, and positive feelings such as joy, harmony, transcendence, and a sense of universal oneness.

In this chapter, we'll take a closer comparative look at these similarities, along with others that are less obvious, though no less intriguing. We'll also explore the most significant differences, some of which are surprisingly specific.

Out-of-Body Experiences, Ascent, and Encountering the Corpse

Out-of-body experiences involve the sensation of separating from the body, then rising and having perceptions from above. This is paralleled in the ancient texts in two ways. First are the repeated references to ascent. This occurs in many forms in all of our cultures: on cremation smoke, rising with stars and planets, dragons, chariots, climbing ladders, or simply the ascent of the soul's spiritual body unaided.

Second is the recurring theme of souls encountering their own corpse. Importantly, as in the NDE, the encounter is often associated with the deceased person's realization that they've survived their own physical death. In other words, they only understand that they're dead when they recognize that they are not their dead body. The theme of deceased gods is related to this, given that souls of the dead are often associated with the divine.

In Egypt, souls of the dead find the corpse of Osiris in Rosetau. Because souls *become* Osiris in death, they are actually encountering their own corpse. This encounter is characterized as the revelation of a "secret," which causes the true realization of death and immortality that enables the deceased to proceed.[1]

In Mesopotamia, Damu's knowledge that beer is being made from his congealed blood in order to facilitate his rebirth makes him realize that he's dead. Enkidu's graphic characterization of the dead body as an "old garment the lice devour" precedes his revelations to Bilgames about the nature of the afterlife. Inana transforms into a corpse prior to her rebirth. In the Atrahasis ascent myth, the divine element in humans is the flesh of a slaughtered god.[2]

In India, out-of-body experiences are described as "shaking off the body" and "rising up from the body." There's also a repeated stress on the realization of one's true immortal nature. The corpse encounter isn't explicit, though the Decay found in the "house infernal" is relevant. The Catholic-Hindu scholar of comparative religions, Raimundo Panikkar, related this Decay to the Vedic principle of "cosmic disintegration"—that "deep within" death and decay is found "the seed of immortality."[3]

In China, OBEs are also overt, including texts intended to call the soul back to the body. While reports of seeing the body during an OBE are absent from the NDE accounts, there are several references to twelve corpses on Mount Kunlun that belonged to divinized humans. A divine corpse encounter appears in the description of shamans who gather around the corpse of the god Ya Yü, who holds the drug of immortality.[4]

In Mesoamerica, each of the multiple deaths and beheadings of the Hero Twins leads to a rebirth. When the Twin sons find the corpse of their merged fathers buried in the underworld, they resurrect him and are then divinized and ascend to the divine realm. Topiltzin Quetzalcoatl seems to understand the nature of death when he sees his own corpse reflected in the mirror, which sets off a series of events culminating in his divine rebirth. The numerous links between bones and creation in the Nahua texts are also relevant here: human remains bringing about life and rebirth.[5]

The revulsion so often expressed by NDE'ers at the sight of their own body and the prospect of returning to it also aligns with the graphic descriptions of the fates of corpses. References to dismemberment or chopping up the body in all our civilizations suggest a recurring shamanic motif of transformation through the death or dismemberment of the body in afterlife realms.[6]

There is, however, a key difference between seeing the body in NDEs and corpse encounters in the ancient texts. The first takes place in this world when the soul leaves the body, while the second takes place in an afterlife realm. But if we allow for a mythologizing of the concept, it's clear that both carry similar meanings: the realization of one's own physical death is also the realization of the survival and transcendence of death—and the means of proceeding into a new spiritualized state of being.

The corpse motif also recalls the Egyptian notion that the *ba* visited the body in the tomb each night to sustain the powers of rebirth. This *could* be a reflection of the "return" element of NDEs, and is experientially similar (from the soul's perspective), though the returning *ba* doesn't reanimate the body or remain in it as would happen in NDEs.

Returning to the body is clear in Chinese poems, such as where the spirit is told by the sun to "turn back."[7] The reluctance to return is also consistent with NDE reports. Only in China is a fear of mistaken identity in the otherworld overtly expressed, though this may be the meaning of some interrogations in other civilizations, too, where the soul is asked, *"Who are you?"* It's surely significant that mistaken identity is the most common reason for return in Chinese NDE testimonies.

A return to the body is a key element in the Sumerian "Death of Bilgames," though the theme is lacking in the Indian and Mesoamerican texts—even in their NDE legends. Logically speaking, however, the return element is presupposed in the texts by their very existence. For the people who valued them as embodying spiritual truths, writings purporting to reveal what happens in the afterlife were surely believed to have originated with someone who had been there and returned. This is attested by the many stories of gods and humans visiting the otherworld.

The idea that the dead have a spiritual "body" of some kind is implicit in all the texts, which is consistent with NDEs. That souls aren't simply pure disembodied consciousness is shown by the many references to the deceased being clothed, the need for nourishment, the possibility of "physical" intimacy, and so on.

It's curious that the corpse encounter theme has been overlooked in the history of religions, despite being evident in afterlife mythologies worldwide. Even the otherwise comprehensive and monumental *Motif-Index of Folk-Literature*, compiled by the American folklorist Stith Thompson, lacks an entry for the theme. Our comparison here highlights its parallel in NDEs, revealing that seeing one's own body while in spirit form is a distinct and important element of the out-of-body experience.

Knowledge and Enlightenment

In all our traditions, knowledge and enlightenment were prerequisites for immortality or a positive afterlife. The realization of having survived death following the corpse encounter is one example of this, though there are many others.

In Egypt, the efflux of Osiris is contained in "the word" that makes one immortal. Those who know the *Book of Two Ways* become like Re and Osiris, invulnerable and immortal. In Mesopotamia, Bilgames obtained secret knowledge from Ziusudra, and Etana hoped for revelations of what is "hidden" in the spiritual realm. In India, "the one who knows" attains liberation, and hell can be avoided by means of "the divine word." The afterlife journeys of Bhrgu are undertaken for the attainment of knowledge. In China, the otherworld is a place to obtain "understanding" and "self-knowledge." In Mesoamerica, the tests the Twins undergo are related to knowledge and ingenuity, and the transformed head of 1/7-Hunahpu imparts the knowledge of spiritual immortality to Blood Moon.[8]

Though not typical of NDEs, in all traditions the evaluation of knowledge and enlightenment in the afterlife is done partly through interrogation. Those who are unable to show the requisite understanding of the association of death with rebirth, or of the true spiritual nature of the self, cannot progress and risk annihilation. Knowing names, being stripped naked, or the changing of clothes also recur in this context.

In Egypt, the interrogations relate to the name, purity, and divinity of the deceased, who are warned not to reveal their true identity. At the same time, only by revealing one's (presumably) earthly identity can the gates of Horus and Osiris be passed. Souls of the dead forget their names at the risk of facial mutilation, and there's a threat from an entity called "Name-Repeater." Other questions concern how many fingers souls have and what they will eat. They are given "dazzling" new clothes to wear as a symbol of spiritual rebirth.[9]

In Mesopotamia, Gilgamesh is questioned by the Scorpion People about his identity and destination. He's allowed to pass when he tells them that he's seeking immortality. Inana is interrogated with the question "Who are you?" While her subsequent undressing is related to stripping her of the seven divine *Me* powers, it may also refer to the shedding of the earthly, enculturated aspects of the self and a return to her original state—particularly considering that many of the accoutrements are of a priestly and royal nature.[10] This stripping is a precondition for her admittance to the underworld. Likewise, Dumuzid is stripped naked prior to Utu bringing about his transformation. When he reaches Dilmun, he's bathed and given new clothes.

In India, the deceased is also asked "Who are you?" in the *Upanishads* and the *Jaiminiya Brahmana*. The correct answer demonstrates a knowledge of *atman* and *brahman*—that the self and transcendent reality are one. The wrong answer is to give one's name, which reveals a lack of awareness of one's true divine nature.

In China, in the *Zhuangzi* the soul is called "Nameless Man." In poems, souls are questioned about what they seek, and when the answer is "the holy way" and "a long life," they are given the means to divinization. A "cloud coat," silk robes, and other wondrous clothing are given to the spirit in other poems.[11]

In Mesoamerica, the Hero Twins are asked their identity and origins by the Lords of the Underworld. Though their claim of ignorance may have been a ruse, it could also reflect loss of ego, or a new state of consciousness in which relations to earthly social identifiers are irrelevant, perhaps reflected in their being dressed as vagabonds. In contrast, knowing the names of the Lords gives the Twins power. Asking their father to name the parts of his face is also a test of identity and self-knowledge. Failure of that test meant that he had to remain in the underworld while the Twins ascended to the heavens. Quetzalcoatl is able to get away from the interrogating sorcerers only when he sheds his worldly goods and tells them that he's seeking the sun.[12]

Judgment and Life Review

Although life reviews seem not to occur in NDEs as much as the popular imagination would suggest, many accounts that lack them nevertheless feature some form of self-evaluation (as seen in chapter 1).

Something very much like a life review is found in Egyptian autobiographical texts, in the *Teaching for King Merikare*, in the deceased's "annals" being read before the gods in the Pyramid Texts, and various confessional and negative-confession inscriptions. The latter list a number of transgressions that the deceased was *not* guilty of in life. In Mesopotamia, Bilgames undergoes a life review when he visits the underworld, and in a text called *A Man and his God*, the deceased declares his sins before the deity. In India, a life review is described in the *Katha Upanishad*. The theme is not explicit in the Chinese or Mesoamerican texts.

In NDEs, the evaluation of the person's earthly life is commonly made by the self with support from a being of light. This is conceptually related to the transformation of souls of the dead into afterlife judges, as found in most of the ancient civilizations. In Egypt, the deceased becomes Osiris among the Ennead. In Mesopotamia, Bilgames and Ur-Namma become underworld judges. Inana is referred to as an Anuna god—that is, one of the very gods who judged her. In India, the deceased "unites" with Yama. Though apparently absent in the Mesoamerican material, self-judgment possibly occurs in the Chinese poem "Qi Jian," when the spirit states that knowing that his acts were "faultless" would enable his happiness.

Perhaps more importantly, in most cases, conduct evaluation or judgment is associated with a deity or being of light, as in NDEs. In Egypt, the merging of Osiris-Re equates a divinity of light with one of judgment. In Mesopotamia, Enki and Utu radiate light as they judge the dead. In India, the seasons descend on rays of light to interrogate the deceased. The connection between light and judgment is less apparent in China, where there are no descriptions of Shangdi's appearance, though the fact that he's a heavenly deity would suggest a radiant appearance. Aztec underworld deities radiate light, and death is "a way for the light to show itself" in the *Popol Vuh*. The dead themselves also become beings of light, often as stars, in all traditions with the possible exception of Mesopotamia. The names of deceased rulers there were written accompanied by a star symbol, however, to indicate their nonearthly status.

Dangers and Perils

Near-death experiences only rarely feature demons, tortures, or perils. In some cases, more typical NDE elements are experienced in frightening ways, such as feeling suffocated by darkness or menaced by a spiritual being. Otherwise, distressing NDEs are not generally consistent with each other, and no specifically negative cross-cultural NDE feature is identifiable.

In contrast, afterlife perils in all traditions include water-crossings, serpents, demons, fire, and abysses. Culturally specific perils are too vast to enumerate—for example, female apes who sever heads in Egypt, not being allowed to sleep in Sumer, a river of blood in India, giant ants in China, and obsidian-bladed winds in Mesoamerica, to name only a very few. Nevertheless, nonexistence or annihilation is the ultimate negative fate in all traditions.[13]

A reversal of the earthly order is a common fear in Egyptian spells against being upside-down, being hunted with nets, and an inversion of the digestion process. In India, there's a warning that the deceased will be consumed by the food they have eaten. In Mesoamerica, food and drink cry out in the otherworld.[14]

Otherworld gates are found in Egyptian, Mesopotamian, and Chinese texts. Solar and lunar doorways occur in India, and different houses are passed through in the *Popol Vuh*, indicating a succession of subexperiences, which is thematically paralleled in NDEs.

Other Realms

The afterlife realm is generally described as an idealized version of Earth—or as just the opposite in the case of hellish realms. Both types are characterized by social hierarchies and earthly "physical" features and institutions. Heavenly realms are lands of plenitude and abundance. These include the Egyptian Marsh of Reeds, the Mesopotamian land of Dilmun, the Indian "pasture," the celestial fields in China, Tlalocan and the nine fields of the underworld in Aztec Mesoamerica. Conversely, there are many earthly-type threats, such as snakes, and perils such as rivers.

While NDE reports sometimes include glimpses of beautiful pastoral lands, specific underworlds and celestial worlds aren't typical. Although there are such realms in all our civilizations, they're not conceptualized in strictly binary terms. In other words, it's not the case that only upper realms are positive and lower realms negative. Instead, the underworld is often *interconnected* with the celestial world, sometimes even located within it, illuminated by the sun when it's night on Earth, or by a sun of its own. It's a place of transformation, renewal, creation, life-giving waters, and deities associated with fertility and rebirth.

These celestial-underworld associations seem to relate to an underlying pantheistic principle common to all the civilizations, connected to the shared themes of transcendence and omnipresence resulting from divinization after death. This is revealed in all the traditions by freedom to travel by thought alone, and multiple transformations into stars and other celestial bodies, birds, animals, elements, concepts, and gods or parts of gods.

More specifically, the idea is expressed in (1) the Egyptian merging of the *ba* and *ka* as a microcosm of the merging of Osiris and Re; (2) the Mesopotamian belief that the soul has divine origins, and in the omnipresence of Damu, who resides in the winds, lighting, tornadoes, and so on; (3) the Indian identification of *atman* with *brahman*, and the soul as microcosm of the sun; (4) the Chinese "universal oneness," becoming identical with the Great Universality, and endlessly wandering the cosmos (strikingly paralleled in the Upanishads); and (5) the Mesoamerican association of the soul with Venus as fragments of the sun, and the union of the Twins and of Quetzalcoatl with the celestial, the earthly, the upper world and the lower world.

Transcendence

In NDEs and in the texts of all our civilizations, life after death entails multiple experiences and intermediate states, with progression to an ultimate transcendence. As seen, attempts to explain such diverse experiences and beliefs in linear "either/or" terms are unsuccessful. Instead, they're best seen in terms of the recurring theme of the metaphysical reconciliation of opposites.

One prominent example is the interassociation of deities such as Osiris-Re, Inana and Ereshkigala, Shangdi and Yo Pei, Mictlantecuhtli and Ometeuctli, among many others. Various deities also have combined afterlife, fertility, and rebirth associations, including Osiris, the Anuna, Dumuzid, Shangdi, and Tlaloc. Likewise, 1-Death and 7-Death are counterparts to the fertility deity 1-Hunahpu and his twin 7-Hunahpu. Underworld gods with celestial associations include Yo Pei and Shangdi, as well as the formerly human Osiris, Bilgames, Ningishzida, Yama, and the Maya Hero Twins—all of whom survived their own deaths to become lords or judges of the underworld.

The reconciliation of opposites is also mirrored in conceptualizations of the human soul having more than one component: the *ba* and *ka* in Egypt, reconciled and divinized as an *akh*; the *asu* and *prana* in India; the *hun, po,* and later *xian* in China; and the *teyolia, tonalli* and *ihiyotl* in Mesoamerica. Only in Mesopotamia does the concept appear to be absent, though it reflects occasional NDE reports that involve dual consciousness. In one example, from 1937, the individual stated, "my consciousness separated from another consciousness which was also me."[15]

Numerologically, pairs and dualities are also common. Two is the most frequently occurring number throughout all the civilizations. The pairs of deities, paths, rivers, realms, and so on align with the concept of transcending duality through dual principles. The afterlife is both in the sky and in the underworld, and it is both the source of all life and the destination of all life. The realm of death is also the realm of renewal, for death without rebirth would be against nature—contrary to the cycles of the sun, the seasons, and the Earth.

Although so many modern scholars have struggled to get to grips with all this, the multivalence of the afterlife was neatly expressed by Diego Durán's Aztec source, as quoted earlier: "where, like a small bird that soars, you have gone to enjoy the Lord of Creation. . . . resting in the shadow of the gloomy meadows of the nine mouths of death, and in the sun's house of resplendent light, where your ancestors are."[16] Note that the quote doesn't say *either* the "sun's house" *or* the "gloomy meadows." Instead, it encompasses both states, either alternately or even simultaneously.

As the Norwegian historian of religions William Brede Kristensen observed, "totality is always linked with death and the realm of the dead."[17] This recalls feelings of transcendence reported by NDE'ers. While literally *becoming* a god is not typical of NDEs, experiencers feel transformed into a spiritualized state with "god-like" abilities that may include universal understanding, clairvoyance, telepathic communication, and movement through the power of thought alone. The idea that there is continuity of identity and selfhood despite unity, transfiguration, and transcendence is also common to both NDEs and the ancient texts.

Further Comparisons with NDEs

One important distinction between the experiences and beliefs is that NDEs mainly concern the afterlife journey, while the texts concern the journey, destinations, and ultimate states beyond NDEs. This means that much of the information about afterlife realms in our sources doesn't *specifically* correspond to NDEs (even if it may conceptually). Likewise, not all elements of NDEs correspond to the texts, because there was no context for their expression. Examples include ineffability, the rather rare and often inaccurate visions of the future,[18] and hearing a doctor or some other person discuss one's death. Positive transformation following the return to the body is also absent (given that the return itself is absent), but it's consistent with the general idea that afterlife realms are places of spiritual knowledge and renewal.

An acceleration of time and thought seems evident in the *Teaching for King Merikare*, when the otherworld judges "regard a lifetime as but an hour" when they place Merikare's earthly actions before him. The reference to ten days passing in seven in "The Death of Ur-Namma" might have a similar meaning. The theme is absent in the other civilizations.

Athough sometimes reported in NDEs, none of the texts seem to involve souls of the dead actively choosing their postmortem fate, whether reincarnation, proceeding to another level, or returning to the body. However, divinization and references to wandering at will in multiple realms, elements, and celestial bodies might presuppose such an ability.

Also absent from the texts is a crashing or buzzing noise, though music features in India, China, and Mesoamerica. The much-debated tunnel experience (see chapter 1) is absent on a literal level, although the paths and waterways serve the same function—of getting the spirit from this world to the next. There are, in any case, numerous descriptions of emerging from darkness into light, coupled with various forms of locomotion in general. The passage of the sun and other celestial bodies through the netherworld also indicates light emerging from darkness.[19] The microcosmic parallel to this is the spirit traveling from a dark underworld to a celestial realm filled with light.

The NDE sensation of rushing through darkness is paralleled by references to falling or being thrown into darkness and pits in the *Rig Veda*, "turning and revolving" in the *Zhuangzi*, and falling into the netherworld in "Bilgames, Enkidu, and the Underworld"—not to mention the many descriptions of descending, ascending, and flying in all the civilizations. The soul is also associated with birds in all the ancient civilizations, though not typically in NDEs.

Symbolism in Afterlife Beliefs across Cultures

Putting NDEs aside for the moment, there are quite a few intriguing—and sometimes mystifying—parallels between the afterlife beliefs of our civilizations. The first concern the symbolic meanings of certain recurring of numbers. While specifying quantity may sometimes have had more to do with attempts at verisimilitude rather than with occult meanings, the more frequently a number occurs the more significance it likely had.

Despite the fact that each culture has its own numerological tradition, seven and nine are particularly prominent in our sources. The significance of nine is likely through an association with birth, in analogy with the human gestation period.[20] Any cross-cultural meaning of the number seven is more questionable. Kristensen wrote that it suggests "totality," though it's unclear why seven would be any more inherently symbolic of totality than, say, three. It more likely has cosmological significance.

In Egypt there are the nine gods of the Ennead, and there are seven rooms, gates, and ferrymen in the underworld. There are also seven gates in Mesopotamia, seven adornments of Inana, seven Anuna gods, and seven underworld deputies and porters, and Bilgames waits seven days before seeking to rescue Enkidu.

In China there are nine entrances to heaven, a nine-headed serpent, a "man with nine heads that can pull up nine thousand trees," the "nine-coiled" deity Yo Pei, and nine heavens, rivers, shores, wells, gates, parts of the sky, and so on. However, there are almost as many instances of the number four in China, and three is also frequently recurrent.

In Mesoamerica there are nine underworlds with nine corresponding deities, nine heavens (though sometimes thirteen), and nine rivers, fields, and "mouths of death." Four and eight are also prominent.

In India the recurring numbers are five and three. There are five heavenly rivers of lotuses and five doorkeepers of heaven. Naraka is "below the three earths," there are three realms of the afterlife (though sometimes six), the deceased's merits split into three parts, and Nachiketas is granted three wishes by Yama.

Many other elements that lack NDE correlations are shared between only some of the traditions. Perhaps most striking are the analogous concepts of *Maat*, *Me*, *Rita*, and *Tien*. Though they're not exclusively afterlife related, as principles of order and rightness that govern the universe, they're important in relation to judgment and the role of the deceased in maintaining cosmic balance.

Only in Mesopotamia, China, and to a lesser extent Mesoamerica are afterlife realms located on mountains. In the first two they link the heavenly and underworld realms. There seems to be no clear counterpart in Mesoamerica, where instead the sacred Maya Yaxche tree connects the upper and lower realms. On the subject of trees, there's also the Maya melon tree, a Soma tree in India, the heavenly Fu-sang and the Illusion Tree in China, among many other references to trees in general.

The ferryman is a key motif in Egypt and Mesopotamia but is lacking in India, China, and Mesoamerica, despite the fact that they all have river crossings. Re's barque and rowers in Egypt are comparable to the charioteer of the sun-god in Mesopotamia, India, and China, and to Venus as the "sun-carrier" in Mesoamerica.

In Egypt, there's a green ferry boat, the deceased becomes a green swan, and Osiris is depicted as having green skin. In China, the immortal Daoists have green feathers and there are green dragons at Mount Kunlun. There is a Maya green path and Green Road, Tlaloc is described as being "bluish green," Mictlan is the "emerald realm," and the deceased becomes a "swan of green places." The color is surely symbolically related to the concept of the underworld being a place of fertility and rebirth—though it's absent in Mesopotamia and India, which also have such associations.

Though there's sometimes a specific afterlife for soldiers who die in battle, only in Mesoamerica is it obviously preferential. In China they become ghosts, and in Mesopotamia they're given to Ur-Namma.

The direction of the otherworld is often west, though this is inconsistent despite common associations between death and the setting sun. In Egypt it's east in the Pyramid Texts, though west in the Coffin Texts, reflecting cyclical interconnections with the sun-god. In Mesopotamia it appears to be east, while China alternates between east and west. The Indian worlds of the gods and Fathers are northeast and southeast, respectively. In Mesoamerica it's usually west but also north and south. This lack of agreement, even within a single civilization, may be due to the conceptual difficulty of trying to situate a supernatural or nonphysical realm within the natural and physical cosmos. Almost by definition, a spiritual realm can't be "located" anywhere in relation to Earth. As the historian of religions Jeffrey Burton Russell wrote, references to afterlife "space" and "time" are really "ontological metaphors referring to something beyond the limits of the human mind."[21]

The "plant of life" in Egypt parallels the plant of rejuvenation, "life-giving plant," and "plant of birth" in Mesopotamia; and the magical-medicinal plants and the sacred herb from the Illusion Tree in China.

In addition to component-souls, and perhaps souls becoming stars, other motifs occur in all civilizations but Mesopotamia. One example is the identification of the Milky Way as a heavenly realm. Another is the lotus as a symbol of rebirth. Canines with dual functions of guard and guide are found in Egypt, India, and China, while in the Aztec afterlife two separate dogs share these functions.

Other motifs are found in only two civilizations, with Egypt and India being the most frequently paired. The two paths to the other-worlds in the Vedas, for example, recall the Egyptian Two Ways. More strikingly because it's so highly specific, Re's sun-boat and the Vedic heavenly boat both undergo member apotheosis, with each component being identified with a different deity. This is also described in relation to Brahma's throne, Re, and the Egyptian deceased themselves. The Sisterly Companions who try to seduce Egyptian souls yet threaten to mutilate them are comparable to Faith and Nonfaith in India. (Inana and Ereshkigala are also underworld sisters, though they are not portrayed as a pair.) Yama was the son of the sun, as was the Egyptian king who became Osiris in death. The association between the Lord of the Dead—Yama and Osiris—and the "son of the sun" in two traditions is remarkable.

Nourishment in the afterlife was a serious concern in Egypt and Mesopotamia, somewhat less so in China, and absent in India and Mesoamerica. The deceased becomes food for gods in India and for the sun in Mesoamerica. Giant tree-barley features in Egypt and China, while owls, bats, and leopards may be found in China and Mesoamerica. The latter two also share with Mesopotamia female Earth-underworld deities: the Queen Mother of the West, Tlaltecuhtli, Tlazoltéotl, and Ereshkigala.

The association between a ball game and a visit to the underworld occurs in "Bilgames, Enkidu, and the Underworld" and in the *Popol Vuh*. In China, a medicine ball was said to be the brain of a god, while severed heads of gods and heroes were prominent in in the Maya *Popol Vuh*. Reincarnation becomes increasingly prominent as time goes on in India, and is mentioned in a few Mesoamerican texts.

Looking beyond our civilizations, there are some simply astonishing, inexplicable parallels with myths from other cultures. One example is the heavenly journey of a horse in the *Rig Veda* and the life review of a horse in an NDE of the famous Oglala Sioux shaman Black Elk.[22]

The myth of the Maya goddess Blood Moon echoes the legend of Nana, an ancient Greek river-nymph. Nana was made pregnant by a fruit of an almond tree that fell into her lap. The tree itself had grown from the castrated genitals of Agdistis, a hermaphrodite deity—just as Blood Moon was made pregnant by the melon tree from which the decapitated head of the transformed sacrificed Twins grew. Nana then gave birth to Attis, who fell in love with Agdistis—who by now had become the goddess Kybele (making Attis, effectively, her son). In a fit of madness, Attis cut off his own genitals and was then himself transformed into a tree.[23] This mirrors how elements of the story of 1-Hunahpu and 7-Hunahpu were reduplicated in the story of their twin sons, Hunahpu and Xblanque. While the Nana myth does not take place in the underworld, the combination of (1) pregnancies caused by trees that incorporate deities; (2) incestuous relationships between the parent and offspring; and (3) the children from those relationships repeating mythic patterns of their parents is highly specific. Perhaps some combination of shared cultural features and cognitive factors could be found to explain such bewildering similarities, but unfortunately, it's beyond our scope to delve into such a complex project here.

Finally, it should be pointed out that there are many dissimilarities between the texts of each individual civilization as beliefs changed over time. Some examples are the loss of an afterlife in the stars in Egypt, the evolving character and function of Yamaloka in India, and the relocations of the otherworld in China.

Making Sense of the Similarities and Differences

Additional similarities and differences could surely be found, but what emerges so far is that the more detailed and specific a theme or idea is, the less it recurs cross-culturally. To put it another way, there are more broad, thematic correlations than there are detailed, specific ones. At the same time, the vastness of the differences makes the similarities of special significance: their very existence requires explanation, while differences are to be expected.

Bruce Trigger had similar findings in his study of the phenomenon of civilization itself. He had expected that the greatest cross-cultural similarities would be related to subsistence, the economy, and social organization, while that the fewest similarities would be in the realm of religions. This was because of his presuppositions regarding the "inflexibility of natural laws which restrict human behavior" on the one hand and "the relative freedom of the human imagination" on the other. What he found, however, was just the opposite: that there was "a basic uniformity of religious beliefs shared by all seven civilizations," despite variations in symbols, mode of expression, and "cultural values." Overall, the similarities occurred more "at the general, structural level" and the differences on a more specific level. [24]

To understand the variations and consistencies across all of our afterlife descriptions, we must first disentangle them to reveal their components. For this it will be useful to turn to the French anthropologist Claude Lévi-Strauss. He used the term "mytheme" to describe the thematic elements of a myth that are combined to form its overall "structure." [25] For example, if the *structure* is a journey to an afterlife realm, elements such as ascent, judgment, and transcendence are *mythemes*. If we add "symbol" to structure and mytheme as a way of specifying culture-specific details, we have a more comprehensive way of organizing and understanding all the various descriptions.

Another way of conceptualizing it might be *language*, *grammar*, and *word*. Words form meaning through the use of grammar in ways that constitute language. Similarly, mythemes are expressed in symbols to make up a narrative's structure. Symbols are culture-specific details, but mythemes and structures indicate some kind of cross-cultural or even universal element that's responsible for the similarities between different socities.

Applying this to our explorations here, the structure "afterlife journey belief" is obviously consistent cross-culturally or this book could not have been written. Mythemes are somewhat consistent, while the symbols utilized in the expression of the mythemes are largely culture specific. Each culture has unique influences from their environment, history, customs, community organization, and so on. This is why social hierarchies in the afterlife reflect particular earthly social hierarchies. The types of animals found in other realms reflect those found in the local environment of the culture: crocodiles in Egypt, lions in Mesopotamia, horses in India, tigers in China, coatis in Mesoamerica. It's also no surprise that we don't find culturally idiosyncratic elements of one civilization's beliefs in another: there are no Indian descriptions of Osiris judging the dead in the underworld, or myths of Inana descending to the Yellow Springs to play football with the Lords of Xibalba.

Instead, we have descriptions of *diverse* methods of ascent and *various* modes of judgment—but all the traditions include the concepts those symbolic descriptions express: the ascent of the soul and evaluation of one's earthly conduct. Other symbols include particular methods of reward and punishment, such as dwelling in an Aztec realm of music and flowers or eating hair in the Indian river of blood, and the numerous specific demons, perils, gates, ferrymen, and paths. Other mythemes include travel between and within realms, borders or limits, divinization, deities, and transformation.

The Romanian historian of religions Mircea Eliade contended that in all afterlife beliefs, we "may be certain that there will be a river and a bridge, a sea and a boat; a tree, and cove, or a precipice; a dog, a demonic or angelic psychopomp or doorkeeper." While we do find most of these themes across our civilizations, few have *all* of them. Although, while Eliade overgeneralized at the symbolic level, if we expand his list to the mythemic level we find that they correspond to the more general elements of getting from this world to the next, barriers and borders, intermediate states, perils, and spiritual beings.[26]

We must also be careful not to overlay our own interpretations onto the meanings of symbols cross-culturally. The American historian of religions Bruce Lincoln, for example, saw rivers in afterlife mythologies as representing oblivion and ferrymen as representing old age.[27] Rather than accepting the meanings that are actually given in the texts, this imposes the reader's own meanings upon them. After all, the texts actually do reveal their own functions and meanings. Depending on the culture, rivers can represent barriers—which may be symbolized in other texts by gates or doors. Along with ferrymen, they can also represent the afterlife journey and the means of embarking on it—which may be symbolized in other texts by paths, ladders, chariots, boats, or ropes.

Although not clearly attested in ancient Maya sources, a self-aware use of symbols to express deeper concepts is characteristic of modern Lacandon Maya afterlife beliefs. Obstacles in the otherworld are seen as illusions intended to test the readiness of the deceased to proceed to higher realms. The river, for example, is symbolic of the tears of grieving friends and relatives, but it's experienced by the deceased as a barrier.[28] A similar meaning could apply to the herb from the Illusion Tree that makes one divine in the Chinese poem "Ballad of Tung Flees." Perhaps the herb allows souls to transcend the illusory aspects of the spiritual realm through divinization. The use of the prison-underworld metaphor in the Sumerian "Hymn to Nungal" also shows that a strictly literal-minded reading of the descriptions can result in misapprehending a text's intended meanings.

Significantly, the NDE itself appears to be a collection of subjectively experienced universal phenomena, interpreted in culture-specific ways. Like afterlife beliefs, it too can be analyzed in terms of structure, mytheme, and symbol.

Nine Core Features

In poring over the ancient texts for quite a number of years, I found that nine of their most consistently recurring mythemes correspond to nine of the most frequently recurring NDE elements. It's as if they were imported whole as a set into the afterlife conceptions of each of the civilizations (with a few minor exceptions), then given symbolic form. Some examples of how each one is expressed in culture-specific ways are summarized below. Keep in mind that they are only representative and that in most cases, the themes are recurrent within each civilization. Further examples may be located by using the index.

1. Out-of-Body Experiences and Ascent

In Egypt, ascent is via a stairway, smoke, a ladder, or celestial boat. The *ba* bird represents the soul outside the body. In Mesopotamia, Damu is in spiritual form when he attempts to interact with people on Earth, and he meets disembodied spirits. There are references to the ascent of Etana and Mami, and in various hymns. In India, the soul "shakes off" the body, and "rises up from" the body. It ascends on cremation smoke and on rays of light. OBEs are recurrent in China, with such remarks as "when I no longer have a body." Ascent is via dragons, chariots, clouds, and unspecified means. In Mesoamerica, the Twins ascend as stars and Quetzalcoatl's ashes and heart ascend as birds.[29]

Out-of-body experiences are also implicit in all our traditions by the very concepts of souls of the dead undergoing experiences after physical death. It was certainly not believed that these experiences took place in the body. Ascent by association with the rising sun or Venus is also common to all.

2. Corpse Encounters

In Egypt, the "efflux" or corpse of Osiris in the underworld is identified with the deceased. In Mesopotamia, the corpse of Inana is resurrected in the underworld and Damu's rebirth is enabled when he sees his own congealed blood. The corpse motif is not explicit in India, though may be related to the "Decay" in the "house infernal." Corpses of divinized humans are found on Mount Kunlun in the Chinese texts, and shamans surround the corpse of the god Ya Yü. In Mesoamerica, there are numerous deaths and rebirths of twins, many involving decapitations. There's also the corpse of the Twins' merged Twin father, and Quetzalcoatl reflected in a mirror as a corpse.[30]

3. Traveling through Darkness

In Egypt there are the underworld paths of Rosetau, the solar boat at night, the Two Ways, and "traveling in darkness." In Mesopotamia, the afterlife is described as a "place of darkness" and the netherworld is dark when the sun is in the celestial realm. India had Paths of Gods and Fathers, "bottomless darkness," "lowest darkness," and pits and abysses. In China, the otherworld is a "dark region," or Dark Palace, reached by unspecified means of descent. Mesoamerican texts describe a path of descent, caverns, and darkness in Xibalba.[31]

References to descent in general reflect traveling through darkness, and both ascent and descent parallel movement through a tunnel.

4. Deceased Relatives and Ancestors

There are numerous references of this kind throughout the texts. In Egypt there are deceased fathers, mothers, brothers, and sisters, as well as friends, servants, concubines, and associates. In Mesopotamia, there's a specific afterlife fate for the parents of those who die in battle. Amashilama joins her brother Damu in the netherworld, and Ur-Namma joins his brother Gilgamesh as underworld judge.[32] In India there is the path of the fathers (i.e. ancestors), as well as references to relatives more generally. Ancestors and relatives commonly feature in China. In Mesoamerica, the Twins meet their father in the otherworld, among other references to parents and relatives.

5. Beings of Light

Among the many examples of beings of light are the sun-gods Re in Egypt, Utu in Mesopotamia, and Vivasvant in India, and the sun itself in

Mesoamerica. In addition, the Sumerian deities Nergal, Enki, Lugalera, and Ishtaran all radiate light. In India, souls ascend on rays of light, there is an "inextinguishable light," and the statement "we have gone to the light." In China there is a "glittering light," as well as radiant divinized ancestors. In Mesoamerica, the Twins "made a way for the light to show itself," and ascend "into the middle of the light." In Aztec poetry, light shines in the House of the Sun.[33]

In addition to beings of light, all traditions feature realms characterized by bright light and the deceased becoming stars (Mesopotamia being a possible exception).

6. Evaluation of Earthly Life

A Herd of Justification is mentioned in Egypt, and the deceased's "annals" are read. Merikare has a life review, and the dead are judged by Osiris and the Ennead. In Mesopotamia, there are numerous underworld judges. They review the life of Bilgames, and Inana also undergoes judgment. In India (as in later depictions in Egypt), souls are judged by being weighed and by encountering Faith, Nonfaith, and Yama. In China, Shangdi "pacifies" or "suppresses" those he judges. Souls are also judged by the deities Yo Pei and Shao si Ming, and there are heavenly palaces for "recompenses and punishments." In Mesoamerica are the Lords and Council of Xibalba and afterlife fates determined by earthly conduct.[34]

7. Barriers and Obstacles

The afterlife descriptions in all our civilizations feature rivers and bodies of water, various perils, trials, demonic beings, and interrogation.[35]

8. Divinization and Transcendence

In Egypt, the deceased becomes Osiris and Re, various other gods, including a composite deity, and multiple gods at once through member apotheosis. In Mesopotamia, Bilgames, Ur-Namma, Damu, Ningishzida, and others all undergo divine transformation. Deceased ancestors become gods in India, and the deceased becomes a golden god who becomes Agni. The concept of *atman* and *brahman* is also relevant, for it means the self and the divine are nondifferent. In China, the ancestors live in realms of gods and there are descriptions of divine transcendence and becoming "godlike." In Mesoamerica, the Twins undergo multiple transformations and divinization. There are references to royalty becoming divine and to everyone who dies becoming gods.[36]

9. Other Realms and a Return to the True State of Being

In Egypt, the afterlife is the origin point and realm of creation, described as "home" and "the place which you know." The same types of descriptions are found in India, China, and Mesoamerica. The theme isn't explicit in Mesopotamia, though is perhaps hinted at in the Atrahasis myth, for if the soul is a fragment of the divine, it may return to a unified state after death.

Nearly all the texts feature both celestial worlds and underworlds. There's also a stress on continual cosmic journeying. Souls go "wandering" in the Daoist and Vedic material, and in all civilizations the deceased joins the sun or Venus on its circuit through the celestial realms and underworlds. These journeys encompass analogues to NDE reports of ascent, darkness, emerging into light, and a being of light—as well as the associated concepts of spiritual rebirth, feelings of oneness, and transcendence.[37]

It's worth stressing again here that the main cross-cultural consistencies are related to the afterlife journey as opposed to destinations, which aligns with NDEs. Indeed, the main function of the texts is to instruct and assist the deceased on the afterlife journey. The ultimate state is often not explicit, though is usually characterized by a complexity of multiple or simultaneous experiences. In all cases, though, it involves becoming divine or divine-like.

To summarize and highlight the key points: the main similarities between the texts occur in sets of elements with remarkable consistency across largely unconnected cultures around the world and of different eras. Rather than a general category such as "belief in life after death," the elements are specifically related to out-of-body afterlife journeys. The set of similar elements is also thematically consistent with some of the most frequently recurring core elements of the NDE.

Our findings here run contrary to certain assumptions about ancient religious beliefs. The British theologian John Bowker, for example, maintained that the "earliest speculations about death did not produce a belief that there is a desirable life with God beyond this life, after death." We have seen that is not the case. While Bowker conceded that "occasionally some heroic individuals"[38] would achieve a more positive state, he didn't consider that their experiences would serve as models for others. Through their own moral, heroic, ritual, or otherwise socially correct behavior, ordinary people may achieve postmortem fates similar to those of "heroic individuals." While there certainly were negative conceptions, there were *always* other alternatives in all of the world's earliest texts about the afterlife.

9

Experiential Origins of the Afterlife

Near-Death Experiences, Shamanism, and Dreams

Although the relationship between NDEs and afterlife beliefs has gone largely unacknowledged in the study of religions, some scholars have recognized more generally that myth and belief have origins in experience. In many ways, myths and beliefs are ways of making sense of our experiences and fitting them into some kind of comprehensible worldview.[1] Such profound, unusual, rare, and transformative experiences as NDEs would be no exception.

When we find similar beliefs around the world, it makes sense to look for common experience types that might explain them. As Wendy Doniger put it, we can approach the problem "by extrapolating from what all the myths have in common, modified in the light of what we can simply observe about the human situation in different cultures."[2] At least since the nineteenth century, a number of scholars have argued for mystical experiences in general as a primary factor in the origins and development of religious beliefs.[3] One was the Victorian Scottish folklorist Andrew Lang, who reached this conclusion by comparing the evidence from psychical research with ethnological reports of supernatural beliefs.[4]

In his classic 1902 study on religious experience, the famous American philosopher and psychologist William James defined the key aspects of religious experience as "the divided self and the struggle," "the change of personal center and the surrender of the lower self," "the appearance of exteriority of the helping power . . . and yet a sense of union with it," "feelings of security and joy," and subsequent positive transformation, which he called the "fruits" of the experience. Specific personal and cultural details, he argued, "reconstruct" the experiences "in their individual forms." A "common core" might be "sifted" out from the discrepancies, and it's this core that might be scientific fact.[5]

While the ancient texts share all of James's typical traits of a religious experience, it's important to be specific about exactly what *kind* of religious beliefs we're talking about and exactly what kind of extraordinary experiences are most relevant to it.

The NDE-Source Hypothesis

Long before the NDE was lodged in the popular consciousness—or even identified as an actual phenomenon—the French author Louis Elbé argued in 1906 that the similarity of ancient afterlife beliefs across cultures indicates "an original revelation, as if primeval man had been favored with an insight into the problem of the invisible world."[6]

The NDE-source theory was perhaps best articulated by the American sociologist James McClenon. He described a "symbiotic process" in which culture and experience influence one another, so that accounts of universal experience types are expressed in culture-specific ways. The cross-cultural similarities of "belief in spirits, souls, heavens, hells" is explained by the fact that NDEs contribute to the formation of religious beliefs. In his comparison of modern NDE reports and return-from-death narratives in medieval China, Japan, and Europe, he concluded that the "universal features" in such narratives support the hypothesis that they share a common "experiential source"—the NDE.[7]

Others have independently reached similar conclusions. Carl Becker, an American scholar of Buddhism and comparative philosophy, suggested that afterlife conceptions in Chinese Pure Land Buddhism were based on near-death experiences. He explained the similarities between the early Japanese and Chinese NDEs and those of the modern West simply in terms of similarity of experience. The British theologian Paul Badham has made similar arguments, with particular focus on the relationship between NDEs and Japanese Pure Land Buddhism, the Tibetan *Bardo Thödol* (*Book of the Dead*), and the late thirteenth-century Jewish mystical text, the Zohar. The Hungarian Classical scholar Jeno Platthy highlighted similarities between modern NDEs, mythical and historical counterparts from ancient Greece and Rome, and afterlife conceptions in the Upanishads, Buddhist sutras, and Zoroastrian beliefs.[8]

Correspondences between the Upanishads and NDEs have also been observed by the scholar of Indian philosophy, William A. Borman, leading him to suggest that the phenomenon might also be useful for understanding other ancient texts relating to the afterlife. The French Egyptologist Ruth Schumann-Antelme identified some common elements between NDEs and the Egyptian *Book of the Dead*, and the psychologist E. J. Hermann noted some compelling similarities between the NDE and *Zhuangzhi*. These include feelings of oneness with the universe, love, joy and peace, ineffability, and so on.[9]

The clearest and most direct historical evidence, however, comes from small-scale societies. In my book *Near-Death Experience in Indigenous Religions,* I examined hundreds of accounts of afterlife beliefs from Africa, Native North America, and Oceania from the seventeenth century to the early twentieth century. Rather than esoteric religious texts, the sources were the records of explorers, missionaries, and anthropologists. There were certainly differences between these broad culture areas. Very few accounts of NDEs were found in Africa, Micronesia, and Australia. Their afterlife beliefs were correspondingly less concerned with spiritual existence in other realms than with the potentially harmful influences of ancestor spirits that remained nearby on Earth. In contrast, I found over a hundred NDE accounts among Native American, Polynesian, and Melanesian societies. They not only tended to valorize NDEs, but their afterlife beliefs and otherworld journey myths were thematically consistent with them.

The really remarkable thing, however—the indisputable evidence—is the existence of *dozens* of statements by indigenous people themselves that their afterlife beliefs derived from accounts of actual individuals who had temporarily died and returned to life. Furthermore, those who had NDEs often became prophets, shamans, or other religious leaders. Badham pointed out that modern medical technology has "democratized" NDEs, explaining not only why they were especially rare in earlier times, but also why those who had them were considered exceptional individuals endowed with religious authority.[10]

A few anthropologists, such as Åke Hultkrantz and Irving Hallowell, distinguished between various types of visionary afterlife experiences: those that originated in dreams, shamanic visions, and apparent temporary deaths. The reason they made such distinctions was because their indigenous sources did. The Winnipeg Salteaux Native Americans, for example, based their afterlife beliefs on dreams, mediumistic communications, and NDEs, with the latter holding the greatest importance and authority. Also relevant is anthropologist Dean Sheils's survey of out-of-body experience beliefs in sixty-seven small-scale societies worldwide. He found that 95 percent believe in the phenomenon and that they're described in remarkably similar ways. This led him to suggest that the belief is based on experience, concluding: "When different cultures at different times and in different places arrive at the same or a very similar out-of-the-body belief we begin to wonder if this results from a common experience of this happening."[11]

That the NDE-source theory is proven for some indigenous societies strengthens the possibility that the afterlife beliefs in our ancient civilizations were also grounded in such experiences. In light of this, it's worth reviewing some of the more *direct* evidence. Leaving aside for the moment the many conceptual and mythological parallels embedded in the texts, with the exception of Egypt, explicit references to an individual dying, returning to life, and undergoing experiences highly reminiscent of NDEs occur in each civilization.

In Mesopotamia, knowledge of NDEs is suggested by the Akkadian term *muballit miti*, "the one who makes the dead to live"—that is, bringing back one who is on the brink of death. Similarly, the afterlife deity Nergal was said to have the power "to carry off and to bring back." Etana's fall from heaven might also suggest the NDE return, particularly as it was in the context of a visionary dream. And as we've seen, "The Death of Bilgames" may be the world's first documented NDE. Lying on his deathbed, he travels to the otherworld, undergoes a life review assisted by beings of light, is reunited with deceased relatives, has a transformative experience in which he becomes godlike, then returns to his body and awakens. The stress on Bilgames's case being exceptional reflects the exceptionality of the occurrence of NDEs.[12]

Near-death experiences are widely attested in ancient India. As far back as the *Rig Veda*, there is a spell to revive those who are at risk of death—"If your mind has gone to the light-beams, the sloping paths to Yama far away"—and return them to consciousness. The "charms to recover a dying man" in the *Atharva Veda* also demonstrate knowledge of NDEs, describing the soul as ascending from the underworld and returning to the body in terms that recall heavenly ascent. Another medical-magical text is intended to retrieve the breath and life from the underworld and restore them to the body. During shamanic journeys, the departure from the body of the "free-soul" (*asu*) that enables consciousness would cause a state of apparent death. The *Jaiminiya Brahmana* contains a reference to people who visited Yamaloka and returned from death. Finally, the otherworld experiences of Bhrgu, Vrsashusma, and Nachiketas were brought about by losing consciousness in contexts associated with death.[13]

In an ancient Chinese poem, the soul reluctantly returns to the body when its path is blocked by a river. Another poem is intended to call the soul back to the body from dangerous afterlife realms. A second contender for the world's first factual NDE account, in the seventh century BCE, Kien-tsze recovered from an illness and reported an enjoyable journey to the home of the Emperor of Heaven, who gave him precognitive information that was later verified. That narrative is embedded in the account of Muh of Ts'in's NDE 150 years later. The NDEs of Dan, an unnamed woman, Du Xie, and Li O span the next 500 years, and numerous further Chinese return-from-death accounts are known from the third century BCE onward.[14]

The NDE of the Mexica princess Quetzalpetlatl includes the thematic elements of an out-of-body journey to another realm, a guide, a sense of joy, other spirits and deceased relatives, an idealized mirror version of Earth, encountering a divine being, precognition, and a return characterized by a positive transformation—the ability to heal the sick on Earth. The fact that the account immediately follows a description of beliefs about the afterlife suggests that Sahagún's sources were relating Quetzalpetlatl's account as proof of Mexica beliefs. Also from Mexico is the prophetic NDE of the Aztec woman from Tenochtitlan.[15]

The Shamanic-Source Hypothesis

Some scholars have suggested that afterlife beliefs stem from shamanic visionary experiences. While there are many kinds of shamanic practices, the variety we are concerned with here involves the consciousness of a spiritual healer traveling temporarily to another realm in order to retrieve the soul of an individual who is in danger of death, or to gain knowledge in the otherworld. Eliade found it likely that "many features of 'funerary geography' as well as some themes of the mythology of death are the result of the ecstatic experiences of shamans." He found similarities between shamanic journey narratives in Central Asia, Siberia, Polynesia, and North America. Hultkrantz similarly argued that ideas of dualism and OBEs stemmed from shamanic experiences. Such practices might also explain concepts of dual souls, for part of the "self" must remain in the body to keep it alive while the "free soul" roams in the other realm.[16]

The shamanic origin theory is not without problems, however. It doesn't explain why there would be cross-cultural similarities of shamanic visions to begin with, particularly when different induction techniques are used in different societies—ranging from drumming, dancing, and chanting to varying types of hallucinogens and extreme forms of self-harm. Different kinds of drugs lead to different kinds of experiences, and drug experiences in general lack the regularity and consistency of NDEs.

Some scholars overgeneralize about shamanic experiences, downplaying their diversity and exaggerating their consistencies with NDEs. Shamanic journeys do not always involve realms of the dead, for example. Unlike spontaneous NDEs, they're deliberately brought about and are therefore more apt to be influenced by expectation.[17]

In fact, there has been little in-depth cross-cultural comparison of the content of shamanic journey experiences, and there's conflicting evidence as to whether shamanic soul-journeys are cross-culturally regular. The anthropologist Michael Winkelman has claimed that shamanic "death-and-rebirth experience" is universal, including "soul journey, flight to lower, middle, and upper worlds; and transformation into animals." While "other realms" and "transformation" are key elements in our comparison, "lower, middle, and upper worlds" and "transformation into animals" are not. Nor are they typical of NDEs. Another allegedly universal shamanic experience related to death and rebirth is dismemberment followed by reconstruction. However, this is unknown for the NDE, and out of all our civilizations it is found only in Egypt—which has the least evidence for shamanism.[18] The beheadings in the Maya *Popol Vuh* are certainly related to death and rebirth, but this is different from dismemberment.

The Australian psychologist Adam J. Rock and his team attempted to identify universal shamanic imagery by inducing visions in American undergraduates using shamanic drumming practices. In addition to the "three worlds," they found a common recurrence of "typical" shamanic cosmography, including rocky ravines, bridges, predatory creatures, and rivers. These similarities are on the symbolic rather than the mythemic level, and though they do feature in some of the ancient texts, their specifics are not cross-culturally consistent. They're also not very typical of NDEs, and it's interesting that other NDE elements—including OBEs—were not reported.[19]

Generally speaking, then, shamanic journeys have more individualistic elements, fewer cross-cultural consistencies, and various idiosyncratic features quite unlike NDEs. Further examples include traveling through time and to earthly places, and seemingly hallucinatory visons such as encountering a man with hair in the shape of a bishop's hat and his heart beating on the outside of his chest, a woman in the moon with a bayonet in her heart, and so on. It's worth noting, too, that the Salteaux Native Americans and others not only distinguish between NDEs and shamanic journeys, but class the latter as dreams and the former as real.[20]

Notwithstanding, many specific examples of shamanic journeys could be given that are consistent with both NDEs and the ancient texts. They certainly *can* include features such as OBE, traveling to a spirit realm, light, joy, ineffability, meeting deities and deceased relatives, barriers, life review or judgment, and return—sometimes after being instructed to do so by a divine being or relative. Peyote experiences reported by the Huichol people of Mexico, whose shamanic practices are believed to be virtually unchanged since pre-Columbian times, include a journey through the Gateway of the Clashing Clouds and along a trail to the origin point "where Our Mother dwells." The inexperienced "walk in darkness," though all are renewed in the bright light emanating from the world beyond the clouds. Dangers include whirlwinds and obstacles placed by sorcerers. The Fang people of Gabon on the west coast of central Africa use the plant *Tabernanthe iboga* to induce otherworld journeys. They described traveling on a "long, multicolored road" or "over many rivers" to the realm of the ancestors who take souls to the "great gods." One man described a forest road leading to "a barrier of black iron" with a bright light beyond, then flying with his deceased father.[21]

Among our ancient civilizations, there's good evidence for shamanism in India, China, and Mesoamerica, where it is generally associated with afterlife journeys. Sahagún described an Aztec ritual involving hallucinogenic mushrooms in which shamans experienced visions of their own deaths and other precognitions. In one shamanic myth, an old man gives Quetzalcoatl a potion, telling him, "You will weep; you will be compassionate. You will think upon your death. And you will think upon the place where you are to go." *Cantares Mexicanos* may have been performed in shamanic rituals, and they include many references to journeying to the otherworld to gather songs. The region where peyote grew was called Mictlan—the same name as the afterlife realm.[22]

As previously mentioned, there are figurines from ancient China that are believed to represent shamans. The *Book of Rites* includes many references to "calling back" the soul, indicating shamanic attempts to restore NDE'ers to their bodies. According to the *Zhuangzi*, hermits undertake soul journeys simply for enjoyment. There are also strong shamanic elements in *Songs of the South*, including references to intoxication by eating valerian root, chrysanthemum petals, and the dew from a magnolia. The "Nine Songs" mention chanting, drumming, various hallucinogenic plants including "spirit hemp," and drinking "cassia-wine and peppered drink." One song describes a man "from the river depths" who descends from a burial mound and says, "Magic fungus is my chariot, dragons are my steeds; I gaze as I wander beyond the four seas." Another song features a shamanic initiate on hallucinogenic mushrooms being led westward by a fairy on a white deer. The Herb of Life referred to on the bronze mirrors might also have shamanic significance, as might the herb of the Illusion Tree in "The Ballad of Tung Flees."[23]

The Canadian scholar of Chinese religions, Jordan Paper, suggested that the similarities between the descriptions of out-of-body ascent in these texts are due to their authors describing similar shamanic experiences.[24] The intermixing of shamanic journeys with afterlife descriptions in the poetry makes it likely that the origins of the descriptions lie in the experiences. Considering that actual NDEs are also attested in ancient

China, it seems that they were regarded as a similar type of experience, so that both may have contributed to afterlife beliefs.

In India, shamanic drug-induced afterlife journeys are suggested by passages in the *Rig Veda* describing Soma as revealing "the abode of immortality," expanding worlds, and showing the Light to those who use it. R. Gordon Wasson, an American ethnomycologist (the study of cultural uses of fungi) argued that Soma was the hallucinogenic fly agaric mushroom. The ritual of sharing it was intended, in part, to provide a foretaste of the otherworld: "We have drunk Soma, we have become immortal. We have reached the light. We have found the gods." The poets of the *Rig Veda* are referred to as "seers" with supernaturally inspired perceptions. They are described as "furious, raging, vibrating, trembling, excited people," probably in reference to their trance states. Another passage describes the poison-induced OBE of a *muni*—a "long-haired, drugged ecstatic." Soma was also associated with the moon, an afterlife realm in the Upanishads. The *Jaiminiya Upanishad Brahmana* mentions a "disembodying chant" that enables the participant to have an OBE. Bodewitz concluded that descriptions of light in the Indian texts reflect actual "visionary experiences" brought about by shamanic techniques, such as drugs, fasting, and meditation.[25]

The existence of Mesopotamian shamanism is more speculative, though the evidence is compelling. Parpola characterized Gilgamesh as a "mystic" who uses "a special technique" to induce visions—including pressing his head between his knees. This, as well as the "prolonged weeping and praying" that brought about the reunion with the deceased Enkidu, are both known mystical practices in Jewish Kabbalistic texts. Indeed, there are other shared cultural elements between the Kabbalah and the *Epic of Gilgamesh*, such as the Tree of Life, and it should be noted that Akkadian was a Semitic language. Gilgamesh is described as an ascetic, wandering the desert dressed in animal skins and with unkempt, wild hair. As with Soma, Wasson suggested that Gilgamesh's plant of life was also a hallucinogenic mushroom. Similar meanings might apply to the "plant of birth sought by Etana" and Inana's life-giving plant and waters. The *muballit miti*, who bring the dead back to life as mentioned above, seems very much a shamanic designation. The American scholar of Mesopotamian religions, Tzvi Abusch, considered references to underworld descent and celestial ascent in a Babylonian incantation to be reflections of shamanic "personal experience" of "transformation, ascent to heaven and mission to the netherworld."[26]

The evidence for Egyptian shamanism is weak. Terrence DuQuesne, a British Egyptologist, speculated that certain Egyptian afterlife conceptions may reveal shamanic origins: transformations into different gods and animals and the deceased being led to the land of the dead by Anubis—whom DuQuesne sees as a shamanic figure. While there are no clear references to shamanic practices, the plant of life in the Pyramid Texts may be relevant. It was also believed that the *ba* could wander in dreams to earthly and supernatural realms.[27]

The Dream-Source Hypothesis

Also worth mentioning is the idea that afterlife beliefs originated with dreams of deceased relatives that were believed to be real. This type of speculation was popular in the nineteenth century among early anthropologists such as E. B. Tylor, John Lubbock, and J. G. Frazer, as well as with Sigmund Freud. The first problem with such notions is that most societies draw a distinction between dreams and other extraordinary visionary experiences. The amateur anthropologist Lord Raglan pointed out that "any sane person, however savage" can distinguish between dreams and waking consciousness—and a virtually universal characteristic of NDEs is that the experiencer is "awake" and lucid.[28]

Raglan also rightly criticized dream-source theories for seeking "to explain the precise and particular by the vague and the general": one cannot extrapolate complex afterlife mythologies across cultures from the notion of dreaming of ancestors. The American psychologist James Hillman combined the dream theory with Jungian perspectives to suggest that dreams and underworld conceptions come from the same "archetypal 'place'"—though this is equally vague. Bowker suggested that the idea of life after death arose from a combination of attempts to understand dreams, memories of the deceased, and genetic resemblance of offspring to their deceased forebears. But this does not address cross-cultural similarities of conceptions, and the latter suggestion is illogical when we consider that offspring also resemble family members while they're still alive. Paper has suggested that the proximity of burial sites to habitation sites in sedentary communities gave rise to dreams of the deceased and thus to afterlife beliefs that helped maintain kinship ties through remembrance of the ancestors. This also does not address cross-cultural similarities, particularly with nonsedentary societies. Finally, no consistency to afterlife dreams, cross-culturally or otherwise, has ever been demonstrated.[29]

In summary, the components of the NDE are more consistent cross-culturally than dreams, hallucinogenic drug experiences, or shamanic visionary journeys. They also correspond more often to afterlife descriptions in the ancient texts.

However, while the NDE seems a more likely experiential source for afterlife conceptions, there is *some* evidence for cross-cultural regularity of shamanic imagery, which corresponds well with certain elements in the texts (and with NDEs). While influence from shamanistic experiences therefore cannot be ruled out—particularly for societies known to have practiced shamanism—the *relative* lack of consistency makes it less satisfying than the NDE hypothesis. There is not enough comparative evidence to suggest that the texts discussed here are more likely to have integrated shamanic than near-death experiences.

Perhaps the most satisfactory approach is to see the two experience types as complementary. As the German ethnopsychologist Holger Kalweit wrote, "when asked about the origins of their knowledge of the Beyond, the members of the various cultures say they gained this knowledge from the experiences of those who have returned [that is,

NDE'ers] and from shamans."[30] Various scholars have seen shamanic otherworld journeying as attempts to replicate the state achieved spontaneously during phenomena such as NDEs, OBEs, and lucid dreaming. We will explore these relationships in greater depth in the next chapter.

10

Crossing Boundaries
Psychology, Neurotheology, and Metaphysics

While we've established that NDEs were likely a common influence on afterlife beliefs across our ancient civilizations, it's worth investigating some other theories, too. None of them alone amount to convincing explanations, though they might help to contribute to a more satisfying and more comprehensive understanding of all the universal, cultural, and individual dimensions of NDEs and afterlife beliefs. They can be grouped roughly into three categories: (1) the psychological, which includes ideas from anthropology; (2) the neurotheological, which encompasses theories based on both the physiology of the brain and on patterns of human cognition; and (3) the metaphysical, which includes philosophical and spiritual arguments that there is an actual afterlife.

Psychology

Jung and the Collective Unconscious
The most widely known attempt to explain cross-cultural similarities of myths is that of the famous Swiss psychiatrist Carl Jung. He

proposed that they're due to universal archetypal symbolism emanating from the collective unconscious of all human beings.[1] In fact, he applied the theory to similarities between Western spiritualist depictions of the afterlife and the intermediate states (*bardos*) described in the *Bardo Thödol*. While attractive in its deceptively simple combination of psychology and spirituality, there are serious limitations and problems with the idea.

The first is that, as the British anthropologist Brian Morris put it, "it simply describes the partly known in terms of the totally unknown."[2] In other words, the collective unconscious itself is speculative rather than a proven fact. This means that, at best, the idea is a way of classifying and naming the phenomena—"archetype" and "symbol"—without actually explaining them. The second objection is that Jung didn't provide a possible mechanism for how the collective unconscious might work. We're not told on what basis and with what sort of process it constructs symbols and archetypes. Why, for example, would encountering barriers be virtually universal but not a ferryman? And why would ferrymen nevertheless be so widely recurrent but the underworld ball game is restricted to two wholly separate civilizations? Ultimately, we're left with a somewhat vague idea of the mind or brain drawing nonuniversal symbols from a hypothetical and unexplained collective unconscious through some unknown process.

The Jungian explanation has been supported by the Czech psychiatrist Stanislav Grof, one of the founders of transpersonal psychology, and his coauthors the psychotherapist Christina Grof and the anthropologist and Zen Buddhist teacher Joan Halifax. They believed it could explain similarities between afterlife beliefs across cultures—including "those which had no demonstrable contact"—and near-death, shamanistic, schizophrenic, and psychedelic experiences. They characterized the visionary imagery experienced in such states as "psychic realities," which sometimes appear "to be from a cultural framework entirely unknown to the subject, or totally alien to his background." In addition to the limitations of the collective unconscious theory, the authors overgeneralize the similarities across a vast range of cultures and experience-types and downplay the many differences. The term "psychic realities" is also vague. Are they real only to the psyche and therefore imaginary, or are they actual realities experienced through psychic means?[3]

It is certainly true that the ancient afterlife conceptions of all our civilizations can be seen as symbolizing the process of individuation—becoming the "whole" true self. This could be one interpretation of the archetypal themes of psychopomp or shaman as guide, a regenerating "descent" into hidden realms of the unconscious as in dreams, nether-world gates that symbolize the point of transformation, and divinization, rebirth, and enlightenment through the attainment of self-knowledge. Eliade viewed hell as symbolizing a return to the origin point, heaven as the transcendence of the physical state and a merging with the sacred and infinite, and death itself as wisdom and enlightenment.[4] With the excep-tion of the origin point being specifically associated with hells, these themes indeed have such associations in the ancient texts. This observa-tion does *not*, however, demonstrate that afterlife beliefs were created to represent the process of individuation. As discussed in chapter 1, simply observing parallels doesn't actually explain anything.

To suggest that afterlife beliefs symbolically refer to a different type of phenomenon than they actually describe also removes them from the culture's own context. It deprives them of their original meanings—the meanings that the very people who created them intended.

All these issues can be resolved if we accept the experiential source hypothesis for NDEs and the ancient civilizations. The experience is spe-cific, widely attested, and particularly relevant to the texts themselves. To argue conversely—that the experience is dependent upon belief—would not address the cross-cultural, cross-temporal, and cross-contextual similarities.

Other types of purely psychological theories are equally problem-atic. Echoing Freud, the Anglican priest and comparative religions scholar S. G. F. Brandon asserted that afterlife beliefs arose from our refusal to accept "the prospect of personal annihilation," and to humans contemplating our place in the universe. He ascribed variations across cultures to "imaginative ingenuity," as influenced by cultural "temperament, environment, and history." While Brandon rightly considered the cross-cultural differences, he didn't actually address the similarities to any substantial degree.[5] The theory is mainly relevant to the mere *fact* that humans have afterlife beliefs at all, as opposed to explaining specific expressions of them.

The British theologian John Hick asserted that beliefs in a positive afterlife were the result of "the emergence of individual self-consciousness and as a correlate of faith in a higher reality." As well as being rather vague, this wrongly assumes a global evolution of "religion" per se, as opposed to individual religions emerging and evolving within separate cultures. It also seems to imply that these concepts did not exist at some identifiable point in human history, which is not the case, as we have seen.[6]

Social Psychology

As long-dominant paradigms in the study of myth, these kinds of theories usually rely on a single social factor or motive to explain afterlife beliefs. That is, the *function* of the beliefs explains their origins, while the beliefs themselves are seen as secondary. As Lévi-Strauss argued, myths are consistent cross-culturally because the basic structures of society are the same and because myths attempt to explain "universal concerns."[7] Many of these types of theories have been repeated for over a century, and some are widely accepted without question. Most of them, however, are more like anthropological literary tropes than fully formed hypotheses. Let's assess the most prominent examples, each in turn.

1. The Afterlife as a Tool of Social Control

The most common theory of this type is that afterlife judgment was invented by the ruling elite to promote good conduct of the populace through the promise of heaven and the threat of hell.[8] As we've seen, however, the earliest afterlife texts were not widely accessible to the general population and indeed were intended for the elite, though they contain references to judgment. Notwithstanding, it's clear that the idea of post-mortem judgment was *manipulated* by the elite over time. In Egypt, India, and China, at least, the increased popularity of funerary texts is accompanied by an increase in vivid descriptions of punishments. This pattern continued in direct proportion to the widening accessibility of the texts, as seen with the Egyptian New Kingdom netherworld guidebooks such as the *Amduat* and the *Book of Caverns*, the Hindu Epics and Puranas in India, and the Buddhist Sutra of Bodhisattva Ksitigarbha in China.

The theory also neglects to consider the differing historical developments of civilizations and their beliefs, treating them all in the same way. In the Upanishads, for example, there's an emphasis on enlightenment over moral or ritual behavior and on *moksha* over heavenly realms. There's no clear social or political reason for this, and it defies a simple reward-and-punishment interpretation. These deeply philosophical, metaphysical concepts are not necessary to the orderly functioning of a society or really even beneficial from a utilitarian standpoint. The concepts didn't *replace* the possibility of heavenly fates but coexisted alongside them. Ultimately, the theory that the origins of afterlife judgment (let alone afterlife beliefs per se) lie in elite control of the populace cannot be applied cross-culturally. In fact, it hasn't been demonstrated convincingly for even a single culture.

What makes more sense given the evidence is that concepts of afterlife judgment originated in human experiences in which it is known to occur—namely, NDEs. The specifics of the judgment process manifested in culture-specific ways—including being subject to manipulations and elaborations by the elite. This argument is also compelling when inverted: if afterlife judgment is a tool of elite control, why would one have judgment-type experiences during a spontaneous, unsought NDE?

2. The Afterlife Determined by Social Organization

Like speculations about a collective unconscious or diffusion from one civilization to another, social psychology theories don't explain why only particular elements would appear cross-culturally, while others would not. The Argentine anthropologist Eva Hunt attempted to address this issue, arguing that there's a combination of factors, including the function of the myth, linguistics, "social projection," "the self-generating quality of social structures," and simple accident. But the limitations of this type of theory are obvious when applied to the present comparison. First, it is inconceivable that the process Hunt described could repeat around the world and result in five separate, largely culturally independent civilizations manifesting the same sets of mythemes for the same type of belief—which just happen to correspond to the NDE. It's equally implausible that a different combination in each society would yield the consistent set of mythemes.

Hunt also argued that agricultural states specifically have similar "religious symbolism" that derives from social factors such as hierarchy, control of crops and animals, and reliance on the annual cycles of the seasons. These states did produce "esoteric knowledge which has no direct social relevance for the masses or for the management of the social system" other than conferring elite status on the "parasitic intellectuals" who possessed it—the "theologians, astrologers, philosophers, poets." These individuals had a "proclivity for making up ideas for their own pleasure." The people would gradually attach "unconscious emotion" to an idea until it became part of their culture, serving to "promote its endurance over time among the members of the community."[9] In other words, Hunt is merely adding "imagination" and "emotion" to her list of factors, so that virtually everything in a culture contributes to the process of creating myths—with the glaring omission of extraordinary experiential phenomena.

Hunt's assertion that hunter-gatherer, nomadic, and other nonstate societies do not have such "dominant paradigms" or archetypes weakens her argument even more. As we've seen, this is demonstrably false in the case of afterlife beliefs and shamanism in small-scale societies, as well as in apparently stateless ancient India. Trigger similarly argued that afterlife expectations in territorial states are more optimistic than those in city-states; and that the upper class's expectation of an afterlife that mirrors their earthly privilege is adopted by the lower classes, who aspire to be like them.[10] This does not, however, explain why this would allegedly not occur in city-states, which are often no less socially stratified.

Furthermore, a link between types of social organization and degrees of afterlife optimism has been largely discredited. The civilizations under consideration here had dissimilarly structured societies, though thematically similar afterlife conceptions. The Indian texts arose from an apparently noncentralized village-based society, and nothing conclusive can be said regarding Vedic afterlife beliefs reflecting social structure. The Egyptian texts appeared in a unified nation-state based on divine kingship, while Mesopotamia and Mesoamerica were composed of city-states governed by extremely powerful rulers. China was characterized by fluctuating degrees of centralization and independent statehood; for example, the Chou period was feudal and the Han was a centralized bureaucracy.[11]

Nor is Trigger's case helped by his repetition of familiar overgeneralizations about ancient afterlife conceptions. The Mesopotamian afterlife is said to be gloomy and vague, while references to light, judgment, and more positive afterlife alternatives are ignored, Utnapishtim is reportedly the "sole exception" to a gloomy fate, and so on. The Mesoamerican afterlife is alleged to be the most negative of all, described as a memoryless, temporary existence as a bird, butterfly, spirit, or demon. The souls of ordinary Maya are said to be "trapped and doomed to oblivion in the underworld"—a notion flatly contradicted in *Relación de las Cosas de Yucatán*. Trigger's claim that across cultures there was a "limited tendency" to link afterlife fates with earthly conduct is clearly insupportable, as is his assertion that in city-states, all the dead became servants to the gods, while in territorial states, the upper class became godlike. In fact, his generalizations are so confusingly full of exceptions that they can only disprove the rule. He states, for example, that a positive afterlife is possible for the Maya upper classes but less so for the lower, although all Maya saw the afterlife as "gloomy," even though Maya conceptions were more optimistic, like those of territorial states than other city-states.

It is true that Mesoamerican and Mesopotamian city-states alone shared a greater focus on Venus and a connection between a ball game and an underworld descent. However, certain elements are also shared exclusively between particular pairs of city-states, territorial states, and India, and thus cannot be explained in terms of similar social structures.[12]

3. The Afterlife Originating in Funerary Rituals

Another common theory among anthropologists is that afterlife beliefs are grounded in funerary rituals and the preparation of corpses. Ascent is said to be associated with cremation and descent with burial.[13] However, all the civilizations considered here had both concepts, regardless of their method of corpse treatment. The Egyptians practiced mummification and burial or entombment, Mesopotamia and China used burial, while India and Mesoamerica used both cremation and burial.

Nor is there any good reason to believe that the situation was not the reverse: that afterlife beliefs dictated funerary rituals. There are, of course, references to ascending on cremation smoke, and associations between corpses and the underworld—and indeed many of the texts had funerary ritual functions. It does not follow, however, that the rituals gave rise to the beliefs. They may instead have been physically enacted expressions of the beliefs, intended to ensure the desired fate. A ritual without an underpinning belief is meaningless, and therefore is unlikely to have preceded the belief.

4. The Afterlife as a Reflection of Nature or Initiation

The observation that afterlife conceptions are paralleled by the death-and-rebirth cycles of nature is popular in Jungian circles.[14] As with the collective unconscious, this is descriptive rather than actually explanatory, for merely identifying a parallel does not explain it. Reducing afterlife beliefs solely to their cycles-of-nature elements also ignores other types of descriptions that can't be confined to such a narrow interpretation, such as beings of light, ancestors, ferrymen, dogs, and much more. Nor can such perspectives account for the theological and metaphysical dimensions of afterlife beliefs, such as out-of-body experiences, transcendence, and encountering spirit beings. The rebirth and fertility themes are merely metaphors for the texts' deeper meanings, and are ways of situating beliefs about human cycles of life and death into the natural world.[15]

A related idea is that afterlife beliefs reflect rites of passage, which concern an "initiatory ordeal" involving "separation, transition, incorporation" and "rebirth" from one condition to another.[16] As with funerary ritual and observations of the natural world, drawing analogies between afterlife conceptions and initiation rites does not explain the origins of either, let alone the results of our comparison. The more likely explanation is that initiatory experiences symbolically enacted afterlife themes, rather than vice versa.

5. Light and Darkness

Yet another similar theory is that the association of light with goodness and height accounts for concepts of ascent and radiant beings.[17] As well as being, once again, merely descriptive, the main assumption is questionable. Light and height are not objectively "better" than darkness and depth. While the sun is required for life and growth, it can also burn and even be deadly during times of drought. Great heights can be terrifying as well as dangerous. Conversely, while darkness may conceal hidden dangers, it's also womb-like, providing safety through concealment and faciliting regenerative sleep. Freshwater springs come from the earth's dark depths, which are also required for growth and life in equal measure to light. The underworld is by no means always a negative place in the texts, and Yamaloka, Duat, Kur, the Yellow Springs, Xibalba, and Mictlan are all realms of rebirth as well as death. The fact that NDE'ers do not usually report feeling afraid during their episode of darkness is also significant.

Ultimately, these types of theories can't explain why two separate categories of human phenomena—ancient afterlife beliefs and NDEs—would bear such similarities. While some afterlife-related symbols are undoubtedly related to social psychology, and certain cross-cultural similarities may be due to similar social and psychological processes, this can't account for each shared afterlife element, or their recurrence as a set, or their relationship to NDEs.

These kinds of theories also severely overgeneralize, characterizing a single *possible* explanation for a belief in *one* society as applicable to all others. Perhaps most seriously, they approach the texts on the scholars' own terms rather than accepting the meanings they hold for the people who created them. In doing so, these scholars reduce philosophical and religious thought to a simple equation that ignores their complexity and sophistication, their cross-cultural recurrence, and the similarities with relevant experiential phenomena.

All in the Mind-Brain

Cognitive Religion

The idea that afterlife beliefs are similar across cultures simply because the human mind works in similar ways has also been argued by a number of scholars. The variety of possible ways of envisioning the afterlife would therefore be limited by common human observation and the logical workings of our minds. In other words, the beliefs are products of the imagination, but the human imagination is constrained by our cognitive processes. For example, concerning similarities of afterlife beliefs between China and other cultures, the Taiwanese scholar of comparative antiquity, Mu-chou Poo, wrote that "human religiosity prescribes elements that are fundamental to every society."[18] This suggests that there is some kind of core panhuman mental "religious" functioning that transcends culture—though it doesn't explain or specify exactly what that might be.

As we have seen, some afterlife symbols simply reflect the local environment. For civilizations near bodies of water, an afterlife journey myth involving a water crossing on a boat "is instinctively right and fitting."[19] The details of the *types* of bodies of water, the ships, the rowers, the ferrymen, the nature of the journey, and the destination are all culture specific. But rather than explaining the origins of beliefs in afterlife water crossings, as with ritual-source theories, the symbols may simply be metaphors for preexisting ideas about the afterlife. Myths are not always intended to explain or reflect nature and can instead use nature to illustrate more abstract concepts and ideas.[20]

Sometimes the reasons for a given culture's use of a particular symbol are more complex. For example, though butterflies exist worldwide, only Mexico conceived of them as souls of the dead. The symbolism was likely related to an association between the transformation of the caterpillar and afterlife rebirth—though why would our other civilizations not make the same analogy? Conversely, in every civilization but Egypt, afterlife dogs act as guides and guards, reflecting the earthly functions of domesticated dogs. While Egypt did have a prominent canine deity, Anubis, he was a jackal, which is not a domesticated animal. The association may instead lie with seeing jackals scavenging for bodies in cemeteries.

While these kinds of associations are reasonable for particular symbols in particular cultures, trying to understand the cognitive processes involved in myth-making across cultures is much more complex. Why would becoming a bird and joining the sun after death be conceptually logical across cultures, but not becoming a fish in an underwater afterlife realm? In no case does ascent involve the human-shaped soul growing wings, though that would perhaps be more conceptually illogical than the idea of ascending on spiritual ladders or chariots. Nor can the theory explain why allegedly panhuman logic processes would apply only to some types of belief and not to others, such as creation myths, which are cross-culturally very different.

The theory also assumes that what is logical in one culture will be logical in all others. Zaleski made the odd claim that "there is simply no other way for the imagination to dramatize the experience of death" than the out-of-body experience. It would be arguably more logical to conceive of consciousness sinking into the underworld with the decomposing of the body, or remaining in the body in a state of suspension awaiting physical resurrection. The few small-scale societies that do *not* have a conception of OBEs, or even of an afterlife, further disprove the claim.[21]

Neurotheology

Neurotheological approaches theorize that universal brain functions can account for similarities in how human beings understand existential questions, such as those regarding the afterlife. A combination of "genetic and cognitive constraints" (the universal elements) and "background conditions" (the culture-specific elements) determine the nature and character of beliefs within a society.[22]

The American psychiatrists Eugene D'Aquili and Andrew Newberg acknowledge the possibility that "mystical experience" also influenced religious beliefs. This is a potentially compelling line of thought because it allows for an extraordinary experiential element *and* for the experience to be affected by cultural and individual factors. They also argue, however, that the NDE itself is the result of "the neural activation of certain archetypes" that are products of "specific neural pathways." As they admit, postulating a neurophysiological basis for Jungian archetypes is highly speculative. It essentially grafts a biological explanation onto the collective unconscious without fully explaining how or why this might work. Equally problematic is the evolutionist Christian bias of their theory, for D'Aquili and Newberg characterize only Western monotheisms as being associated with total functioning of the brain. Their characterization of the NDE is also flawed, for they treat the experience as a Western phenomenon. They claim that both positive and negative archetypes are generally "activated" in a single experience but that people are not prepared to acknowledge "such grisly horrors." Their statement that thoughts move in "slow motion" during NDEs is also not supported by the evidence, which actually describes thoughts speeding up. Finally, they neglect the significance of reports of veridical OBEs and the evidence that NDEs can happen when no brain function is possible.[23]

In Winkelman's neurotheological study of shamanism, he argued that:

> The universality of the death-and-rebirth experience reflects neurognostic processes of self-transformation, a natural response to overwhelming stress and intrapsychic conflicts. This breakdown of ego structures is experienced in "autosymbolic images" of bodily destruction, which activate innate drives toward psychological integration.[24]

By "neurognostic" he means the ways in which the brain processes and organizes information.

The first issue here is Winkelman's a priori reasoning, for he assumes that universality necessarily indicates a biological origin. In fact, many psychological and metaphysical theories are also built around the "universality of the death-and-rebirth experience."

Second, most people experience "overwhelming stress and intrapsychic conflicts" at some point in their lives, but "self-transformation" through extraordinary experiences is limited to comparatively few individuals. Furthermore, NDEs are associated with the *end* of life when self-transformation would be irrelevant. From an evolutionist perspective, "psychological integration" is functionally useless to a dying brain.

Winkelman also argues that OBEs and soul journeys are "symbolic" of transcendence of the self and of the capacity for self-referentiality—that is, seeing yourself as others see you. It seems unintelligible, however, to suggest that an experience is symbolic of what it actually *is*. Is laughing an experience of laughter, or is it merely symbolic of laughter? Regardless of whether the experience has metaphysical or biological origins, surely it is *effectively* a transcendence of the self and the ultimate realization of self-referentiality.

The purpose of such a scenario is also obscure, notwithstanding Winkelman's argument that "Evolution of the human brain has produced a modular structure with specialized subsystems, which result in a fragmentation of consciousness. Shamanic traditions have produced an integration of consciousness through community-bonding rituals."[25] How undergoing a symbolic experience might repair a hard-wired "fragmentation of consciousness" isn't explained. Nor is it clear how an individual's extraordinary experience would have a profound effect on community members who do not undergo the experience, especially considering that only shamans become "psychologically integrated." Finally, the claim that shamanic experiences and dreaming both stem from the same neurobiological system only raises the question of why there would be some cross-cultural consistency of shamanic experiences but not of dreams.

Bruce Trigger argued that some of the cross-cultural similarities he discovered in his study of early civilizations "reflect little-understood tendencies of the human mind to produce particular types of analogies." The origins of these "tendencies" he believed would be found in the fields of biology, neuroscience, and evolutionary psychology, for "only a materialist evolutionary approach is sustainable." Effectively, he assumed that a particular type of unproven theory would be correct—prior to it even being formulated—because the alternative would be a challenge to such a theory. Interestingly, although Trigger briefly considered the possibility that shamanism spread from Siberia to China to Mesoamerica, he did not consider the possibility that shamanic experiences could explain some of the cross-cultural similarities he found.[26] While Trigger did acknowledge that a "broader spectrum of factors must be taken into account to explain similarities and differences among early civilizations than is fashionable in most current theorizing," the limitations he imposed on his own theorizing ultimately led him to a dead end in this regard.

Ultimately, as the American historian of religions Luther H. Martin wrote, there is as yet no naturalistic or cognitive science–based "complete theory for a competent comparing of religions that has been fully 'tested' against the cross-cultural and historical data."[27]

Metaphysical Hypotheses

So far, we've skirted the issue of whether or not the ancient texts and NDEs could relate to an actual afterlife. The cross-cultural recurrence of a belief or experience obviously doesn't mean it's true. After all, "a large part of the human race at one time believed that mankind is descended from melon seeds," as Arthur Waley put it.[28] However, people do not have experiences associated with that belief, and it's difficult to imagine how it could be potentially indicative of an identifiable type of direct experience. Significantly, cross-cultural comparisons of creation myths do not yield consistent similarities the way afterlife journey myths do. In contrast, the parallels with ancient, medieval, and modern NDEs make the similarities between the ancient texts of special significance.

While the question of the survival of consciousness after death is marginal to the basic claim that afterlife conceptions are often grounded in NDEs, it does have some bearing on how we might understand the relationships between belief and experience. Afterlife beliefs are an unavoidably metaphysical issue. To deny this is to remove the subject from its own cultural and religious context and to transplant it into a modern Western academic one. To automatically assume that our own "scientific" explanations for another culture's beliefs or experiences is superior to theirs is an ethnocentric dismissal of the meanings and values they hold for the people who relate them.

Various scholars have argued for a common metaphysical basis of religions in general, based on cross-cultural similarities of concepts of the divine or ultimate reality. A few have noted specifically the similarities between NDEs and afterlife conceptions across cultures and have concluded that they indicate a genuine postmortem reality.[29] Here we'll evaluate some of the metaphysical ideas that could help explain the results of our comparison.

A Mind-Dependent Afterlife

The Welsh philosopher H. H. Price developed an ingenious model for what life after death might actually be like. He posited what he called an "intersubjective" afterlife, created by the person's mind in conjunction with the collective minds of others in groups of compatible souls.

Individuals would retain the capacity for personal observations and actions, and they would not only contribute to the creation of the shared group-afterlife, but also manifest their own idiosyncratic elements. The deceased effectively becomes a godlike creator being, integrating with a select collective of consciousnesses in a communal "dreaming" of reality. The nature of the experience would therefore be largely determined by the psychological state of the participants, influenced by subconscious factors such as repressed fears, which would manifest as negative experiences; wish-fulfillment, which would manifest as positive experiences; and self-perception, which could manifest as either. The result would not be a single afterlife experience for everyone but multiple afterlives depending on a person's culture and nature.[30]

Lucid dreaming offers a useful analogy. In this phenomenon, a person is conscious and "awake" during a dream, and fully aware that they're dreaming. While the dream can be deliberately manipulated by the lucid dreamer, it's also partly determined by the subconscious, which creates and maintains the consistent "background" environment. As with any dream, it's self-created—though lucid dreamers experience their dream surroundings, events, sensations, and indeed their own "body" as objective reality. Memory, the sense of self and personal identity, spatial orientation, touch, sight, and sound are all replicated in dreams. Activities of the mind such as doubt, insight, fear, and joy interact with, and directly influence, the "reality" of the dream. Likewise, in the afterlife state, as the philosopher David H. Lund put it,

> Imagining would replace the perceiving which is normally caused by stimulation of the sense organs. Imagining would perform the function which perceiving performs now, namely, the function of providing us with objects which engage our thought and attention and about which we can have emotions and desires.[31]

NDE reports sometimes read remarkably like lucid dreams. The French actor Daniel Gélin, for example, described stirring up "a cloud of fine, gleaming dust" during his NDE. The dust made him think of stardust, an association that seemed to bring into being "a preternaturally clear" blue sky. He also recounted that when he tried to embrace the spirit of his deceased son, everything he had been perceiving "vanished like a mirage." The French ballet dancer and choreographer Janine Charrat reported a hellish NDE in a realm of flames, which she was able to deliberately reduce to a soothing translucent rosiness after she became lucid. When she felt lonely and began looking around for company, she met her grandmother.[32] Interestingly, both these accounts are French and were reported by a French author. It's rare to find such explicit descriptions of control over the NDE environment, and when it is reported it seems idiosyncratic and dreamlike.

The American psychologist J. Timothy Green identified a number of similarities that can occur between lucid dreams and NDEs. He gave examples in which the dreamer described an out-of-body experience, a journey through darkness and into light, and feelings of calm and peace. Lucid dreamers typically describe the experience as a spiritual state of extreme clarity, with a sense of euphoria and freedom, transcendence of the self, and entering a state of expanded consciousness. They also feel elation when they become aware of the paradox of being conscious while *unconscious*.[33] This recalls the impact upon NDE'ers of seeing their own "corpse"—realizing the paradox of being *alive* outside of their own "dead" body.

In the Tibetan Buddhist practice of dream yoga, practitioners have lucid dreams in order to direct their "consciousness towards the clear light of death." As observed by the sociologist Raymond L. M. Lee, this recalls descriptions of bright light and beings of light in NDEs. In the Tibetan tradition, the light is said to be a manifestation of the mind, though it's *perceived* as being external by the inexperienced lucid dreamer unfamiliar with dream yoga. Merging with the light brings about the realization of nonduality and "liberation from egocentric consciousness."[34] The light is thus a symbolic manifestation of "enlightenment," which is both real and subjective, for there is no meaningful difference between subjectivity and reality in a mind-dependent world. If we combine this philosophy with telepathic communication between dreamers, for which there is alleged evidence,[35] the parallel with Price's theory is even stronger.

While a mind-dependent afterlife could hypothetically account for variations between NDE reports, it doesn't address the issue of shared elements beyond the confines of each group of souls. If like-minded souls are drawn together, it would make sense that afterlives would be based upon culture-specific beliefs, resulting in an Egyptian group, a Mesopotamian group, and so on. Why these separate group-created realities would have so many similarities as seen in chapter 8 remains a puzzle. Nor does the mind-dependent hypothesis account for the "otherness" described for deceased relatives and beings of light. Such elements do not *seem* cocreated by NDE'ers, who consider them to be external realities.

On the other hand, if we accept that the NDE actually *is* a process of souls surviving the dying process and journeying to a mind-dependent realm, this can resolve the issue. The cross-cultural similarities of NDEs might indicate that the transitional experience of leaving the body and going to the other world is universal. But upon arrival, souls merge with groups and cocreate their separate realities. Bowker's objection that the diversity of beliefs in the afterlife "cannot possibly all be true" can be resolved if we conceptualize the NDE as a transition made up of the elements that the ancient beliefs all hold in common, followed by a post-NDE mind dependent existence. Without the NDE core, the mind-dependent hypothesis means that any description of the afterlife would be equally real—from the human-devouring "earth cricket" that looks like a ram to "a centaur with the face of Jesus" riding a chariot.[36] The way to determine what is subjective and what is objective is through comparison, which in our case leads to a recurring set of NDE elements.

An afterlife created by group souls could also include "real" features. John Hick suggested that there might be a genuine divine element or that individuals could even exist *within* a transcendent "divine consciousness."[37] Regardless, if we dispense with the group souls altogether and adapt Price's hypothesis to the idea of an individual-*universal* cocreation, we then arrive at a solution that can accommodate all the issues of similarity and difference. Features of the near-death experience such as OBE, deceased relatives, and the being of light could all be genuine though *experienced* differently according to a person's cultural and individual makeup.

It's important to remember here that regardless of cultural differences, NDEs are not greatly influenced by a person's conscious expectations. Some people even have experiences that run contrary to their hopes and beliefs and they may wonder why they were not met by a particular deity or expected deceased loved one. Conversely, atheists who have NDEs are typically convinced of the reality of the experience.

Becker suggests that we're so accustomed to experiencing and comprehending things visually and symbolically that we construct imagery around objectively real but nonphysical states and beings. We project form onto them in a way that makes them comprehensible, even perceivable. But we're limited by our own individual background, knowledge, and experience, which provides us with orientation, "just like the imagery we project in our dreams."[38] Thus, as outlined earlier, there may be objective, possibly universal aspects to the NDE, which are given form by our own individual psychology, culture, and memory processes.

This model is also borne out in some of our ancient sources. The concept of a mind-dependent afterlife occurs repeatedly in the Vedas. Yamaloka is reached via the "chariot of the mind," which can travel in all directions. Ancestors become creator-gods, and the soul of the dead "wanders as his nature wills." Svargaloka is "a projection of the mind," an intermediate state to be transcended by achieving *moksha*. It's also reached "by means of the mind." The mind is equated with the moon, which is Brahma, which is "utter freedom." When the moon asks the deceased, "Who are you?" the answer required for liberation is "I am you." When Brahma asks the same question, the correct reply is, "the self of every being. What you are, I am, all that is The Real." The *atman* is the "inner controller, the immortal," and "whatever world a man ponders with his mind, and whatever he covets; that very world, those very desires, he wins."[39]

Dreaming and even lucid dreaming are seen as analogous to the afterlife state in India. Sleep is the "minister of Yama," the *atman* is "that person who, as one sleeps, roams about in dreams," and Pitrloka is compared to the dream-state. "This world and the other" meet in the world of dreams, which "serves as an entryway to the other world. When earthly terrors appear in dreams, and one, as a god thinks 'I alone am this world! I am all!' That is his highest world." The dreaming self is "the maker" who creates every aspect of the dream and may go "wherever he wishes for he is a god." He "is the ultimate reality."[40] The goal of realizing that *atman* is *brahman* (or the being of light in the form of the sun) is essentially the transcendence of illusory separateness—a realization of universal oneness, which is analogous to a realm cocreated with other souls.

Though not evident in the ancient Maya texts, the modern Lacandon Maya believe in an illusory afterlife that tests the readiness of the deceased to transcend it.[41] The Aztec notion that the deceased, associated with Venus, is a fragment of the sun, and that reunification with the sun is the afterlife goal, is conceptually similar to the principle of *atman* and *brahman* and the idea of merged consciousnesses in the otherworld.

Notwithstanding identifications of the deceased with creator-deities, becoming both Re and Osiris, and having godlike abilities, the idea of a mind-dependent afterlife is not clear in Egypt. Associations between dreams and the afterlife occur in Mesopotamia, where the dream-god Sissig "lights up" the netherworld for Bilgames, and the dream-goddess Nanshe is the wife of underworld deity Niminur.[42] In China, the conception of Shangdi as the collectivity of deceased ancestors recalls the notions of group souls, and "the mind penetrates into the depths of creation."[43]

In addition, the ancient texts facilitate a mind-dependent afterlife interpretation when we consider the recurring importance placed on (1) self-awareness and the realization of the reality of the spiritual self; and (2) the constant associations between souls of the dead and the divine, including creator-deities. Throughout all this, despite all the transformations, divinizations, and transcendence, souls seem to retain their discrete identity. As Becker wrote, "death may represent the end of all personal limits and boundaries, without necessarily being the end of conscious experience."[44] This is also reflected in NDEs when individuals describe the experience as happening to *them*—a conscious individual self—despite feelings of universal oneness. Important to both conception and experience is the realization of the self as microcosmic part of the macrocosmic whole.

Similar concepts can also be found in other traditions, including Zoroastrian, Jewish, Sikh, Christian, Sufi, Japanese Pure Land Buddhist, and in shamanic experiences.[45] The afterlife is perhaps most clearly mind-dependent in sixteenth-century Chinese Pure Land Buddhism. As Becker wrote, "the fact that everyone at death seems to report essentially similar imagery demonstrates that the Pure Land is indeed intersubjective and substantial rather than hallucinatory or illusory." It "shares certain intersubjective features for all its 'inhabitants,' has various regions suited to various types of consciousness, and responds in its minor events to the thoughts and wills of its 'inhabitants' or experimenter/creators." The tradition also addresses issues regarding conflicting wills and wishes of the cocreators. For example, if someone desires to see a particular person, that person cannot be forced to appear. Only objects, not people, are mind-dependent, and individuals retain separate consciousness and free will. Deceased relatives can thus be seen as genuine, and not illusory.[46]

As discussed earlier, the *Bardo Thödol* states that the being of light will be perceived according to the individual's cultural and religious background and beliefs. Other images seen in the dying process would be mind-dependent manifestations of personal hopes, fears, desires, and so on. In Winnebago Native American conceptions, psychological and emotional factors contribute to determining the nature of the afterlife experience, for the soul must be free of fear and doubt when undergoing afterlife trials. As Kalweit wrote, such barriers and perils are "culturally conditioned visions of an ego which is still caught in the grip of social and cultural models of the imagination and has not yet learned to adapt to the new environment." They represent "our primordial consciousness confronted by our thoughts." Such experiences are "an attempt to make the surviving consciousness aware of the fact that it itself constitutes the world of the Beyond."[47]

To summarize, if we view the NDE as a genuine afterlife journey that culminates in a mind-dependent state, this could explain both the similarities and differences across cultures and between NDEs. In addition, mind-dependence could account for the concept that the individual becomes divine or divine-like, with supernatural and creative powers. It could also explain the descriptions of multiple realms and experiences in each tradition. Feelings of oneness are consistent with the notion of becoming part of the unified consciousness.[48]

Quantum Mysticism

Some writers, such as theoretical physicist Amit Goswami, have enlisted quantum physics alongside the notion of a collective unconscious to try to explain the nature of survival after death. Put very simply, quantum mechanics suggests that observation brings about actuality from infinite possibility—a process called "wave collapse." In other words, consciousness literally brings form and matter into existence. This is achieved through a consensual process in which the collective unconscious creates our shared universe. "Quantum objects" such as photons appear to be interconnected, for they can influence one another "even when separated by vast distances"—a phenomenon known as "nonlocality." This may suggest a *monistic* universe, meaning that the independent existence of "selves" or individual consciousness is essentially meaningless.[49] Thus, if there is a consensual belief in an afterlife, the collective unconscious will actualize an experience that corresponds to it. The similarities between cultures, and the correspondences to the core NDE elements, would be due to the fact that they are all universally cocreated.

A number of problems are left unexplained by these speculations, however, such as the role of the individual in relation to the universality, and most importantly the reasons for the variations of experience and conflicting conceptions. How could individuals with *different* beliefs collapse the necessary waves to form a *consensual* afterlife reality—particularly when many people don't believe in an afterlife at all? As with the neurotheology theory discussed above, the hypothesis merely proposes a mechanism for the functioning of a Jungian collective unconscious and does not explain why or how supposedly consensual afterlife ideas and experiences arose in the first place. The idea essentially states that all objectivity—in this world and the next—is merely an illusion created by universal subjectivity. In which case, why would there be any difference between "life" and "afterlife" in the first place?

The biologist and philosopher John Poynton has criticized Goswami's ideas for misapplying theories that address "position and movement in physical space and time" to human observers and consciousness. He argues that applying the behavior of protons to consciousness is unjustifiable; and that extrapolating an interconnected realm of pure consciousness "that transcends space and time" from the theory of wave collapse is unsupportable. Goswami himself admits that evidence from parapsychology (particularly OBEs) is problematic, for it implies mind-body dualism rather than the monism he requires for his theory.[50] Finally, although he supports Tibetan Buddhist ideas of conscious dying and recognizing the pure light, he also states that what remains of the "self" after death "is devoid of any subject-object experience." This is contradictory to the extent of being unintelligible.

Quantum theory thus does not provide a compelling explanation for the results of our comparison, nor does it contribute in any meaningful or intelligible way to the mind-dependence hypothesis.

The main drawback to the mind-dependence hypothesis is that it's almost wholly speculative. It requires a leap of faith into abstract ideas that are unproven by current empirical science. Adam Rock and his team have, however, found correlates between shamanic vision imagery and emotional states, levels of awareness, and "autobiographical memories." These occur in combination with certain recurring landscape features that do not appear to be culturally conditioned.[51] Of course, mental and emotional states also affect our dreams.

In any case, the fact that a hypothesis is unproven does not invalidate it for the present purpose, which is to evaluate the ability of competing models to explain the results of the comparison. Our ability to fully explain natural processes and phenomena is not a prerequisite for their existence—and if consciousness does in fact survive bodily death, it must be considered "natural."

A Holistic View
of the Afterlife

Given all the competing theories reviewed above, with all their strengths and weaknesses, how can we best understand afterlife beliefs across cultures? Before answering that question, let's first have a quick recap and synthesis of what we've learned from our comparison of the ancient civilizations and NDEs.

There were significant chronological and geographical distances between our civilizations, a lack of noteworthy cultural contact, and many differences between the types of texts in which afterlife descriptions appear. Despite all this, their beliefs in the experiences of souls after death show a consistent set of thematic elements shared across the traditions. This particular set of elements also corresponds to some of the most recurrent features of cross-cultural, historical, and modern near-death experiences. The clear connection between NDEs and afterlife conceptions in the ancient texts suggests that such experiences influenced the beliefs cross-culturally. The beliefs encompass representations of NDEs, according to cultural and individual interpretations and elaborations.

Because NDEs are also *experienced* in real time according to cultural and individual symbols and beliefs, they not only contribute to new afterlife ideas, but also reflect existing ones. Culture and experience have a symbiotic relationship, mutually influencing one another and playing equally vital roles in the evolution of beliefs about the afterlife.

The very existence of the cross-cultural similarities shows that the experiences preceded the beliefs. To argue the reverse—that NDEs didn't occur prior to people having afterlife beliefs—can't explain how a set of similar afterlife ideas could be independently invented across cultures. Nor can it explain *how* exactly those beliefs could create spontaneous, unsought NDEs. Near-death experiences are not caused by intention or deliberate action. While they might be used for political, social, or religious purposes,[1] their spontaneous and unpredictable nature means that they don't arise out of some intrinsic social or political function. Nor are NDEs a biological necessity, making no contribution to the survival of the species.

Likewise, transcendental beliefs such as *moksha*, multiple divine transformations, and cosmic wanderings don't correspond to any particular economic, social, or political functions. They don't try to explain observable phenomena in the natural world, and they aren't necessary for providing comfort to the bereaved. Nor are they required to encourage good behavior, or for a coherent afterlife doctrine. But these kinds of concepts in the texts *do* share metaphysical meanings with NDEs. Both are characterized by these technically "unnecessary" ideas of spiritualization and the transcendence of the earthly self. The texts are imbued with the spiritual significance of the experiences, while the experiences are given authority by parallels in texts that were sources of spiritual meaning. Again, the symbiotic relationship is clear.

Reconciling the Opposites

In the Hellenistic period of the ancient Greek and Roman world, a philosophy known as Eclecticism developed during the second century BCE. The basic principle was to combine selected ideas and theories from a number of philosophical schools and synthesize them in a new way that would lead to more thorough modes of analysis and understanding. At the heart of such thinking is the recognition that theories that rely on only a *single* explanation often fail—such as those reviewed in the previous chapter. Eclectic approaches are unpopular in many academic circles, partly because they question "received wisdom" and partly because it's human nature to want simple, clear-cut answers. The problem is that human behaviors, beliefs, and experiences are anything but simple and clear-cut. Complex, nuanced, *eclectic* phenomena would seem to require complex, nuanced, eclectic explanations. As Bowker wrote, the diversity of beliefs means that "no single theory will be able to eliminate all others as being itself a sufficient and complete account." For example, psychological interpretations such as wish-fulfillment or fear of death "are not in competition with each other; they are complementary."[2]

As we have seen, the relationships between the experiences and beliefs can't be convincingly explained by any of the usual theories, from the collective unconscious to social psychology, to cognitive science and neurotheology. In fact, it's puzzling that attempts to explain cross-cultural similarities of afterlife beliefs so rarely mention NDEs or shamanism as contributing factors. They unjustifiably ignore *the* most directly relevant human phenomenon. Instead they rely entirely on a single factor relating to their social or biological function.

While such theories *alone* can't adequately explain the results of our comparison, it can be illuminating to explore how social structure, economy, environment, psychology, and biology contribute to the formation and expression of certain elements of afterlife conceptions. If we incorporate some of those elements *with* the NDE-source hypothesis, we arrive at a more satisfying, comprehensive explanation of the origins and development of afterlife beliefs in cultures around the world. This is especially appropriate when we remember that afterlife beliefs have different layers of meaning: individual, cultural, and experiential. As with NDEs, multifaceted beliefs require multifaceted theories.

All the theories considered in the previous chapter agree that there must be some kind of universal factor to explain the similarities, and culture-specific factors to explain the differences. Although the precise nature of these elements varies between the social, psychological, neurophysiological, and metaphysical, they're not necessarily mutually exclusive, and an eclectic combination of factors makes the most sense.

For example, on the psychological level, the impetus to create afterlife texts may lie in a desire to resolve existential feelings about death, such as the fear of dying and coping with loss. Realms of opulence and beauty may be influenced by Freudian wish-fulfillment. There are limited ways of conceptualizing otherworlds, even allowing for the vast powers of the imagination.

Such ideas are also influenced by the cognitive processes of the human mind. It's conceptually logical to visualize the afterlife realm as an idealized version of the only realm we know, so that the descriptions mirror familiar earthly landscapes, including rivers, mountains, and trees. Sometimes other realms are symbolized by observable celestial features, such as the Milky Way being conceptualized as an afterlife river. The otherworld also reflects earthly social structures, including bureaucracy, judgment, and social hierarchies. Beliefs that the land of the dead is also a realm of rebirth have parallels in the cycles of planets and stars, as well as the earthly cycles of nature and life-giving springs—symbols that are woven into afterlife beliefs. Human physical needs and desires were also often seen as persisting in the otherworld, including an abundance of food, music and dancing, and the possibility of sexual intimacy. Conversely, in the case of negative realms some of these features could be inverted as afterlife counterparts to the hardships and perils of Earth, such as a concern for proper nourishment, fear of wild animals, and so on.

The specifics of expression obviously differ because each civilization has different physical environments, social organization, value systems, languages, modes of expression, and symbolic associations—as well as differences in what was considered to be conceptually logical. Another reason our civilizations shared many similarities is likely due to the fact that they all had polytheistic religions with prominent pantheistic and transcendental features. All were characterized by exceptionally interassociated webs of concepts, deities, and metaphors. In addition, sociopolitical manipulations by the elite of ideas about afterlife judgment have cross-cultural dimensions, as well as culture-specific ones. These are evident in the varying descriptions of opposing rewards and punishments and the different kinds of earthly conduct that they're based on.

At the same time, it's also conceptually logical to base afterlife beliefs on the testimonies of people who were nearly or temporarily dead, then revived and recounted their unusual experiences. When it happens to more than one person in a society over time, accounts of experiences will affirm one another while also contributing new knowledge about the afterlife.

On the neurophysiological level, the brain may help to assign recognizable form or identity to each element of the experience, generating imagery, sensations, and perceptions that are relevant to individuals and their cultures. There is a universal human tendency to anthropomorphize and to mentally construct identifiable objects out of abstract forms, such as clouds. It may be the same with giving form and meaning to ineffable experiences. This would occur both during the NDE and afterward when it is being described. This is not to say that the brain *creates* the experience—especially in cases of temporary actual clinical death—but that it clothes the experience in ways that help the person to make sense of it according to one's cultural and personal background.[3]

Some features of NDEs might support the existence of a genuine metaphysical element. The perceived "otherness" of the being of light and deceased relatives, assessment of earthly conduct, and especially claims of veridical perceptions during OBEs and precognitive elements of NDEs have not been adequately explained in "dying-brain" terms. The mind-dependence theory incorporates all these universal elements—and the concept of mind dependence itself may have an experiential basis in lucid dreaming and NDEs.

In addition to providing a well of symbols with which to express ideas, experiences, and emotions, culture and environment also impose limitations on expression. There was no narrative genre for the recording of documentary NDEs in any of the civilizations but China, for example.

And there was, of course, no possibility of Egyptian crocodiles or a celestial counterpart to the Nile appearing in Aztec otherworlds. The human brain also imposes cognitive constraints, limiting conceptions to what's comprehensible within a given culture. Finally, it's important to remember that experiencers and authors of the texts were *individuals*, and that personal interpretation, emotion, and imagination play a role in experiences and in processing and describing them.

A few other scholars have also been led to propose eclectic theories to explain cross-cultural afterlife phenomena. The British theologian John G. Bishop noted consistencies in underworld descent myths in Mesopotamia, ancient Greece, Japan, Scandinavia, Siberia, and small-scale societies in Polynesia and North America. Writing before widespread knowledge of NDEs, he suggested that the myths could be accounted for partly by dreams and shamanic underworld journeys. Such experiences were later elaborated upon in the formation of afterlife beliefs, supplemented by cultural and psychological factors. Likewise, McClenon wrote that in addition to NDEs, similar social and cultural features "contributed to the commonalities within Buddhist and Christian images of the afterlife."[4]

Not all attempts at eclectic explanations have been as successful, though. The Romanian historian of religions Ioan Couliano wrote that otherworld journey accounts arise from a combination of cognitive processes, diffusion, and shamanism. He suggested that "a simple set of rules would generate similar results in the minds of human beings." These "rules" would be: "There is another world; the other world is located in heaven; there is a body and soul; the body dies and the soul goes to the other world." Couliano suggested these rules had roots in shamanism rather than NDEs—though as discussed, the consistency of shamanic journey experiences hasn't been established. At the same time, he suggested that diffusion of myths and ideas played a role, but as we have seen, this is unlikely to have been a significant factor between our ancient civilizations. Finally, there's also some confusion arising from Couliano's seemingly contradictory statements that afterlife conceptions are universal *and* that they originate in the minds of individuals.[5]

A Macrocosmic Whole

The NDE-source hypothesis doesn't automatically suggest either a materialist *or* a metaphysical explanation for the experience. In fact, the ultimate nature of NDEs is largely irrelevant to the question.

Nevertheless, seeing the NDE as a genuine out-of-body postmortem journey leading to a shared mind-dependent afterlife state has the benefit of addressing all the issues at hand. It can account for the differences and the similarities in all our times, places, and contexts, in descriptions of both the journeys and the destinations, in beliefs, and in extraordinary experiences.

While acceptance of a metaphysical component requires a leap of faith, the other theories we've reviewed also require acceptance of the unproven—as well as of the inadequate, for none can comprehensively account for the results of our comparison. This goes for everything from the collective unconscious to diffusion, neurophysiology, fear of death, elite control, wish-fulfillment, and so on. Whether one particular leap of faith is somehow more or less valid than another is a matter of individual perspective, for these are all unproven culturally situated paradigms. This is not to suggest that these other theories are less *empirically plausible* than an actual mind-dependent afterlife, but from a philosophical perspective, explanatory force may hold more weight than empirical plausibility.

At the same time, a satisfactory eclectic explanation need not include an actual afterlife—as long as it allows for the inclusion of near-death and perhaps shamanic experiences, whatever their nature. Though seen by some as unorthodox, there is more evidence for the NDE-source hypothesis than there is for any of the others discussed abbove. Ultimately, our comparison points to a specific type of experiential "reality," which may or may not indicate an actual metaphysical reality.

The fact that documented NDEs occur cross-culturally, historically and in the present day, in all types of societies, demonstrates that they are a universal human experience. The claim that the ancient texts in our five civilizations reflect this universal human experience should therefore be uncontroversial. There's little difference between this and a claim that culture-specific humor in ancient texts reflects the universal subjective human experience of being amused, though we may lack empirical proof of it.

To summarize, the recurring set of elements revealed in our comparison suggests that NDEs informed ancient afterlife conceptions. Cross-cultural elements that do not have a parallel in NDEs can be explained by an eclectic addition of theories concerning similarities in social structure, cognition, psychology, and brain function. Environmental and cultural differences account for the dissimilarities, as do the personalities, histories, and psychologies of the individuals who had the experiences and those who composed the texts. Some degree of prehistoric diffusion cannot be entirely ruled out, nor can limited diffusion between adjacent civilizations—particularly Egypt and Mesopotamia. Even if that were the case, however, the *original* myth or belief could still have been rooted in an NDE or shamanic experience.

Mircea Eliade also supported this type of hypothesis—and even used the phrase "experiential source." He wrote that certain types of beliefs "have concrete experiences as their basis," citing "metaphysic phenomena" such as mediumship, clairvoyance, and other "miracles"—some of which he accepted as proven. The beliefs did not arise from "fantastic creations" but from "concrete facts" that were learned from extraordinary experiences. Where anomalous experiences had not occurred, he added, diffusion would explain the spread of such beliefs—but he stressed that "the *initial fact* is an experience, and we cannot insist enough on this point." He cautioned that "It is not a matter here of 'believing' blindly in all popular legends and superstitions, but of not rejecting them *en bloc* as delusions of the primitive spirit."[6]

Though we have surveyed only selected ancient civilizations here, afterlife beliefs in other societies around the world also include some of the main thematic elements of the NDE. As discussed in chapter 9, there are many historical accounts of people in indigenous societies stating outright that their afterlife beliefs derived from the experiences of people who apparently died and returned to life.

There are, of course, exceptions, and even a very few societies without any beliefs in an afterlife at all.[7] This may be partly due to the fact that none of their members have had experiences such as NDEs. Badham argued along these lines to explain changes in Jewish afterlife beliefs appearing concurrently with descriptions of religious experience.[8] Some indigenous societies, however, showed knowledge of NDEs but did not find them meaningful sources of information about the afterlife. This was due to cultural particularities surrounding ideas of death, dying, sorcery, taboo, and funerary practices that often prevented NDEs from occurring or prohibited people from talking about them.[9]

This book, together with my others on cross-cultural and historical NDEs, demonstrates that extraordinary experiences are essential to a thorough understanding of the origins and development of beliefs about life after death. They show conclusively that afterlife beliefs and conceptually related experiences are intimately intertwined—effectively rewriting a chapter in the history of religions.

Notes

Introduction

1. Pyr. N249
2. Kristensen, *Life Out of Death*, 20.
3. Bottéro, *Mesopotamia*, 270.

Chapter 1: Near-Death Experiences

1. Fenwick, "Science and Spirituality," 2.
2. See, for example, the International Association for Near-Death Studies website and The Near-Death Experience Research Foundation website, which claims that 774 NDEs occur daily in the United States alone.
3. Ring, *Life at Death*; Fox, *Religion, Spirituality*, 31.
4. Fox, *Religion, Spirituality*, 139; McClenon, "Content Analysis," 163; Kellehear, *Experiences Near Death*, 32.
5. Fenwick, "Science and Spirituality," 2; Moody, *Life After Life*; Greyson, "A Typology."
6. Zaleski, *Otherworld Journeys*, 123.
7. Blackmore, *Dying to Live*.
8. Paterson, *Philosophy and the Belief*, 139–49.
9. Among the numerous examples, see Serdahely, "Pediatric," 38; Delacour, *Glimpses*, 20; Ring, *Life at Death*, 207–8; McClenon, *Wondrous Events*, 173; Parnia, *What Happens*, 83ff; Sartori, *A Prospective Study*, 296.
10. Fenwick, "Science and Spirituality," 4.
11. Parnia et al., "AWARE."
12. Sartori, *Near-Death Experiences*
13. Becker, "The Centrality of Near-Death Experiences," 154; Ring, *Life at Death*, 136; Long and Long, "A Comparison of Near-Death Experiences," 29.

14. Bush, "The Near-Death Experience in Children," 177; Fox, *Religion, Spirituality*, 216–18.

15. Bremmer, *Rise and Fall*, 92–3.

16. Zhi-ying and Jian-xun, "Near-Death Experiences," 46.

17. Murphy, "Near-Death Experience in Thailand," 170, 172, 175–76.

18. Zaleski, *Otherworld Journeys*, 7, 131, 136, 138, 187–8.

19. Fenwick and Fenwick, *Truth in the Light*, 239; Fox, *Religion, Spirituality*, 318; Campany, "Return-from-Death Narratives," and "To Hell and Back"; Wade, "In a Sacred Manner"; Lundahl, "Near-Death Experiences of Mormons," 167ff.

20. Platthy, *Near-Death Experiences in Antiquity*, 92; Bremmer, *Rise and Fall*, 95; Murphy, "Near-Death Experience in Thailand."

21. Zaleski, *Otherworld Journeys*, 28, 31, 75ff.; Osis and Haraldsson, *At the Hour of Death*, 152–3, 192; Pasricha, "Near-Death Experiences in South India"; Pasricha, "A Systematic Survey."

22. Murphy, "Near-Death Experience in Thailand," 175.

23. Zaleski, *Otherworld Journeys*, 6, 27; Gardiner, *Visions of Heaven and Hell*, xiv.

24. Lundahl, "Near-Death Experiences of Mormons,"166ff.

25. Campany, "Return-from-Death Narratives," 102–04; Campany, "To Hell and Back," 35.

26. McClenon, *Wondrous Events*, 170.

27. Wade, "In a Sacred Manner," 94–5; Shushan, *Indigenous Religions*, 48.

28. Fontana, *Is There An Afterlife*, 403.

29. Zaleski, *Otherworld Journeys*, 7, 187–8, 136ff.

30. Campany, "Return-from-Death Narratives," 124.

31. Ring, *Life at Death*, 193.

32. Fenwick and Fenwick, *The Truth in the Light*, 231; Kellehear, *Experiences Near Death*, 28.

33. Price, "Survival," 31–2.

34. Vicente et al., "Advanced Interplay."

35. Kellehear, *Experiences Near Death*, 32, 334; Shushan, *Indigenous Religions*, 222–23, 235.

36. Murphy, "Near-Death Experience in Thailand," 172.

37. Jung, *Jung On Death and Immortality*, 136–8.

38. Delacour, *Glimpses of the Beyond*; Hampe, *To Die is Gain*; Tylor, *Primitive Culture*, 50–2; cf. Kellehear, *Experiences Near Death*, 31; Shushan, *Indigenous Religions*.

39. Bremmer, *Rise and Fall*, 101.

40. Counts, "Near-Death and Out-of-Body Experiences," 115–16, 130.

41. Green, "Near-Death Experience in a Chamorro Culture"; Wade "In a Sacred Manner," 101–2, 105–8; Shushan, *Indigenous Religions*, 221–22, 242, passim.

42. Kellehear, *Experiences Near Death*, 36–7.

43. Moody, *Life After Life*, 32ff.; Kellehear et al., "The Absence of Tunnel Sensation," 111–12.

44. Bremmer, *Rise and Fall*, 102.

45. Audette, "Historical Perspectives," 31.

46. Kellehear, *Experiences Near Death*, 37–8, 40.

47. Wade "In a Sacred Manner," 110; Counts "Near-Death and Out-of-Body Experiences," 121; Shushan, *Indigenous Religions*.

48. Moss, *Life After Death in Oceania*, 2–3, 38; Hultkrantz, *Religions of the American Indians*, 132, 134–5. See Part II of the present book for "archaic" religions.

49. Zaleski, *Otherworld Journeys*, 127.

50. Nichelson, "The Luminous Experience," 204; cf. Fox, *Religion, Spirituality*, chap. 3.

51. Evans-Wentz, *The Tibetan Book of the Dead*, 94, 2n; cf. Badham, "Religion and Near-Death Experience," 11.

52. Becker, "Views from Tibet," 3; Badham, *Near-Death Experiences*.

53. Zaleski, *Otherworld Journeys*, 193.

54. Becker, "Views from Tibet," 17.

55. Zaleski, *Otherworld Journeys*, 195.

56. For a fuller discussion of these issues, see Shushan, *The Next World*, Appendix I.

57. Stroebe and Stroebe, *Bereavement and Health*, 53–4.

58. Bremmer, *Rise and Fall*, 93.

59. McClenon, *Wondrous Events*, 172.

60. Kellehear, *Experiences Near Death*, 28; Stevenson and Greyson, "Near-Death Experiences: Relevance to the Question of Survival," 203–4.

61. Osis and Haraldsson, *At the Hour of Death*, 182.

62. Kellehear, *Experiences Near Death*, 29-30.

63. Serdahely, "Variations from the Prototypic," 194.

64. Zaleski, *Otherworld Journeys*, 203.

65. Zaleski, *Otherworld Journeys*, 54–5.

66. Kellehear, "An Hawaiian Near-Death Experience," 34.

Chapter 2. Early Civilizations

1. Trigger, *Early Civilizations: Ancient Egypt*, 6–7.

2. Trigger, *Early Civilizations: Ancient Egypt*, 87.

3. Jorgensen, "On Continuous Area and Worldwide Studies," 200-201.

4. Littleton, *The New Comparative Mythology*, 4–6; cf. Lincoln, *Death, War, and Sacrifice;* Shushan, *Conceptions of the Afterlife*, ch. 1; and Shushan, "Rehabilitating the Neglected 'Similar.'"

5. Roux, *Ancient Iraq*, 202.

6. Bodde, *Festivals in Classical China*, 36.

7. Davies, *Death, Burial and Rebirth*, 63–4; Currid, *Ancient Egypt and the Old Testament*.

8. Driver, *Comparative Studies*, 110.

9. Roux, *Ancient Iraq*, 140.

10. Trigger, *Early Civilizations: Ancient Egypt*, 13; *Understanding Early Civilizations*, 38–9.

11. Mark, *From Egypt to Mesopotamia*, 115.

12. Mark, *From Egypt to Mesopotamia*, 115, 120; see also 10–20; see also Arnett, *Predynastic Origins*.

13. Meeks and Favard-Meeks, *Daily Life*, 49.

14. Kuhrt, *The Ancient Near East*, 12, 22, 26; Pollock, *Ancient Mesopotamia*, 6, 94, 114.

15. For example, Dalley, "Occasions and Opportunities," 14–15.

16. Lal, "Aryan Invasion of India," 69–71.

17. Schaffer and Lichtenstein, "South Asian Archaeology," 93-94; Witzel, "Indocentrism," 375.

18. Lahiri, *Archaeology of Indian Trade Routes*, 409.

19. Liu, *Ancient India and Ancient China*, 2–3.

20. O'Callaghan, *Aram Naharaim*, 63.

21. Astour, "Mitanni," 423.

22. Liu, *The Chinese Neolithic*, 57, 88, 91.

23. Mair, "Old Sinitic," 36; cf. Liu, *The Chinese Neolithic*, 93 on the earlier figurines.

24. Boltz, "Language and Writing," 84, 87.

25. Coe, "Iconology of Olmec Art," 10.

26. Trigger, *Understanding Early Civilizations*, 38; Crawford, *Origins of Native Americans*, 25, 30–1; Trigger, *Early Civilizations: Ancient Egypt*, 20–1.

27. Herodotus, *Histories*, II.75.

28. Hultkrantz, *Religions of the American Indians*, 162.

29. Carr, "Mortuary Practices."

30. Parker Pearson, "The Return of the Living Dead," 1047–8.

31. Ucko, "Ethnography and the Archaeological Interpretation," 264–5, 270

32. Mithen, *Prehistory of the Mind*, 175.

33. Witzel, "Vala and Iwato," 63–4.

34. Doniger, *Implied Spider*, 133.

35. Lévi-Strauss, *Structural Anthropology*, 248, 264.
36. Chang, *Shang Civilization*, 357.

Chapter 3. Egypt

1. Allen, *Ancient Egyptian Pyramid Texts*, 4.
2. Assmann, *Death and Salvation*, 248ff.
3. Allen, "Funerary Texts," 48; Trigger, *Understanding Early Civilizations*, 537; Hays, "Death of the Democratization"; Smith, *Following Osiris,* 167ff.
4. All quotations from the Pyramid Texts are from James P. Allen's translation, *The Ancient Egyptian Pyramid Texts*, abbreviated here as Pyr. All of my summaries are also based on Allen's translations. The text reference numbers adhere to his system, with letters referring to the specific versions of the texts as found in particular pyramids. For ease of reading, the citations to the relevant text numbers have been grouped by paragraph, in the order of the quoted or summarized passage. Thus, the references to the "honored ones" and "clean ones" are Pyr. P467 and P465.
5. Allen, *The Book of the Dead*, 2.
6. Assmann, *Death and Salvation*, 240ff; Allen, *Pyramid Texts*, 2, 10–11.
7. Pyr. W139–45.
8. Hornung, *Conceptions of God*, 42.
9. Pyr. W146, W135, P511, N910.
10. Pyr. Nt242, W147.
11. Allen, "Cosmology of the Pyramid Texts," 4.; Quirke, *Ancient Egyptian Religion*, 159.
12. Pyr. W155.
13. Pyr. W148, N305.
14. Pyr. W149, W155, P38, P476, P324, P466, P42–45, P155, N350.
15. Pyr. T17, T9, T20.
16. Pyr. W150.
17. Pyr. W151–52, P30, T144, W472, N412, W155.
18. Pyr. W158, W159.
19. Pyr. P521, W320, P4, T181, W160–161.
20. Assmann, *Search for God*, 67.
21. Pyr. W158, W162, W170, P327.
22. Pyr. T185, P507, T187, Nt244, T220, P321, P321, Nt243, P31.
23. Pyr. W172, W173, W180a, Nt242; for the Milky Way, see Allen, "Cosmology of the Pyramid Texts," 7–8.
24. Pyr. T227, T225, P31.
25. See Davis, "The Ascension Myth."

26. Pyr. W174, W206, W176, P357, P458, W175, T8, P502, W155, P289, P320, W164, N564, P324

27. Pyr. W180.

28. Pyr. N564, W165.

29. Pyr. W205, P453, P450, W209.

30. Pyr. P510, W170, W207, P450, D548, P476.

31. Pyr. W167–8, P353, W171, W210, P469, P460, P484, P495.

32. Pyr. W219, P495, W220, P495, W218, P450; Meeks and Favard-Meeks, *Daily Life*, 44.

33. Pyr. Nt253, P376, T286, P463, W224.

34. Pyr. W178–179, W182–204, W226, P481.

35. Assmann, *Death and Salvation*, 74.

36. *Merikare*, §50–60; Simpson, *Literature of Ancient Egypt*, 158–9.

37. See examples in Simpson, *Literature of Ancient Egypt*; cf. Coffin Texts VII; Robinson, "As for Them Who Know Them," 148.

38. All quotations from the Coffin Texts are from Raymond O. Faulkner's translation, *The Ancient Egyptian Coffin Texts*, abbreviated here as CT. All of my summaries are also based on Faulkner's translations. The text reference numbers adhere to his system, with Arabic numerals referring to the spell number and roman numerals (where relevant) referring to the specific line of the spell. For ease of reading, the citations to the relevant text numbers have been grouped by paragraph, in the order of the quoted or summarized passage. The descriptions cited in this paragraph are from CT 548, II.367, 1007, IV.364, V.335, I.161, and II.213.

39. CT 901, I.226.

40. CT II.48, 342, 424f, 440, 441, 335, IV.327, 343, VI.237.

41. CT III.160, 175, III.99.

42. Mueller, "An Early Egyptian Guide," 120–1.

43. CT 203, 398.

44. CT V.174, V.81–3

45. CT VII.26, 336, IV.325–8.

46. CT V.105, I.369, 404, IV.296.

47. CT I.158, V.209, I.197, VI.452; Hornung, "Black Holes," 316.

48. CT II.388.

49. Faulkner, Coffin Texts, 154 n.3; III.78, 466, II.161, 576, 472.

50. CT I.130, 34.

51. CT 1052, 1130, VII.458, VII.276.

52. CT 1034, 1072, VII.282, 1036.

53. CT 1080, VII.366, 1050, VII.283, 1082.

54. CT VII.459, 1045, 1056f, 1059, 1054, 1043, 1062–66.

55. CT 1041, 1044, 1037–8.

56. CT 1100–3, 1108-10, 1107; Quirke, *Ancient Egyptian Religion*, 108, 151.

57. CT 1132, VII.476, VII.479–81.

58. CT VII.494-5, VII.376–7, 1146.

59. CT 1139, 1156, 56, 268–78, 285-97, II.161, 84–5.

60. Murnane, "Taking It with You," 42–4; Allen, "Cosmology," 1.

61. Lesko, *Ancient Egyptian Book of Two Ways*, 136, 134.

62. Hornung, *Conceptions of God*, 252.

63. Allen, Pyramid Texts, 8; Allen, *Genesis in Ancient Egypt*, 56.

64. Assmann, *Search for God*, 174.

65. Beaux, "La douat," 6.

66. cf. Allen, Pyramid Texts, 9.

67. Smith, *Following Osiris*, 144ff, 163, 165; 377.

68. Hornung, *Conceptions of God*, 127, 253.

69. Assmann, *Search for God*, 182.

70. *Man Who Was Weary*, §131–49; Simpson, *Literature of Ancient Egypt*, 168.

71. Fischer-Elfert, "Der Pharao."

72. Herodotus, *Histories* 2.122, 423.

73. Liotsakis, "Following the King," 141-45, 148 n50.

74. Simpson, *Literature of Ancient Egypt*, 472ff.

75. Betz, "Fragments," 288, 294.

76. Shushan, *Indigenous Religions*, 86, 104, 195, 198, 201, 211ff.

Chapter 4. Mesopotamia

1. Black et al., *Literature of Ancient Sumer*, 223 (1.1.3), 126; Foster, *Before the Muses*, 19n3.

2. "The Death of Bilgames" may be found in George, *Epic of Gilgamesh*. The Old Babylonian and Standard Versions of the *Epic of Gilgamesh* are in George, *Babylonian Gilgamesh Epic*. Quotations from most other Sumerian texts are from University of Oxford's *Electronic Text Corpus of Sumerian Literature* (Black et. al. 1998–), abbreviated here as *ETCSL*. My summaries are based on these translations. The text reference numbers adhere to the *ETCSL* system, and all are available online at the *ETCSL* website, hosted by the Faculty of Oriental Studies, University of Oxford. For ease of reading, the citations to the relevant text numbers have been grouped by paragraph, in the order of the quoted or summarized passage. The references in this paragraph are to *ETCSL* c.5.5.2, 2.4.1.1, and t.5.7.3.

3. George, *Babylonian Gilgamesh Epic*, 128.

4. George, *Epic of Gilgamesh*, 197ff.

5. Black et al., *Literature of Ancient Sumer*, ix, xlvii.

6. Dalley, *Myths from Mesopotamia*, 1, 42.

7. Foster, *Before the Muses*, 81.

8. George, *Epic of Gilgamesh*, 179.

9. George, *Babylonian Gilgamesh Epic*, 900.

10. Lambert, "The Theology of Death," 60; Katz, *Image of the Netherworld*, 176; *ETCSL* t.4.80.1.

11. George, *Epic of Gilgamesh*, 183–84.

12. George, *Epic of Gilgamesh*, 186–95.

13. Katz, *Image of the Netherworld*, 199.

14. Foster, *Epic of Gilgamesh*, 228.

15. *ETCSL* t.1.1.1.

16. *ETCSL* t.4.80.1; see also the Sumerian lament "Ershemma of Ninhursaga," in Katz, *Image of the Netherworld*, 19.

17. Foster, *Epic of Gilgamesh*, 67; George, *Babylonian Gilgamesh Epic*, 283.

18. Contra George, *Babylonian Gilgamesh Epic*, 494.

19. George, *Babylonian Gilgamesh Epic*, 500–1; 275, 281.

20. George, *Babylonian Gilgamesh Epic*, 493.

21. Parpola, "Assyrian Tree of Life," 192–3; Foster, *Epic of Gilgamesh*, xxi; George, *Babylonian Gilgamesh Epic*, 523.

22. cf. Parpola, "Assyrian Tree of Life," 195.

23. Katz, *Image of the Netherworld*, 126, 149–51.

24. cf. "Dumuzid's Dream," *ETCSL* 1.4.3.

25. Katz, *Image of the Netherworld*, 174; *ETCSL* t.4.15.2.

26. Jacobsen, *Treasures of Darkness*, 62–3; *ETCSL* 1.4.1

27. Jacobsen, *Treasures of Darkness*, 51; Katz, *Image of the Netherworld*, 203.

28. Jacobsen and Alster, "Ningiszida's Boat-Ride," 326; Jacobsen, *Harps That Once*, 59.

29. Jacobsen, *Harps That Once*, 63; Katz, *Image of the Netherworld*, 23.

30. Jacobsen, *Harps That Once*, 51ff; Heimpel, "The Sun at Night," 148.

31. Jacobsen and Alster, "Ningiszida's Boat-Ride," 334.

32. *ETCSL* t.1.7.3, t.4.80.1, t.4.19.1; Jacobsen and Alster, "Ningiszida's Boat-Ride," 331.

33. *ETCSL* 2.4.1.1; Black et al., *Literature of Ancient Sumer*, 58–60.

34. Black et al., *Literature of Ancient Sumer*, 103–6, 1.2.1; *ETCSL* t.4.05.01.

35. *ETCSL* c.2.1.1; Dalley, *Myths from Mesopotamia*, 189.

36. *ETCSL* c.5.5.2; George, *Babylonian Gilgamesh Epic*, 129; VII.202.

37. Foster, *Before the Muses*, 534, 552ff.; Parpola, "Assyrian Tree of Life," 198.

38. George, *Babylonian Gilgamesh Epic*, 510; Foster, *Before the Muses*, 250.

39. *ETCSL* c.2.5.3.1.

40. *ETCSL* t.6.2.3; *ETCSL* t.5.5.3.

41. Veldhuis, "Entering the Netherworld," 1, 2, 4.

42. Veldhuis, "Entering the Netherworld," 3; Sladek, *Inanna's Descent*, 58.

43. *ETCSL* t.6.1.01; *ETCSL* c.5.5.2.

44. cf. Katz, *Image of the Netherworld*, 212ff; *ETGSL* t.5.7.3; Black et al., *Literature of Ancient Sumer*, 159–61; *ETCSL* 2.5.2.1.

45. Jacobsen in Frankfort et al., *Before Philosophy*, 239–40; Bottéro, *Religion in Ancient Mesopotamia*, 222; Bottéro, *Mesopotamia*, 286

46. Katz, *Image of the Netherworld*, 199, cf. xviii–xix; Cooper, "Fate of mankind," 26.

47. See, for example, Job 10:21, Ps. 6:5, Ps. 94:17.

48. Brandon, *Judgment of the Dead*, 55.

49. Bottéro, *Religion in Ancient Mesopotamia*, 109; Bottéro, *Mesopotamia*, 278–9; Crawford, *Sumer and the Sumerians*, 122.

50. Katz, *Image of the Netherworld*, 183, 191.

51. *ETCSL* t.2.5.4.13; Jacobsen, *Harps That Once*, 122–3; *ETCSL* t.4.06.1.

52. Black et al., *Literature of Ancient Sumer*, 339-42, 4.28.1; Jacobsen, *Harps That Once*, 82.

53. *ETCSL* c.5.5.2; Katz, *Image of the Netherworld*, 224.

54. *ETCSL* t.5.2.4.

55. cf. Kramer, "Death and the Netherworld," 66; Crawford, *Sumer and the Sumerians*, 123.

56. *ETCSL* t.2.4.2.21; Jacobsen, *Harps That Once*, 122–3; *ETCSL* t.2.4.5.2.

57. Katz, *Image of the Netherworld*, 223f.; Heimpel, "The Sun at Night," 146, 148–49; *ETCSL* c.5.5.2.

58. Spronk, *Beatific Afterlife*, 99; using the example of Standard Version, George, *Babylonian Gilgamesh Epic*, III.iv.47; Spronk, *Beatific Afterlife*, 118; Dalley, *Myths from Mesopotamia*, 318.

59. Bottéro, *Religion in Ancient Mesopotamia*, 106, 107, 109, 274; cf. Roux, *Ancient Iraq*, 98; Bottéro, *Mesopotamia*, 269; Katz, *Image of the Netherworld*, 246.

60. Bottéro, *Religion in Ancient Mesopotamia*, 37; Bottéro, *Mesopotamia*, 278.

61. Evers, *Myth and Narrative*, 98; Black et al., *Literature of Ancient Sumer*, 91; 2.5.4.11.

62. Kirk, *Myth*, 104–5.

63. Black et al., *Literature of Ancient Sumer*, 263, 2.5.3.1; Foster, *Before the Muses*, 227; George, *Epic of Gilgamesh*, xi; Bottéro, *Mesopotamia*, 272; Bottéro, *Religion in Ancient Mesopotamia*, 62.

64. Smith, "Wisdom's Place,"; cf. Evers, "Myth and Narrative," 71; Katz, *Image of the Netherworld*, 113.

65. Heimpel, "The Sun at Night," 140.

Chapter 5. India

1. Except where alternative readings are noted, all summaries and quotes from the *Rig Veda* are from the translation by Jamison and Brereton, *The Rigveda*, abbreviated here as *RV*. The text reference numbers adhere to the traditional system. For ease of reading, the citations to the relevant text numbers have been grouped together, often by paragraph, in the order of the quoted or summarized passage. The reference in this paragraph is to *RV* X.135, 1, 3, 7; Jamison and Brereton, *The Rigveda*, 1618–20.

2. Eggeling, *Satapatha Brahmana*, XI.VI.1.4; Panikkar, *The Vedic Experience*, 624. For later similar descriptions of Yama, see *Markandeya Purana* 11.22–32. See also *Mahabharata* 1.3.146–75; O'Flaherty, *Tales of Sex and Violence*, 37.

3. O'Flaherty, *Tales of Sex and Violence*, I.43; 39; cf. Bodewitz, *Jaiminiya Brahmana*, I.42; 100.

4. O'Flaherty, *Tales of Sex and Violence*, *Jaiminiya Brahmana*, I.42, 37, 42; Bodewitz, *Jaiminiya Brahmana*, I.44.

5. Bodewitz, *Jaiminiya Brahmana*, I.43–44

6. O'Flaherty, *Tales of Sex and Violence*, *Jaiminiya Brahmana*, II.160-61; 44.

7. Olivelle, *The Early Upanishads, Katha Upanishad*, I.1-I.17 .

8. Olivelle, *The Early Upanishads, Katha Upanishad*, I.18-I.25.

9. Olivelle, *The Early Upanishads, Katha Upanishad*, I.20-I.29.

10. Olivelle, *The Early Upanishads, Katha Upanishad*, II.15-II.18.

11. Olivelle, *The Early Upanishads, Katha Upanishad* III.8; III.15; IV.1.

12. O'Flaherty, *Tales of Sex and Violence*, 45–47.

13. *RV* X.57–60, X.161; Jamison and Brereton, *Rigveda*, 1468; Whitney, *Atharva Veda*, VIII.1–2; VII.53.3.

14. Bodewitz, *Jaiminiya Brahmana*, I.167.

15. Malamoud, "Religion and Mythology," 27; Jamison and Brereton, *The Rigveda*, 349, 1397.

16. *RV* IX.113.7–11; Jamison and Brereton, *The Rigveda*, 1364–65.

17. *RV* VIII.48.3; *RV* IX.104, 14.

18. *RV* VII.88; *RV* V.II.88; Bodewitz, "Life after Death," 37; Bodewitz, "Light, Soul and Visions," 19, 21.

19. *RV* X.16.2–5, 9; with modifications from O'Flaherty, *The Rig Veda*; Butzenberger, "Ancient Indian Conceptions," 95, 97; Jamison and Brereton, *The Rigveda*, 1395.

20. *RV* X.16.1, 5; on a physical afterlife in the body, see De Mora, "On Death," 468; Butzenberger, "Ancient Indian Conceptions," 71; contra Werner, "The Vedic Concept," 278–9; and Bodewitz, "Yonder World," 109.

21. *RV* X.136.

22. *RV* X.17.3–5; *RV* I.125.5–6; *RV* X.XVI.1; for Pushan see *RV* VI.53.1, VI.55.3, and VI.159.2.

23. *RV* X.56.1–2.

24. *RV* X.154.

25. *RV* X.14.8–12.

26. *RV* X.58; *RV* X.68.11; *RV* VIII.48.13; *RV* X.15.2, 6–11; MacDonell, *Vedic Mythology*, 170.

27. *RV* I.154.5; O'Flaherty, *The Rig Veda*, 227.

28. *RV* II.29.6; *RV* X.98.16; *RV* IV.25.6; *RV* I.121.13, *RV* X.97.16; *RV* X.95.15; *RV* VII.104.3–11 Bodewitz, "The Dark and Deep Underworld," 215, 218; Mehr, *Yama*, 108, 136; Bodewitz, "Yonder World," 215.

29. *RV* I.35.6.

30. *RV* I.163.2–10.

31. Panikkar, *The Vedic Experience, Atharva Veda (AV)* VIII.1.3, 1.9–11, 19, 2.10, 24; Bodewitz, "Dark and Deep," 219; Whitney, *Atharva Veda AV* VIII.1.12.

32. Panikkar, *The Vedic Experience, AV* II.14.3; *AV* V.19.3; *AV* VI.118A; Whitney, *Atharva Veda AV* VIII.4.9; Bodewitz, "Yonder World," 110–11; Bodewitz, "Pits, Pitfalls," 111.

33. Whitney, *Atharva Veda AV* XI.1.37; *AV* IX.5.1; *AV* XVIII.2.21–6; *AV* XII.3.16–17; *AV* X.5.1, 7, 11.

34. Panikkar, *The Vedic Experience, AV* XII.4.36; XII.5.64; Bodewitz, "Distance and Death," 103, 105.

35. Panikkar, *The Vedic Experience, AV* IV.34.5–6; *AV* VI.120.1, 3; Whitney, *Atharva Veda AV* IV.34.2–4; *AV* V.4.4–5; *AV* XII.3.41.

36. Keith, *Veda of the Black Yajus, Krishna Yajur Veda* III.3.8; V.4.1; V.7.3.

37. Keith, *Veda of the Black Yajus, Krishna Yajur Veda* VII.3.5; VI.1.8; V.4.11; II.6.2.

38. Eggeling, *Satapatha Brahmana*, XI.2.7; XII.9.1; I.9.3.2; XII.9.1.8; IX.2.3.29; I.6.1.11; III.4.4.4; 2.1.23; 4.2.5.

39. Eggeling, *Satapatha Brahmana*, IX.2.3.24; XIII.2.12; X.5.2.3; XII.8.1.19; III.6.1.13–14; XIII.4.3.9; Bodewitz, "Yonder World," 218.

40. Eggeling, *Satapatha Brahmana*, VI.5.4.8; I.9.3.11; IX.4.2.5; X.1.4.12; VIII.6.1.21.

41. Eggeling, *Satapatha Brahmana*, XIII.3.5.1.d; X.1.4.12; Butzenberger, "Ancient Indian Conceptions."

42. Bodewitz, *Jaiminiya Brahmana*, I.18; 52–3.

43. Bodewitz, *Jaiminiya Brahmana*, I.291; Bodewitz, "The Dark and Deep Underworld," 215.

44. Bodewitz, *Jaiminiya Brahmana*, 52, 118; O'Flaherty, *Tales of Sex and Violence, Jaiminiya Brahmana*, I.46.
45. Borman, "Upanishadic Eschatology," 99; Olivelle, *The Early Upanishads*, 4.
46. Olivelle, *The Early Upanishads, Katha Upanishad* III.10–11, IV.13, V.2, V.8, V.7, IV.10–11, VI.5.
47. Olivelle, *The Early Upanishads, Mundaka Upanishad* 1.2.11, 3.10.
48. Olivelle, *The Early Upanishads, Chandogya Upanishad* VIII.12.1–2, 8.15.
49. Olivelle, *The Early Upanishads, Chandogya Upanishad* VIII.6.4–5, V.10.1; VIII.5.3, III.13.6.
50. Olivelle, *The Early Upanishads, Kausitaki Upanishad* I.2–3; Bodewitz, *Light, Soul and Visions*, 24.
51. Olivelle, *The Early Upanishads, Kausitaki Upanishad* I.3-4
52. Olivelle, *The Early Upanishads, Kausitaki Upanishad* I.4; Bodewitz, *Light, Soul and Visions*, 26.
53. Olivelle, *The Early Upanishads, Kausitaki Upanishad* I.4; 585; Bodewitz, *Light, Soul and Visions*, 26.
54. Olivelle, *The Early Upanishads, Kausitaki Upanishad* I.5–7; IV.15ff.
55. Olivelle, *The Early Upanishads, Brhadaranyaka Upanishad* IV.3.7–8; III.2.13.
56. Olivelle, *The Early Upanishads, Brhadaranyaka Upanishad* III.1.6; III.7.3ff., V I.2.15–16, IV.3.7-8, V.10, BU 5.15.1.
57. Olivelle, *The Early Upanishads*, 519; *Prashna Upanishad* I.6–10.
58. Olivelle, *The Early Upanishads*, 528; *Prashna Upanishad* V.4.4.
59. Olivelle, *The Early Upanishads, Brhadaranyaka Upanishad* VI.2.2; IV.4.9–10; *Isa Upanishad* 3; Roebuck, *The Upanishads, Maitri Upanishad* IV.2.
60. O'Flaherty, *Tales of Sex and Violence*, 42.
61. Bodewitz, "The Dark and Deep Underworld," 221.
62. Butzenberger, "Ancient Indian Conceptions," 93, 97, 64–5 passim.
63. Butzenberger, "Ancient Indian Conceptions," 84; Jamison and Brereton, *The Rigveda*, 32; cf. Werner, "The Vedic Concept," 280.
64. Eggeling, *Satapatha Brahmana* XIII.8.4.7; Panikkar, *The Vedic Experience, Atharva Veda*, XII.5.64.
65. Bodewitz, "The Dark and Deep Underworld," *Jaiminiya Upanishad Brahmana* IV.5.1–2, 103; Bodewitz, *Jaiminiya Brahmana*, I.42; Jamison and Brereton, *The Rigveda*, 1381.
66. Jamison and Brereton, *The Rigveda*, I.164; 8.58, etc.; Panikkar, *The Vedic Experience, Taittiriya Aranyaka* III.11.1, 660; Borman, "Upanishadic Eschatology," 91.

Chapter 6. China

1. De Groot, *Religious System* IV, *Shiji*, 113–15.
2. Harper, "Resurrection," 14, 22; Arbuckle, "Chinese Religions," 111.
3. Harper, "Resurrection," 13.
4. Arbuckle, "Chinese Religions," *Shenxian Zhuan*, 109–110.
5. Kao, *Classical Chinese Tales, Souchen Ji*, 87–89.
6. Hawkes, *Songs of the South*, "Ai shi ming" ("Alas, That My Lot Was Not Cast"), 337.
7. Campany, "Return-from-Death Narratives," 91–2; De Groot, *Religious System*, 123.
8. Yü, "O Soul, Come Back," 363.
9. Chan, *A Sourcebook, Analects* XI.11, 36; Watson, *Hsün Tzu*, 96–111; Xinzhong Yao, pers. comm. 16 November 2004.
10. Yü, "O Soul, Come Back," 382; Needham, *Science and Civilization*, 81; Poo, *Personal Welfare*, 4, 16.
11. Ching, *Chinese Religions*, 19, 34; Poo, *Personal Welfare*, 28; Yü, "O Soul, Come Back," 378.
12. Waley, *The Book of Songs, Shijing* Songs #214, 242, 276, 284, 276, 279; Eno, *Confucian Creation*, 188; Erkes, "God of Death," 188, 191.
13. Legge, "*The Shu King, etc.,*" 153; Poo, *Personal Welfare*, 160.
14. Erkes, "God of Death," *Chunqiu* 1.18a, 188–9.
15. Thompson, *Chinese Religion, Zuo Zhuan* I.I, VIII.V, 29, 31; Berling, "Death and Afterlife," 183; Needham, *Science and Civilization*, 81, 84; Poo, *Personal Welfare*, 158.
16. Thompson, *Chinese Religion, Zuo Zhuan* X.VII.
17. Legge, *The Li Ki, Li ji* VII.I.7, IX.III.17, II.II.1.34, II.II.1.22; Needham, *Science and Civilization*, 86; Loewe, *Ways to Paradise*, 60; Poo, *Personal Welfare*, 62.
18. Legge, *The Li Ki, Li ji* XXVIII.1.44; Chan, *A Sourcebook*, 220.
19. Chan, *A Sourcebook*, 265.
20. Lao, *Lao Tzu, Dao de jing* I.XIII.30a; *Wenzi*; Cleary, *Further Teachings*, 33, 120, 172.
21. Watson, *Hsün Tzu*, 85–8.
22. Watson, *Hsün Tzu*, 46, 81-82, 93; Paper, *Spirits Are Drunk*, 133–4.
23. Paper, *Spirits Are Drunk*, 33; 54–5.
24. Needham, *Science and Civilization*, 71, 81.
25. Morgan, *Tao the Great Luminant*, 33, 34, 44-45, 253 44n.
26. Morgan, *Tao the Great Luminant*, 58, 66, 74; Seidel, "Tokens of Immortality," 108.

27. Hawkes, *Songs of the South*, 60; 325, 327; Loewe, *Ways to Paradise*, 52, 87, 111.

28. Hawkes, *Songs of the South*, 73, 334, 337, 339.

29. Hawkes, *Songs of the South*, 74, 77–8, 90, 94, 327, 334.

30. Hawkes, *Songs of the South*, 223–24.

31. Hawkes, *Songs of the South*, 191, 195, 196, 201–2.

32. Hawkes, *Songs of the South*, 197–8

33. Hawkes, *Songs of the South*, 255.

34. Hawkes, *Songs of the South* Song VI, 9, 109, 111–12; Erkes, "God of Death," *Shijing* 27, 2a; 25, 27.

35. Hawkes, *Songs of the South*, Song VII, 112–13; Waley, *Nine Songs*, 46.

36. Hawkes, *Songs of the South*, Song VIII, 114–15.

37. Hawkes, *Songs of the South*, 302.

38. Hawkes, *Songs of the South*, 275–6.

39. Birrell, *Popular Songs*, "The Ballad of Tung Flees," 6, 70.

40. Birrell, *Popular Songs*, 98, 193 20n.

41. Birrell, *Popular Songs*, "Walking Out of Hsia Gate," 75.

42. Birrell, *Classic of Mountains and Seas*, 23–4.

43. Birrell, *Classic of Mountains and Seas*, xv, 140; Birrell, *Chinese Mythology*, 183.

44. Birrell, *Chinese Mythology*, 184; Birrell, *Classic of Mountains and Seas*, 141, 209.

45. Harper, "Warring States Religion," 869; Seidel, "Traces of Han Religion," 25, 32, 45; Poo, *Personal Welfare*, 173–5.

46. Loewe, *Ways to Paradise*, 60, 83, 198.

47. Yü, "O Soul, Come Back," 387, 389ff.

48. Hawkes, *Songs of the South*, 255.

49. Thompson, "Prehistory of Hell," 37–8.

50. Poo, *Personal Welfare*, 211.

51. Dudbridge, *Legend of Miaoshan*, 45, 54.

Chapter 7. Mesoamerica

1. Sahagún, *Primeros Memoriales*, 182; Léon-Portilla, *Native Mesoamerican Spirituality*, 36.

2. Sahagún, *Florentine Codex* Book 8, 3; Sullivan in Sahagún, *Primeros Memoriales*, 181, 20n.

3. Coe, *Mexico*, 162; Tedlock, *Popol Vuh*, 251.

4. Tedlock, *Popol Vuh*, 91, 92, 139.

5. Tedlock, *Popol Vuh*, 93.

6. Tedlock, *Popol Vuh*, 94–5.

7. Tedlock, *Popol Vuh*, 96–7.

8. Tedlock, *Popol Vuh*, 97, 99, 225; Hultkrantz, *Religions of the American Indians*, 226.

9. Tedlock, *Popol Vuh*, 102.

10. Tedlock, *Popol Vuh*, 192–93, 261, 272.

11. Tedlock, *Popol Vuh*, 116–17, 119.

12. Tedlock, *Popol Vuh*, 120–23.

13. Tedlock, *Popol Vuh*, 124–26, 275.

14. Tedlock, *Popol Vuh*, 127; 276.

15. Tedlock, *Popol Vuh*, 128–30.

16. Tedlock, *Popol Vuh*, 131–3.

17. Tedlock, *Popol Vuh*, 134–6.

18. Tedlock, *Popol Vuh*, 137–8.

19. Tedlock, *Popol Vuh*, 140–2, 287.

20. Coe, "The Hero Twins," 180, 259; Tedlock, *Popol Vuh*, 39, 77–81, 150, 207, 279.

21. Coe, "Death and the Ancient Maya," 91; Tedlock, *Popol Vuh*, 139, 239; Coe, "The Hero Twins," 167.

22. Coe, Death and the Ancient Maya, 89; Landa, *Relación de las Cosas*, 131–2.

23. Roys, *Book of Chilam Balam*, 6, 99 3n; López Austin, *Tamoanchan, Tlalocan*, 262; Love, *Paris Codex*, 82.

24. Bierhorst, *History and Mythology of the Aztecs, Legend of the Suns* 76: 22–39.

25. Bierhorst, *History and Mythology of the Aztecs, Legend of the Suns* 76:42–54; Bierhorst, *Four Masterworks*, 19–20;

26. Bierhorst, *Four Masterworks*, 19–20, 22–24; n.16, 17, 23; Séjourné, *Burning Water*, 59–60.

27. Bierhorst, *History and Mythology*, 5:9ff, 5:39, 5:42, 5:45–6, 7:14, 7:27, 7:37; Bierhorst, *The Hungry Woman*, 36.

28. Graulich, "Afterlife in Ancient Mexican Thought," 172; illustration in Codex Magliabechiano, see Klein, "Post-Classic Mexican Death Imagery," 78; Klein, "Wild Women in Colonial Mexico," 255; cf. Klein, "The Devil and the Skirt," 258–9.

29. References to *History of the Things of New Spain* are abbreviated here as *HNS*. They may be found in Sahagún, *The Florentine Codex*. This reference is at III: 201–10.

30. *HNS*, III: 79–80, 178–9.

31. *HNS* VI: 81, 163; VI: 38; Sahagún, *Primeros Memoriales*, 178.

32. *HNS* II: 178, 224–5; I: 9, 80; VI: 48, 36, 115.

33. *HNS* VI: 115; Léon-Portilla, *Native Mesoamerican Spirituality*.

34. Sahagún, *Primeros Memoriales* 176–7.

35. Sahagún, *Primeros Memoriales*, 175, 177; López Austin, *Human Body and Ideology*, 112.

36. *HNS* II: 224–5; III: 41–2; VII: 21; Léon-Portilla, *Native Mesoamerican Spirituality*, 44.

37. *HNS* VI: 152, 190, etc., VI: 27; Sahagún, *Primeros Memoriales* VII: 4.

38. *HNS* VI: 20, 27, 171; Léon-Portilla, *Native Mesoamerican Spirituality*, 72; López Austin, *Human Body and Ideology*, 318.

39. *HNS* III: 2–6; 62; VII: 14.

40. Léon-Portilla, *Native Mesoamerican Spirituality*, 191 1n, 55; Sahagún, *Primeros Memoriales*, "Song of Tlaloc" 6.

41. Léon-Portilla, *Native Mesoamerican Spirituality*, 44, 57; Bierhorst, *Cantares Mexicanos*, 181, 184, 251, 258–9; XVIII: 30, XVIII: 30.

42. Bierhorst, *Cantares Mexicanos*, 186; III: 5; LXXXVIc: 18.

43. Bierhorst, *Cantares Mexicanos*, XVIII: 50; V: 2–3; XVI II; I: 4; II: 1–2; XVII: 44; LXXXVIc: 40; IX: 11; II: 5; Léon-Portilla, *Native Mesoamerican Spirituality*, 187; López Austin, *Tamoanchan, Tlalocan*, 270.

44. Bierhorst, *Cantares Mexicanos*, LIVb: 5, 7; LIVb: 3–4; LIVc: 6; LXXXVIc: 40.

45. Bierhorst, *Cantares Mexicanos*, XVIII: 6; LXIXc: 25; LXXXIIIa: 1.

46. Haly, "Bare Bones," 278, 281, 283 (Codex Tudela, fol. 52).

47. Hunt, *Transformation of the Hummingbird*, 68 (Codex Boturini); Haly, "Bare Bones," 287; Brotherston, *Painted Books*, 136 (Laud Codex); Bassie-Sweet, "Corn Deities," 5.

48. Graulich, "Afterlife in Ancient Mexican Thought," 166; Léon-Portilla, *Aztec Thought*, 127; Furst, "To Find Our Life," 26; Nicholson, "Religion in Pre-Hispanic Mexico," table 2; Léon-Portilla, *Native Mesoamerican Spirituality*, 201.

49. López Austin, *Human Body and Ideology*, 330.

50. López Austin, *Human Body and Ideology*, 318; Furst, *Natural History of the Soul*, 177.

51. López Austin, *Tamoanchan, Tlalocan*, 194, 265

52. Bierhorst, *The Hungry Woman*, 81, 48n; 37.

53. Graulich, "Afterlife in Ancient Mexican Thought," 180.

54. López Austin, *Human Body and Ideology*, 337.

55. López, "De profecía a leyenda"; for Native American political dimensions of NDEs, see Shushan, *Near-Death Experience in Indigenous Religions*.

Chapter 8. Comparing Otherworld Journeys

1. Faulkner, Coffin Texts, IV.95.

2. Katz, *Image of the Netherworld*, "In the Desert by the Early Grass"; George, *Epic of Gilgamesh*, "Bilgames, Enkidu, and the Underworld" XII.97.

3. Bodewitz, *Jaiminiya Brahmana*, 115, I.46; Olivelle, *Early Upanishads* 285, *Chandogya Upanishad* VIII.12.1–2; Panikkar, *The Vedic Experience*, 627, *Atharva Veda* II.14.3 Panikkar, *The Vedic Experience*, 616.

4. Birrell, *Classic of Mountains and Seas*, 184, 209.

5. Tedlock, *Popol Vuh, passim*; Bierhorst, *History and Mythology*, Annals of *Cuauhtitlan* 7:37.

6. Moody, *Life After Life*, 40–41; Kalweit, *Dreamtime and Inner Space*, 104ff.

7. Hawkes, *Songs of the South*, 197–8.

8. Faulkner, Coffin Texts 1087, VII.471; Panikkar, *The Vedic Experience, Atharva Veda* VIII.1.3; Olivelle, *The Early Upanishads, Brhadaranyaka Upanishad* VI.2.1; *Shatapatha Brahmana, Jaiminiya Brahmana*; *Songs of the South*; *Popol Vuh.*

9. Pyramid Texts, Coffin Texts.

10. Sladek, *Inanna's Descent*, 84.

11. Birrell, *Popular Songs*, 70.

12. Tedlock, *Popol Vuh*, 133; Sahagún, *Florentine Codex, History of the Things of New Spain*, III: 2–6.

13. For Egypt, see Horning, "Black Holes"; Zandee, *Death as an Enemy*. For India, see Brown, "The Rigvedic Equivalent for Hell."

14. Bodewitz, *Jaiminiya Brahmana*, 115, I.46; Roys, *Book of Chilam Balam*, 99.

15. Bodewitz, "Light, Soul and Visions," 40ff; Audette, "Historical Perspectives," 33.

16. López Austin, *The Human Body*, 330.

17. Kristensen, *The Meaning of Religion*, 338.

18. Shushan, *The Next World*, ch. 2.

19. Stephen Quirke, pers. comm. 11 July 2004.

20. López Austin, *Tamoanchan, Tlalocan*, 262; Kristensen, *The Meaning of Religion*, 162.

21. Russell, *A History of Heaven*, 12.

22. DeMallie, *The Sixth Grandfather*, 259; Shushan, *Indigenous Religions*, 50.

23. Pausanias, *Description of Greece* 7.19, 9–12.

24. Trigger, *Early Civilizations: Ancient Egypt*, 86, 109; cf. Driver, *Comparative Studies*, 44; Eliade, "Methodological Remarks," 104.

25. Lévi-Strauss, *Structural Anthropology*, 210–12.

26. Eliade, "Mythologies of Death," 19.

27. Lincoln, *Death, War, and Sacrifice*, 14.

28. Bierhorst, *History and Mythology*, 155.

29. Faulkner, Coffin Texts 1130; Pyramid Texts W178, W174, W149; Katz, *Image of the Netherworld*, "In the Desert by the Early Grass" 51ff.; O'Flaherty, *Tales*

of Sex and Violence, Jaiminiya Brahmana I, 46; Olivelle, *Early Upanishads, Chandogya Upanishad* VIII.12.1–2, III.13.6; *RV* X.16.2–5; Eggeling *Satapatha Brahmana* X.5.2.3; Watson, *Hsün Tzu, Zhuangzi*; Hawkes, *Songs of the South*; oracle bones; Waley, *The Book of Songs*, 242; Tedlock, *Popol Vuh* 141–2; Bierhorst, *History and Mythology, Annals of Cuauhtitlan* 7:37.

30. Faulkner, Coffin Texts VII.283, 1082; *ETCSL* 1.4.1; Katz, *Image of the Netherworld*, "In the Desert by the Early Grass" 51ff.; Panikkar, *Vedic Experience, Atharva Veda* II.14.3; Birrell, *Classic of Mountains and Seas* 184, 209; Tedlock, *Popol Vuh*, 140–42. Bierhorst, *History and Mythology, Legend of the Suns* 5:45–6.

31. Faulkner, Coffin Texts 1034; Pyramid Texts W170; George, *Epic of Gilgamesh*, "The Death of Bilgames"; *Rig Veda* X.14.9–10, VII.104; Panikkar, *The Vedic Experience, Atharva Veda* VIII.1.10–11; Legge, *Li ji*, IX.III.17; Watson, *Hsün Tzu, Zhuangzi*, 81–82.Waley, *The Book of Songs*, 214; Tedlock, *Popol Vuh* 96; Bierhorst, *Cantares Mexicanos* LXXXVIc: 40; IX:11.

32. Faulkner, Coffin Texts V.335; George, *Epic of Gilgamesh*, "Bilgames, Enkidu, and the Underworld"; Katz, *Image of the Netherworld*, "In the Desert by the Early Grass" 51ff.; *Rig Veda* X.14.3; Olivelle, *Early Upanishads, Chandogya Upanishad* VIII.12.1–2; Waley, *Book of Songs*, 199; Watson, *Hsün Tzu, Zhuangzi*, 191; Thompson, *Chinese Religion, Zuo Zhuan* I.1, funerary documents; Tedlock, *Popol Vuh*, 140–1; Sahagún, *The Florentine Codex, History of the Things of New Spain* VI:27; Durán, *History of the Indies of New Spain*; Bierhorst, *Cantares Mexicanos* XVIII:30.

33. *ETCSL* t.2.4.2.21, t.2.4.5.2; Katz, *Image of the Netherworld*, "In the Desert by the Early Grass" 51ff.; *Rig Veda* VII.88, IX.113.7–11, VIII.48.3; Eggeling, *Satapatha Brahmana*, X.5.2.3; Olivelle, *Early Upanishads, Chandogya Upanishad* III.13.6; Keith, *Veda of the Black Yajus, Krishna Yajur Veda* II.6.2; Hawkes, *Songs of the South*, 339; 198; Waley, *The Book of Songs, Shijing* 242; Legge, *The Li Ki, Li ji, Book of Rites* II.II.1.22; Tedlock, *Popol Vuh*, 102, 141–2; Durán, *History of the Indies of New Spain*.

34. Pyramid Texts P510; P450; Faulkner, Coffin Texts VI.452; "The Death of Bilgames"; *ETCSL* t.5.2.4; *Rig Veda* XI.2.7; XII.9.1; Eggeling, *Satapatha Brahmana*, 12–13; Waley, *The Book of Songs, Shijing* 279; Erkes, "God of Death," *Spring and Autumn Annals* 1, 18a; Hawkes, *Songs of the South*; Morgan, *Tao the Great Luminant, Huainanzi* 108; Tedlock, *Popol Vuh*, 94–5; Sahagún, *The Florentine Codex, History of the Things of New Spain*: VI:163; de Landa, *Relación de las Cosas*, 131–2.

35. Pyramid Texts P476; Faulkner, Coffin Texts 398; Bodewitz, *Jaiminiya Brahmana*, I.18; Birrell, *Popular Songs*, "Ballad of Tung Flees"; Tedlock, *Popol Vuh*, 133; Sahagún, *The Florentine Codex, History of the Things of New Spain* III: 2–6.

36. Faulkner, Coffin Texts 56, 268–78; Pyramid Texts W472, W146, 148; *Rig Veda* X.15.8–11, 68.11, X.1.4.12; VIII.6.1.21; Olivelle, *Early Upanishads, Katha Upanishad* IV.15; Legge, *The Li Ki, Li ji, Book of Rites* XXVIII.1.44; Watson, *Hsün Tzu, Zhuangzi*, 48; *Popol Vuh* 131–2; 141–2; Sahagún, *The Florentine Codex, History of the Things of New Spain* III: 201–10; Sahagún, *Primeros Memoriales*, "Song of Tlaloc" 6.

37. Pyramid Texts; Faulkner, Coffin Texts IV.296; *Rig Veda* X.17.3; Waley, *The Book of Songs, Shijing* 242; *Wenzi*; Cleary, *Further Teachings*, 172; Morgan, *Tao the Great Luminant*, 69; *The Florentine Codex, History of the Things of New Spain* 6:20; Bierhorst, *Cantares Mexicanos* III: 5.

38. Bowker, *Meanings of Death*, 29–30.

Chapter 9. Experiential Origins of the Afterlife

1. Frankfort et al., *Before Philosophy*, 11; cf. Eliade, "Methodological Remarks," 102.

2. Doniger, "Minimyths and Maximyths," 56, 113.

3. See, for example, D'Aquili and Newberg, *The Mystical Mind*, 14; James, *Varieties of Religious Experience*; Otto, *Idea of the Holy*; Wach, *Types of Religious Experience*; Almond, *Mystical Experience*; Hufford, "Beings without Bodies"; Davis, *Evidential Force of Religious Experience*; Hick, *Interpretation of Religion*; Yandell, *Epistemology of Religious Experience*; Smart, *Dimensions of the Sacred*.

4. Lang, *The Making of Religion*, 322ff.; cf. Shushan, *Near-Death Experience in Indigenous Religions*, 5–7.

5. James, *Varieties of Religious Experience*, 507–10; cf. James, *Mind-Dust and White Crows: The Psychical Research of William James*.

6. Elbé, *The Future Life*, 4.

7. McClenon, *Wondrous Events*, 151, 168.

8. Becker, "The Centrality of Near-Death Experiences," 159; Becker, "The Pure Land Revisited," 64; Badham, *Near-Death Experiences*; Badham, "Religion and Near-Death Experience," 134; Platthy, *Near-Death Experiences in Antiquity*, 60ff., 105; cf. MacGregor, *Images of Afterlife*, 193; Ma'súmián, *Life After Death*, ch. 10; Collins and Fishbane, *Death, Ecstasy and Otherworldly Journeys*, ix–x.

9. Borman, "Upanishadic Eschatology," 97ff.; Schumann-Antelme and Rossini, *Becoming Osiris*, 110; Hermann, "The Near-Death Experience," 181, 176–7.

10. Shushan, *Near-Death Experience in Indigenous Religions*; Badham, "Religious Experience," 10.

11. Hultkrantz, *North American Indian Orpheus Tradition*; Hallowell, "Spirits of the Dead," 29; Kalweit, *Dreamtime and Inner Space*, 70; Sheils, "A Cross-Cultural Study," 607, 699.

12. Heidel, *Gilgamesh Epic*, 208; Black et al., *Literature of Ancient Sumer*, 159–61; 2.5.2.1.

13. *RV* X.57–58; Jamison and Brereton, *Rigveda*, 1468; Panikkar, *The Vedic Experience, Atharva Veda* VIII.1–2, VII.53.3; cf. Bodewitz, "The Dark and Deep Underworld"; Bodewitz, *Light, Soul and Visions*, 40; *Jaiminiya Brahmana* I.167.

14. Hawkes, *Songs of the South*, "Ai shi ming," cf. "Yuan You"; de Groot, *Religious System* IV, 113–14, 123; cf. Harper, "Resurrection," 14; Campany, "Return-from-Death Narratives," 91–2.

15. Sahagún, *Primeros Memoriales*, 179n3; Sahagún, *The Florentine Codex*, HNS IX:3, II:498; 181, 20n.

16. Eliade, "Mythologies of Death," 17; cf. Eliade, *Shamanism*, 500ff.; Hultkrantz, *Religions of the American Indians*, 132.

17. Fox, *Religion, Spirituality*, 328; Rock et al., "Experimental Study of Ostensibly Shamanic Journeying."

18. Winkelman, "Shamanism as the Original Neurotheology," 196, 205.

19. Rock et al., "Experimental Study of Ostensibly Shamanic Journeying."

20. Wasson, "The Divine Mushroom," 197–8; Fernandez, "Tabernathe Iboga," 252; Hallowell, "Spirits of the Dead," 29; cf. Wade, "In a Sacred Manner," 97.

21. Kalweit, *Dreamtime and Inner Space*, 41; Doore, "Journeys to the Land of the Dead"; Furst, "To Find Our Life," 162–3; Fernandez, "Tabernathe Iboga," 251; cf. Eliade, *Shamanism*.

22. Sahagún, *The Florentine Codex*, HNS IX: 38–9; XI: 129; Léon-Portilla, *Native Mesoamerican Spirituality*, 154; Bierhorst, *The Hungry Woman*, 42; Bierhorst, *Cantares Mexicanos*, 18.

23. Legge, *The Li Ki, Li ji, Book of Rites* I.II.1.32; cf. II.I.1.20; Hawkes, *Songs of the South*, 42, 67, Song V, Song I; Waley, *The Nine Songs*, 23; Birrell, *Popular Songs*, 66, 68.

24. Paper, *The Spirits Are Drunk*, 57.

25. *RV* 9.94.2, X.119, VIII.48, IX.113, X.136; Wasson, "What Was the Soma of the Aryans," 202; Panikkar, *The Vedic Experience*, 633, 892; Bodewitz, *Light, Soul and Visions*, 14, 16, 18; O'Flaherty, *Tales of Sex and Violence*, 46.

26. Wasson, "The Divine Mushroom," 212; Parpola, "Assyrian Tree of Life," 191–2, 194; Tab. IX.1–14; Abusch, "Ascent to the Stars," 17.

27. DuQuesne, *Jackal at the Shaman's Gate*, 12–13; Trigger, *Understanding Early Civilizations*, 535.

28. See Kirk, *Myth*, 268–74; Bartel, "A Historical Review," 36; Sheils, "A Cross-Cultural Study," 732; Raglan, *Death and Rebirth*, 11.

29. Hillman, *The Dream and the Underworld*, 3, 68; Bowker, *Meanings of Death*, 34; Paper, *The Deities Are Many*, 60–1; cf. Hertz, *Death, and the Right Hand*, 77.

30. Kalweit, *Dreamtime and Inner Space*, 70; Eliade, *Shamanism*, 486; Walsh, *The Spirit of Shamanism* 148–9; Kalweit, *Shamans, Healers, and Medicine Men*, 40, 263; Green, "Near-Death Experiences, Shamanism," 209.

Chapter 10. Crossing Boundaries

1. Jung, *Jung On Death and Immortality*, 29, 35.

2. Morris, *Anthropological Studies of Religion*, 17; cf. Grof and Halifax, *Human Encounter With Death*, 177.

3. Grof and Grof, *Beyond Death*, 13–14, 20ff, 31; cf. Grof and Halifax, *Human Encounter With Death*, ch. 8; Grof, *Books of the Dead*, 6–7; Huxley, *Heaven and Hell*.

4. Hornung, *Idea Into Image*, 95; DuQuesne, *Jackal at the Shaman's Gate*, 12; Eliade, *Birth and Rebirth*, 98.

5. Brandon, *Man and His Destiny*, 384–5, 375.

6. Hick, *Death and Eternal Life*, 73.

7. Lévi-Strauss, *Structural Anthropology*, 210–12; cf. Malinowski, *Magic, Science and Religion*, 51.

8. See, for example, Weber, *Sociology of Religion*, 140–1; Brandon, *Judgment of the Dead*, 193.

9. Hunt, *Transformation of the Hummingbird*, 251.

10. Trigger, *Understanding Early Civilizations*, 684, 539.

11. Carr, "Mortuary Practices"; Flood, *Introduction to Hinduism*, 50; Bodde, *Festivals in Classical China*, 35.

12. Trigger, *Understanding Early Civilizations*, 526f, 531, 539, 540, 647.

13. Butzenberger, "Ancient Indian Conceptions," 71

14. Eliade, *Birth and Rebirth*, 230–1.

15. Evers, "Myth and Narrative," 70.

16. Eliade, *Birth and Rebirth*, 230–1.

17. Bodewitz, *Light, Soul and Visions*, 1.

18. Poo, *Personal Welfare*, 218.

19. Davidson, "The Ship of the Dead," 73.

20. Lévi-Strauss, *The Savage Mind*, 95.

21. Zaleski, *Otherworld Journeys*, 62–3; Sheils, "A Cross-Cultural Study," 732.

22. Boyer, *The Naturalness of Religious Ideas*, 12–21.

23. D'Aquili and Andrew Newberg, *The Mystical Mind*, 14, 122, 131, 134, 139, 142; Paper, *The Mystic Experience*, 66; Parnia et. al., *AWARE*.

24. Winkelman, "Shamanism as the Original Neurotheology," 205.

25. Winkelman, "Shamanism as the Original Neurotheology," 200–203, 213.

26. Trigger, *Understanding Early Civilizations*, 685–7.

27. Martin, "Comparison," 55.

28. Waley, *Book of Songs*, 246.

29. Smith, "Methodology, Comparisons," 179–80. For arguments on a metaphysical basis for religions per se, see, for example, H. Smith, *Forgotten Truth*; W. C. Smith, *Toward a World Theology*; Ward, *Images of Eternity*; and Reat and Perry, *A World Theology*. For NDE-source arguments see, for example, Hick, *Death and Eternal Life*; Grosso, "Jung, Parapsychology," 34–5; Platthy, *Near-Death Experiences in Antiquity*, 60ff, 105; Grof, *Books of the Dead*, 6–7; Ma'súmián, *Life After Death*, ch. 10; Badham, "Religious Experience as the Common Core."

30. Price, "Survival"; Paterson, *Philosophy and the Belief in Life After Death*, 205–8; cf. Grof and Grof, *Beyond Death*, 14; Hick, *Death and Eternal Life*, 456–82.

31. Lund, *Death and Consciousness*, 43.

32. Delacour, *Glimpses*, 4, 7, 17.

33. Green, "Lucid Dreams," 52–3.

34. Lee, "Reimagination of Death," 221.

35. Ullman et al., *Dream Telepathy*; cf. Hart, *Enigma of Survival*, 236; Ducasse, *Critical Examination*.

36. Bowker, *Meanings of Death*, 209; Birrell, *Classic of Mountains and Seas*, 23–24; Zaleski, *Otherworld Journeys*, 135.

37. Hick, *Death and Eternal Life*, 275.

38. Becker, *Paranormal Experience*, 167, 178–9.

39. *RV* X.135; *RV* I.164.30; Panikkar, *The Vedic Experience*, 633; Olivelle, *The Early Upanishads*, *Brhadaranyaka Upanishad* III.1.6; *Katha Upanishad* I.2.2; I.5.6; *Mundaka Upanishad* 3.10, XVI.5.1–6.

40. Olivelle, *The Early Upanishads*, *Katha Upanishad* IV.3.13, 15; II.5.8; *Brhadaranyaka Upanishad* IV.3.9–14,18; O'Flaherty, *Textual Sources*, 44.

41. Bierhorst, *History and Mythology of the Aztecs*, 155.

42. George, *Epic of Gilgamesh*, "The Death of Bilgames."

43. Paper, *The Deities Are Many*, 64; Morgan, *Tao the Great Luminant, Huainanzi*.

44. Becker, *Paranormal Experience*, 185.

45. Badham, "Death and Immortality," 119, 121; Badham, *Near-Death Experiences*, 18; Harner, *Way of the Shaman*, 21.

46. Becker, "The Pure Land Revisited," 61, 65–6.

47. Evans-Wentz, *The Tibetan Book of the Dead*, 94; Kalweit, *Dreamtime and Inner Space*, 64, 66–67; Shushan, *Near-Death Experience in Indigenous Religions*, 234.

48. Badham, *Near-Death Experiences*, 14–15; Gier, "Humanistic Self-Judgment," 10–11.

49. Goswami, *Physics of the Soul*, 13–14, 30.

50. Poynton, "What Survives?" 143, 145; Goswami, *Physics of the Soul*, 77ff, 134, 204.

51. Rock et al., "Experimental Study," 79–80.

Chapter II. A Holistic View of the Afterlife

1. See Shushan, *Near-Death Experience in Indigenous Religions*, 204–06, 243–44.

2. Bowker, *Meanings of Death*, 29.

3. Lund, *Death and Consciousness*.

4. Bishop, "The Hero's Descent to the Underworld," 112, 120; McClenon, *Wondrous Events*, 169, 184.

5. Couliano, *Out of this World*, 6–9.

6. Eliade, "Folklore as an Instrument of Knowledge," 36.

7. Haley, "Death and After Death," 2.

8. Badham, "Religion and Near-Death Experience," 8–9.

9. Shushan, *Near-Death Experience in Indigenous Religions*.

Bibliography

Abusch, Tzvi. "Ascent to the Stars in a Mesopotamian Ritual: Social Metaphor and Religious Experience." In *Death, Ecstasy, and Other Worldly Journeys*, edited by J. J. Collins and M. A. Fishbane, 15–38. Albany: SUNY Press, 1995.

Allen, James P. "Funerary Texts and Their Meaning." In *Mummies and Magic*, edited by S. D'Auria, P. Lacovara, & C. H. Roehrig, 38–49. Boston: Museum of Fine Arts, 1988.

———. *Genesis in Ancient Egypt: The Philosophy of Ancient Egyptian Creation Accounts*. New Haven: Yale University Press, 1988.

———. "The Cosmology of the Pyramid Texts." In *Religion and Philosophy in Ancient Egypt*, edited by W. K. Simpson, 1–28. New Haven: Yale Egyptological Studies 3, 1989.

———. *The Ancient Egyptian Pyramid Texts*. Atlanta: SBL, 2005.

Allen, Thomas G. *The Book of the Dead, or Going Forth by Day*. Chicago: Chicago University Press, 1974.

Almond, Philip C. *Mystical Experience and Religious Doctrine*. Berlin: Mouton, 1982.

Arbuckle, Gary. "Chinese Religions." In *Life After Death in World Religions*, edited by H. Coward. New York: Orbis, 1997.

Arnett, William S. *The Predynastic Origins of Egyptian Hieroglyphs*. Washington, DC: University Press of America, 1982.

Assmann, Jan. *The Search for God in Ancient Egypt*. Translated 2001. Ithaca: Cornell University Press, 1984.

———. *Death and Salvation in Ancient Egypt*. Translated 2005. Ithaca: Cornell University Press, 2001.

Astour, Michael C. "Mitanni." In *The Oxford Encyclopædia of Ancient Egypt*, edited by D. Redford, 422–24. Oxford: Oxford University Press, 2001.

Audette, J. R. "Historical Perspectives on Near-Death Episodes and Experiences." In *A Collection of Near-Death Research Readings*, edited by C. Lundahl, 21–47. Chicago: Nelson-Hall, 1982.

Badham, Paul. *Near-Death Experiences, Beliefs About Life After Death, and the Tibetan Book of the Dead*. Tokyo: Tokyo Honganji International Buddhist Study Center, 1990.

———. "Death and Immortality: Towards a Global Synthesis." In *Beyond Death: Theological and Philosophical Reflections on Life After Death*, edited by D. Cohn-Sherbok and C. Lewis, 119–25. London: Macmillan, 1995.

———. "Religion and Near-Death Experience in Relation to Belief in a Future Life." *Mortality* 2, no. 1 (1997): 7–20.

———. "Religious Experience as the Common Core of the World Religions." *The Christian Parapsychologist* 15, no. 7 (2003): 202-14.

Bartel, Brad. "A Historical Review of Ethnographical and Archaeological Analyses of Mortuary Practice." *Journal of Anthropological Archaeology* 1 (1982): 32–58.

Bassie-Sweet, Karen. "Corn Deities and the Complementary Male/Female Principle." Paper presented at La Tercera Mesa Redonda de Palenque, Palenque, Chiapas, July 1999. Revised September 2000, Mesoweb.

Beaux, Nathalie. "La douat dans les textes des pyramides." *BIFAO* 94 (1994): 1–6.

Becker, Carl. B. "The Centrality of Near-Death Experiences in Chinese Pure Land Buddhism." *Anabiosis* 1 (1981): 154–74.

———. "The Pure Land Revisited: Sino-Japanese Meditations and Near-Death Experiences of the Next World." *Anabiosis* 4 (1984): 51–68.

———. "Views from Tibet: Near-Death Experiences and the Book of the Dead." *Anabiosis* 5, no. 1 (1985): 3–20.

———. *Paranormal Experience and Survival of Death*. Albany: SUNY Press, 1993.

Berling, Judith. A. "Death and Afterlife in Chinese Religions." In *Death and Afterlife: Perspectives of World Religions*, edited by H. Obayashi. New York: Greenwood, 1992.

Betz, Hans Dieter "Fragments from a catabasis ritual in a Greek Magical Papyrus." *History of Religions* 19, No. 4 (1980): 287-295.

Bierhorst, John. *Four Masterworks of American Indian Literature*. New York: Farrar, Straus, Giroux, 1974.

———. *The Hungry Woman: Myths and Legends of the Aztecs*. New York: Quill, 1984.

———. *Cantares Mexicanos*. Stanford: Stanford University Press, 1985.

———. *History and Mythology of the Aztecs: The Codex Chimalpopoca*. Tucson: University of Arizona Press, 1992.

Birrell, Anne. *Popular Songs and Ballads of Han China*. London: Unwin Hyman, 1988.

———. *Chinese Mythology*. Baltimore: Johns Hopkins, 1993.

———. *The Classic of Mountains and Seas*. London: Penguin, 1999.

Bishop, J. G. "The Hero's Descent to the Underworld." In *The Journey to the Other World*, edited by H. R. E. Davidson, 109–25. Cambridge: Brewer, 1975.

Black, Jeremy A., Graham Cunningham, Eleanor Robson, and Gábor Zólyomi eds. *The Literature of Ancient Sumer.* Oxford: Oxford University Press, 2004.

Black, Jeremy A., Graham Cunningham, Jarle Ebeling, Esther Flückiger-Hawker, Eleanor Robson, Jon Taylor, and Gábor Zólyomi. *The Electronic Text Corpus of Sumerian Literature.* 1998–.

Blackmore, Susan J. *Dying to Live: Near-Death Experiences.* London: Grafton, 1993.

Bodde, Dirk. *Festivals in Classical China.* Princeton: Princeton University Press, 1975.

Bodewitz, Hendrik Wilhelm (1973) *Jaiminiya Brahmana* 1, 1–65. Leiden: Brill, 1973.

———. "Light, Soul and Visions in the Veda." In *Professor P. D. Gune Memorial Lectures (fifth series).* Poona: Bhandarkar Oriental Research Institute, 1991.

———. "Life after Death in the Rigvedasamhita." *Wiener Zeitschrift für die Kunde Südasiens* 38 (1994): 23–41.

———. "Pits, Pitfalls and the Underworld in the Vedas." *Indo-Iranian Journal* 42, no. 3 (July 1999): 211–26.

———. "Yonder World in the Atharva Veda." *Indo-Iranian Journal* 42, no. 2 (April 1999): 107–20.

———. "Distance and Death in the Veda." *Asiatische Studien* 54 (2000): 103–17.

———. "The Dark and Deep Underworld of the Vedas." *Journal of the American Oriental Society* 122, no. 2 (April–June 2002): 213–24.

Boltz, Willian G. "Language and Writing." In *Cambridge History of Ancient China,* edited by M. Loewe and Shaughnessy. Cambridge: Cambridge University Press, 1999.

Borman, William A. "Upanishadic Eschatology." In *Perspectives on Death and Dying,* edited by A. Berger, P. Badham, A. H. Kutscher, J. Berger, M. Perry, and J. Beloff, 89–100. Philadelphia: Charles, 1989.

Bottéro, Jean *Mesopotamia: Writing, Reasoning, and the Gods.* Chicago: University of Chicago Press, 1992.

———. *Religion in Ancient Mesopotamia.* Chicago: University of Chicago Press, 2001.

Bowker, John *Meanings of Death.* Cambridge: Cambridge University Press, 1991.

Boyer, Pascal. *The Naturalness of Religious Ideas: A Cognitive Theory of Religion.* Berkeley: University of California Press, 1994.

Brandon, S. G. F. *Man and His Destiny in the Great Religions.* Manchester: Manchester University Press, 1962.

———. *The Judgment of the Dead.* London: Weidenfeld & Nicholson, 1967.

Bremmer, Jan N. *The Rise and Fall of the Afterlife.* London: Routledge, 2002.

Brotherston, Gordon. *Painted Books from Mexico.* London: British Museum Press, 1995.

Brown, William N. "The Rigvedic Equivalent for Hell." *Journal of the American Oriental Society* 61 (1941): 76–80.

Bush, Nancy E. "The Near-Death Experience in Children: Shades of the Prison House Reopening." *Anabiosis* 3 (1983): 177–93.

Butzenberger, Klaus. "Ancient Indian Conceptions on Man's Destiny after Death: The Beginnings and the Early Development of the Doctrine of Transmigration I." *Berliner Indologische Studien* 9 (1996): 55–118.

———. "Ancient Indian Conceptions on Man's Destiny after Death: The Beginnings and the Early Development of the Doctrine of Transmigration II." *Berliner Indologische Studien*, vol. 9 (1998): 11–12, 1–84.

Campany, Robert. F. (1990) "Return-From-Death Narratives in Early Medieval China." *Journal of Chinese Religions* 18 (1990): 90–125.

———. "To Hell and Back: Death, Near-Death, and Other Worldly Journeys in Early Medieval China." In *Death, Ecstasy, and Other Worldly Journeys*, edited by J. J. Collins and M. Fishbane, 343–60. Albany: SUNY Press, 1995.

Carr, Chrisopher. "Mortuary Practices: Their Social, Philosophical-Religious, Circumstantial and Physical Determinants." *Journal of Archaeological Method and Theory* 2 (1995): 105–99.

Chan, Wing-tsit, trans. *A Sourcebook in Chinese Philosophy*. Princeton: Princeton University Press, 1963.

Chang, Kwang-Chih. *Shang Civilization*. New Haven: Yale University Press, 1980.

Ching, Julia *Chinese Religions*. London: Macmillan, 1993.

Cleary, Thomas. *The Further Teachings of Lao Tzu*. Boston: Shambhala, 1991.

Coe, Michael. "The Iconology of Olmec Art." In *The Iconography of Middle American Sculpture*. New York: Metropolitan Museum of Art, 1973.

———. "Death and the Ancient Maya." In *Death and the Afterlife in Pre- Columbian America*, edited by E. P. Benson, 69–85. Washington, DC: Dumbarton Oaks, 1975.

———. "The Hero Twins: Myth and Image." In *The Maya Vase Book*, vol. 1, edited by J. Kerr, 161–84. New York: Kerr, 1989.

———. *Mexico: From the Olmecs to the Aztecs*. Rev. ed. London: Thames & Hudson, 2002.

Collins, John. J., and Michael. Fishbane. *Death, Ecstasy and Otherworldly Journeys*. SUNY Press, 1995.

Cooper, Jerrold S. "The Fate of Mankind: Death and Afterlife in Ancient Mesopotamia." In *Death and Afterlife: Perspectives of World Religions*, edited by H. Obayahsi, 19–34. New York: Praeger, 1992.

Couliano, Ioan. P. *Out of This World: Otherworldly Journeys from Gilgamesh to Albert Einstein*. Boston: Shambhala, 1991.

Counts, Dorothy A. "Near-Death and Out-of-Body Experiences in a Melanesian Society." *Anabiosis* 3 (1983): 115–35.

Crawford, Harriet *Sumer and the Sumerians*. Cambridge: Cambridge University Press, 1991.

Crawford, Michael H. *The Origins of Native Americans*. Cambridge: Cambridge University Press, 1998.

Currid, John D. *Ancient Egypt and the Old Testament*. Grand Rapids: Baker, 1997.

Dalley, Stephanie. *Myths from Mesopotamia*. Oxford: Oxford University Press, 1989.

———. "Occasions and Opportunities I: To the Persian Conquest." In *The Legacy of Mesopotamia*, edited by S. Dalley, 9–34. Oxford: Oxford University Press, 1998.

D'Aquili, Eugene, and Andrew B. Newberg. *The Mystical Mind*. Minneapolis: Fortress, 1999.

Davidson, Hilda R. E. "The Ship of the Dead." In *The Journey to the Other World*, edited by H. R. E. Davidson, 73–89. Cambridge: Brewer, 1975.

Davies, Jon. *Death, Burial and Rebirth in the Religions of Antiquity*. London: Routledge, 1999.

Davis, Caroline F. *The Evidential Force of Religious Experience*. Cambridge: Cambridge University Press, 1989.

Davis, Whitney M. "The Ascension Myth in the Pyramid Texts." *Journal of Near Eastern Studies* 36, no. 3 (1977): 161–79.

De Groot, J. J. M. *The Religious System of China*, I. Leyden: Brill, 1892.

Delacour, Jean-Baptiste. *Glimpses of the Beyond*. London: Harwod Smart, 1973. Translated 1974.

DeMallie, Raymond, ed. *The Sixth Grandfather: Black Elk's Teachings Given to John G. Neihardt*. Lincoln: University of Nebraska, 1984.

De Mora, Juan Miguel. "On Death and Other Subjects in the Rigveda" In *Sanskrit and World Culture: Proceedings of the Fourth World Sanskrit Conference of the International Association of Sanskrit Studies, Weimar, May 23–30, 1979* edited by Wolfgang Morgenroth, 467–470. Berlin, Boston: De Gruyter, 1986.

Doniger, Wendy "Minimyths and Maximyths and Political Points of View." In *Myth and Method*, edited by L. L. Patton and W. Doniger, 109–27. Charlottesville: University of Virginia Press, 1996.

———. *The Implied Spider*. New York: Columbia University Press, 1998.

Doore, Gary. "Journeys to the Land of the Dead: Shamanism and Samadhi." In *What Survives?: Contemporary Explorations of Life After Death*, edited by G. Doore. Los Angeles: Tarcher, 1990.

Driver, Harold. E. *Comparative Studies by Harold E. Driver and Essays in His Honour*. Edited by J. G. Jorgensen. New Haven: HRAF, 1974.

Ducasse, C. J. A. *A Critical Examination of the Belief in a Life After Death*. London: Thomas, 1961.

Dudbridge, Glen. *The Legend of Miaoshan*. Rev. ed. Oxford: Oxford University Press, 2004.

DuQuesne, Terence. *Jackal at the Shaman's Gate*. *Oxfordshire Communications in Egyptology III*. Oxford: Darengo, 1991.

Durán, Diego. *The History of the Indies of New Spain*. Translated by D. Heyden. Norman: University of Oklahoma Press, 1994. First published 1581.

Eggeling, Julius, trans., ed. *Satapatha Brahmana*. 5 vols. Sacred Books of the East XII, XXVI, XLI, XLIII, XLIV. Oxford: Clarendon, 1882–1900.

Elbé, Louis. *The Future Life in Light of Ancient Wisdom and Modern Science*. London: Chatto & Windus, 1906.

Eliade, Mircea. "Folklore as an Instrument of Knowledge." In *Mircea Eliade: A Critical Reader*, edited by B. Rennie, 25–37. London: Equinox, 2006. First published 1937.

———. *Birth and Rebirth*. New York: Harper, 1957. Reprinted 1975.

———. "Methodological Remarks on the Study of Religious Symbolism." In *The History of Religions*, edited by M. Eliade and J. Kitagawa. Chicago: Chicago University Press, 1959.

———. *Shamanism: Archaic Techniques of Ecstasy*. Rev. ed. Princeton: Princeton University Press, 1964.

———. "Mythologies of Death: An Introduction." In *Religious Encounters with Death*, edited by F. E. Reynolds and E. H. Waugh. Penn State University Press, 1976.

Eno, Robert. *The Confucian Creation of Heaven*. Albany: SUNY Press. 1990.

Erkes, Eduard. "The God of Death in Ancient China." *T'oung Pao* 35 (1940): 185–210.

Evans-Wentz, W. Y. *The Tibetan Book of the Dead*. 3rd ed. Oxford: Oxford University Press, 1927.

Evers, John. D. *Myth and Narrative: Structure and Meaning in Some Ancient Near Eastern Texts*. Alter Orient und Altes Testament, Band 241. Neukirchener Verlag, Neukirchin-Vluyn, 1995.

Faulkner, R. O. *The Ancient Egyptian* Coffin Texts. 3 vols. Warminster: Aris and Philips, 1973. Reprinted 1977, 1978.

Fenwick, Peter. (2005) "Science and Spirituality: A Challenge for the 21st Century." *Journal of Near-Death Studies* 23, no. 3 (2005).

Fenwick, Peter, and Elizabeth Fenwick. *The Truth in the Light*. London: Headline, 1995.

Fernandez, James W. "Tabernathe Iboga: Narcotic Ecstasies and the Work of the Ancestors." In *Flesh of the Gods: The Ritual Use of Hallucinogens*, edited by P. T. Furst, 237–60. Prospect Heights, IL: Waveland, 1972. Reprinted 1990.

Fischer-Elfert, Hans-Werner. "Der Pharao, die Magier und der General: Die Erzählung des Papyrus Vandier. In *Bibliotheca Orientalis*, Band 44, S. 5–21. 1987.

Flood, Gavin. *An Introduction to Hinduism*. Cambridge: Cambridge University Press, 1996.

Fontana, David. *Is There an Afterlife?* Ropley: O Books, 2005.

Foster, Benjamin. R. *Before the Muses: An Anthology of Akkadian Literature*. 3rd ed. Bethesda: CDL Press, 2005.

———. *The Epic of Gilgamesh*. New York: Norton Critical Editions, 2001.

Fox, Mark. *Religion, Spirituality and the Near-Death Experience*. London: Routledge, 2003.

Frankfort, Henri, John A. Wilson, Thorkild Jacobson, and William A. Irwin. *Before Philosophy: The Intellectual Adventure of Ancient Man, An Essay on Speculative Thought in the Ancient Near East*. Harmondsworth: Penguin, 1946. Reprinted 1949.

Furst, Jill L. M. *The Natural History of the Soul in Ancient Mexico*. New Haven: Yale University Press, 1995.

Furst, Peter T. "To Find Our Life: Peyote among the Huichol Indians of Mexico." In *Flesh of the Gods: The Ritual Use of Hallucinogens*, edited by P. T. Furst, 136–84. Prospect Heights, IL: Waveland, 1972. Reprinted 1990.

Gardiner, Eileen. *Visions of Heaven & Hell Before Dante*. New York: Italica, 1989.

George, A.R. *The Babylonian Gilgamesh Epic*. 2 vols. Oxford: Oxford University Press, 2003.

———. *The Epic of Gilgamesh*. Rev. ed. London: Penguin, 2003.

Gier, Nicholas F. "Humanistic Self-Judgment and After-Death Experience." In *Immortality and Human Destiny*, edited by G. MacGregor, 3–20. New York: Paragon, 1985.

Goswami, Amit. *Physics of the Soul*. Charlottesville: Hampton Roads, 2001.

Graulich, Michel. "Afterlife in Ancient Mexican Thought." In *Circumpacifica: Festschrift für Thomas S. Barthel*, vol. I, edited by B. Illius and M. Laubscher, 165–89. Frankfurt am Main: Lang, 1990.

Green, J. Timothy. "Near-Death Experience in a Chamorro Culture." *Vital Signs* 4, no. 1–2 (1984): 6–7.

———. "Lucid Dreams as One Method of Replicating Components of the Near-Death Experience in a Laboratory Setting." *Journal of Near-Death Studies* 14, no. 1 (1995): 49–59.

———. "Near-Death Experiences, Shamanism and the Scientific Method." *Journal of Near-Death Studies* 16, no. 3 (1998): 205–22.

Greyson, Bruce. "A Typology of Near-Death Experiences." *American Journal of Psychiatry* 142 (1985): 967–9.

Grof, Stanislav. *Books of the Dead: Manuals for Living and Dying*. London: Thames & Hudson, 1994.

Grof, Stanislav, and Christina Grof. *Beyond Death*. London: Thames and Hudson, 1980.

Grof, Stanislav, and Joan Halifax. *The Human Encounter with Death*. New York: Dutton, 1977.

Grosso, Michael. "Jung, Parapsychology and the Near-Death Experience: Toward a Transpersonal Paradigm." *Anabiosis* 3 (1983): 3–38.

Haley, S. "Death and After Death." In *The Loved Body's Corruption: Archaeological Contributions to the Study of Human Mortality*, edited by J. Downes and T. Pollard. Glasgow: Cruinthe Press, 1999.

Hallowell, A. Irving. "Spirits of the Dead in Salteaux Life and Thought." *Journal of the Royal Anthropological Institute* 70 (1940): 29–51.

Haly, Richard. "Bare Bones: Rethinking Mesoamerican Divinity." *History of Religions* 31, no. 1 (1992): 269–304.

Hampe, Johann C. *To Die is Gain*. Santa Fe: Afterworlds Press, 1975. Translated 1979. Reprinted 2022.

Harner, Michael. *The Way of the Shaman*. 3rd ed. New York: Harper Collins, 1990.

Harper, Donald. (1994) "Resurrection in Warring States popular religion." *Taoist Resources* 5 (2.1), 13–28.

———. "Warring States Religion and Occult Thought." In *The Cambridge History of Ancient China*, edited by M. Loewe and E. L. Shaughnessy, 813–84. Cambridge: Cambridge University Press, 1999.

Hart, Hornell N. *The Enigma of Survival*. London: Rider, 1959.

Hawkes, David. *Songs of the South*. Rev. ed. Harmondsworth: Penguin, 1985.

Hays, Harold. M. "The Death of the Democratisation of the Afterlife." In *Old Kingdom, New Perspectives: Egyptian Art and Archaeology 2750-2150 BC*, edited by N. Strudwick and H. Strudwick, 115–130. Oxford: Oxbow, 2011.

Heidel, Alexander. *The Gilgamesh Epic and Old Testament Parallels*. 2nd ed. Chicago: University of Chicago Press, 1949.

Heimpel, Wolfgang. "The Sun at Night and the Doors of Heaven in Babylonian Texts." *Journal of Cuneiform Studies* 38 (1986): 27–151.

Hermann, E. J. "The Near-Death Experience and the Taoism of Chuang Tzu." *Journal of Near-Death Studies* 8 (1990): 175–90.

Herodotus. *Histories*. Trans. A. D. Godley, *Herodotus with an English Translation*. Cambridge, MA: Harvard University Press, 1920.

Hertz, Robert. *Death, and The Right Hand*. Translated by Rodney and Claudia Needham. London: Cohen & West, 1960. First published 1907.

Hick, John. *Death and Eternal Life*. London: Collins, 1976.

———. *An Interpretation of Religion*. London: Macmillan, 1989.

Hillman, James. *The Dream and the Underworld*. New York: Harper & Row, 1979.

Hornung, Erik. *Conceptions of God in Ancient Egypt*. London: Routledge & Kegan Paul, 1983.

———. *Idea into Image: Essays on Ancient Egyptian Thought*. Translated by E. Bredeck. New York: Timken, 1992.

———. "Black Holes Viewed from Within: Hell in Ancient Egyptian Thought." *Diogenes* 165 (1994): 133–56.

Hufford, David J. "Beings without Bodies: An Experience-Centered Theory of the Belief in Spirits." In *Out of the Ordinary: Folklore and the Supernatural*, edited by B. Walker. Boulder: Utah State University Press, 1995.

Hultkrantz, Åke. *The North American Indian Orpheus Tradition: Native Afterlife Myths and Their Origins*. Santa Fe: Afterworlds Press. 1957. Reprinted 2022.

———. *The Religions of the American Indians*. Berkeley: University of California, 1967.

Hunt, Eva. *The Transformation of the Hummingbird*. Ithaca: Cornell University Press, 1977.

Huxley, Aldous. *Heaven and Hell*. Harmondsworth: Penguin, 1959.

Jacobsen, Thorkild. *The Treasures of Darkness: A History of Mesopotamian Religion*. New Haven: Yale University Press, 1976.

———. *The Harps That Once*. New Haven: Yale University Press, 1987.

Jacobsen, Thorkild., and Bendt Alster. "Ningiszida's Boat-Ride to Hades." In *Wisdom, Gods and Literature: Studies in Assyriology in Honour of W. G. Lambert*, edited by A. R. George and I. L. Finkel, 315–44. Winona Lake: Eisenbrauns, 2000.

James, William. *The Varieties of Religious Experience*. Rev. ed. London: Longmans, 1902.

———. *Mind-Dust and White Crows: The Psychical Research of William James*. Edited by Gregory Shushan. Guildford: White Crow, 2023.

Jamison, Stephanie W., & Joel P. Brereton. *The Rigveda: The Earliest Religious Poetry of India*. Oxford and New York: Oxford University Press, 2014.

Jorgensen, Joseph. G. "On Continuous Area and Worldwide Studies in Formal Comparative Ethology." In *Comparative Studies by Harold E. Driver and Essays in His Honour*, edited by J. G. Jorgensen. New Haven: HRAF, 1974.

Jung, C. G. *Jung On Death and Immortality*. Edited by J. Yates. Encountering Jung. Princeton: Princeton University Press, 1999.

Kalweit, Holger. *Dreamtime and Inner Space: The World of the Shaman*. Translated 1988. Boston: Shambhala, 1984.

———. *Shamans, Healers, and Medicine Men.* Boston: Shambhala, 1992.

Kao, Karl. S. Y., ed. *Classical Chinese Tales of the Supernatural and Fantastic: Selections from the Third to Tenth Century,* 87–89. Translated by Michael Broschat. Bloomington: Indiana University Press, 1985.

Katz, Dina. *The Image of the Netherworld in the Sumerian Sources.* Bethesda: CDL, 2003.

Keith, Arthur B. The *Veda of the Black Yajus School Entitled Taittiriiya Sanhita.* Cambridge: Harvard University Press, 1914.

Kellehear, Allan. *Experiences Near Death.* Oxford: Oxford University Press, 1996.

———. "An Hawaiian Near-Death Experience." *Journal of Near-Death Studies* 20, no. 1 (2001): 31–5.A

Kellehear, Allan, Ian Stevenson, Satwant Pasricha, and Emily Cook. "The Absence of Tunnel Sensation in Near-Death Experiences from India." *Journal of Near-Death Studies* 13 (1994): 109–13.

Kirk, Geoffrey S. *Myth: Its Meanings & Functions in Ancient and Other Cultures.* Berkeley: University of California Press, 1970.

Klein, Cecilia. F. "Post-Classic Mexican Death Imagery as a Sign of Cyclic Completion." In *Death and the Afterlife in Pre-Columbian America,* edited by E. P. Benson, 69–85. Washington, DC: Dumbarton Oaks, 1975.

———. "Wild Women in Colonial Mexico." In *Reframing the Renaissance: Visual Culture in Latin America 1450–1650,* edited by C. Farago, 244–63. New Haven: Yale University Press, 1995.

———. "The Devil and the Skirt." *Ancient Mesoamerica* 11 (2000), 1–26.

Kramer, Samuel N. "Death and the Netherworld according to the Sumerian Literary Texts." *Iraq* 22 (1960): 59–68.

Kristensen, W. Brede. *Life Out of Death: Studies in the Religions of Egypt and of Ancient Greece.* Translated 1992. Louvain: Peeters, 1949.

———. *The Meaning of Religion: Lectures in the Phenomenology of Religion.* The Hague: Nijhoff, 1960.

Kuhrt, Amelie. *The Ancient Near East.* 2 vols. New York: Routledge, 1995.

Lahiri, Nayanjot. *The Archaeology of Indian Trade Routes up to 200 BC.* Oxford: Oxford University Press, 1992.

Lal, B. B. "Aryan Invasion of India: Perpetuation of a Myth." In *The Indo-Aryan Controversy,* edited by E. F. Bryant, and L. L. Patton, 50–74. London: Routledge, 2005.

Lambert, W. G. "The Theology of Death." In *Death in Mesopotamia,* edited by B. Alster, 53–66. Copenhagen: Akademisk Förlag, 1980.

Landa, Diego de. *Relación de las Cosas de Yucatán.* Translated by A. M. Tozzer. Cambridge: Harvard College Museum, 1941. First published 1566.

Lang, Andrew. *The Making of Religion*. London: Longman's Green, 1898.

Lee, Raymond. L. M. "The Reimagination of Death: Dream Yoga, Near-Death, and Clear Light." *Journal of Near-Death Studies* 22, no. 4 (2004): 221–34.

Legge, Jame. *The Sacred Books of China; The Texts of Confucianism. Part I: The Shu King, etc.* Sacred Books of the East. Delhi: Banarsidass. 1879. Reprinted 1967.

———. The *Sacred Books of China: The Texts of Confucianism. Part III and IV: The Li Ki*. Sacred Books of the East. Delhi: Banarsidass, 1885. Reprinted 1967.

León-Portilla, Miguel. *Aztec Thought and Culture*. Norman: University of Oklahoma Press, 1963.

———. *Native Mesoamerican Spirituality*. Mahwah, New Jersey: Paulist, 1980.

Lesko, Leonard. H. *The Ancient Egyptian Book of Two Ways*. Berkeley: University of California, 1972.

Lévi-Strauss, Claude. *Structural Anthropology*, vol. I. London: Penguin, 1963. Reprinted 1993.

———. *The Savage Mind*. Chicago: University of Chicago Press, 1966.

Lincoln, Bruce. *Death, War, and Sacrifice: Studies in Ideology and Practice*. Chicago: Chicago University Press, 1991.

Liotsakis, Vasileios. "Following the King to the Underworld: The Tale of Rampsinitus (*Hdt*. II 122) and Ancient Egyptian Tradition." *Eikasmos* XXIII (2012), 139–158.

Littleton, C. Scott. *The New Comparative Mythology: An Anthropological Assessment of the Theories of Georges Dumézil*. Berkeley: University of California Press, 1966. Revised 1982.

Liu, Li. *The Chinese Neolithic*. Cambridge: Cambridge University Press, 2004.

Liu, Xinru. *Ancient India and Ancient China*. Delhi: Oxford University Press, 1988.

Loewe, Michael. *Ways to Paradise: The Chinese Quest for Immortality*. London: Allen & Unwin, 1979.

Long, Jeffrey P., and Jody A. Long. "A Comparison of Near-Death Experiences Occurring before and after 1975." *Journal of Near-Death Studies* 22, no. 1 (2003): 21–32.

López Austin, Alfredo. *The Human Body and Ideology: Concepts of the Ancient Nahuas*. Salt Lake City: University of Utah Press, 1988.

———. *Tamoanchan, Tlalocan: Places of Mist*. Translated by B. R. Ortiz de Montellano and T. Ortix de Montellano. Niwot: University Press of Colorado, 1997.

López, David. C. "De profecía a leyenda: invención y reinvenciones de la princesa Papantzin, 1558–1921." *Historia Mexicana* 71/2, no. 282 (October–December 2021). Online version Accessed 25 March 2023.

Love, Bruce. *The Paris Codex*. Austin: University of Texas Press, 1994.

288 ◆ Bibliography

Lundahl, Craig R. "Near-Death Experiences of Mormons." In *A Collection of Near-Death Research Readings*. Chicago: Nelson Hall, 1982, 165–79.

Lund, David H. *Death and Consciousness*. Jefferson: McFarland, 1985.

MacDonell, Arthur. A. *Vedic Mythology*. Strassburg: Verlag, 1897.

MacGregor, Geddes. *Images of Afterlife*. New York: Paragon, 1992.

Mair, Victor H. "Old Sinitic **Myag*, Old Persian *Magu*, and English *Magician*." *Early China* 15 (1990): 27–47.

Malamoud, Charles. "The Religion and Mythology of Vedic India." In *Asian Mythologies*, edited by Y. Bonnefoy, 25–9. Translated 1991. Chicago: University of Chicago Press, 1981.

Malinowski, Bronislaw. *Magic, Science and Religion*. New York: Doubleday, 1948.

Mark, Samuel. *From Egypt to Mesopotamia*. London: Chatham, 1998.

Martin, L. "Comparison." In *Guide to the Study of Religion*, edited by W. Braun and R. T. McCutcheon. London: Cassell, 2000a.

Ma'súmián, Farnáz. *Life After Death: A Study of the Afterlife in World Religions*. Oxford: Oneworld, 1995.

McClenon, James. *Wondrous Events: Foundations of Religious Belief*. Philadelphia: University of Pennsylvania Press, 1994.

———. "Content Analysis of a Predominantly African-American Near-Death Experience Collection." *Journal of Near-Death Studies* 23, no. 3 (2005): 159–81.

Meeks, Dimitri, and Christine Favard-Meeks. *Daily Life of the Egyptian Gods*. London: Pimlico, 1996.

Mehr, Kusum. P. *Yama: The Glorious Lord of the Other World*. New Delhi: D. K., 1996.

Mithen, Steven. *The Prehistory of the Mind: A Search for the Origins of Art, Religion and Science*. London: Thames and Hudson, 1996.

Moody, Raymond A. *Life After Life*. New York: Bantam, 1975.

Morgan, Evan S. *Tao the Great Luminant*. Shanghai: Kelly & Walsh, 1933.

Morris, Briar. *Anthropological Studies of Religion*. Cambridge: Cambridge University Press, 1987.

Moss, Rosalind L. B. *The Life After Death in Oceania and the Malay Archipelago*. Oxford: Oxford University Press, 1925.

Mueller, Dieter. "An Early Egyptian Guide to the Hereafter." *Journal of Egyptian Archaeology* 58 (1972): 99–125.

Murnane, William J. "Taking It with You: The Problem of Death and Afterlife in Ancient Egypt." In *Death and Afterlife: Perspectives of World Religions*, edited by H. Obayashi, 35–48. New York: Praeger, 1992.

Murphy, Todd. "Near-Death Experience in Thailand." *Journal of Near-Death Studies* 19, no. 3 (2001): 161–78.

Needham, Joseph. *Science and Civilization in China*, Vol. V, Pt. II. Cambridge: Cambridge University Press, 1974.

Nichelson, Oliver. "The Luminous Experience and the Scientific Method." *Journal of Near- Death Studies* 8, no. 4 (1990): 203–6.

Nicholson, Henry B. "Religion in Pre-Hispanic Mexico." In *Handbook of Middle American Indians*, vol. X, edited by G. F. Eckholm and I. Bernal , 395–446. Austin: University of Texas Press, 1971.

O'Callaghan, Roger. T. *Aram Naharaim: A Contribution to the History of Upper Mesopotamia in the Second Millennium BC*. Rome: Pontificium Institutum Biblicum, 1948.

O'Flaherty, Wendy Doniger. *The Rig Veda*. London: Penguin, 1981.

———. *Tales of Sex and Violence: Folklore, Sacrifice and Danger in the Jaiminiya Brahmana*. Chicago: University of Chicago Press, 1985.

———. *Textual Sources for the Study of Hinduism*. Totona: Barnes & Noble, 1988.

Olivelle, Patrick. *The Early Upanishads*. Oxford: Oxford University Press, 1999.

Osis, Karlis, and Erlendur Haraldsson *At the Hour of Death*. New York: Avon, 1977.

Otto, Rudolph. *The Idea of the Holy*. Oxford: Oxford University Press, 1923.

Panikkar, Raimundo. *The Vedic Experience*. London: Darton, Longman and Todd, 1977.

Paper, Jordan D. *The Spirits Are Drunk*. Albany: SUNY Press, 1995.

———. *The Mystic Experience*. Albany: SUNY Press, 2004.

———. *The Deities Are Many*. Albany: SUNY Press, 2005.

Parker Pearson, Mike. "The Return of the Living Dead: Mortuary Analysis and the New Archaeology Revisited." *Antiquity* 69 (1995): 1046–8.

Parnia, Sam. *What Happens When We Die*. London: Hay, 2005.

Parnia, Sam., Ken Spearpoint, Gabriele de Vos, Peter Fenwick, Diana Goldberg, Jie Yang, Jiawen Zhu, et al. "AWARE—AWAreness during REsuscitation: A Prospective Study." *Resuscitation* 85, no. 12 (2014): 1799–1805.

Parpola, Simo. "The Assyrian Tree of Life: Tracing the Origins of Jewish Monotheism and Greek Philosophy." *Journal of Near Eastern Studies* 52, no. 3 (1993): 161–208.

Pasricha, Satwant. "Near-Death Experiences in South India: A Systematic Survey in Channapatua." *National Institute of Mental Health and Neuro-Sciences Journal* 10 (1992): 111–18.

———. "A Systematic Survey of Near-Death Experiences in South India." *Journal of Scientific Exploration* 7 (1993): 161–71.

Paterson, R. W. K. *Philosophy and the Belief in Life After Death*. London: Macmillan, 1995.

Pausanias. *Description of Greece*. Trans. W.H.S. Jones. Cambridge, MA: Harvard University Press, 1918.

Platthy, Jeno. *Near-Death Experiences in Antiquity*. Santa Claus, IN., Federation of International Poetry Associations of UNESCO, 1992.

Pollock, Susan. *Ancient Mesopotamia*. Cambridge: Cambridge University Press, 1999.

Poo, Mu-chou. *In Search of Personal Welfare: A View of Ancient Chinese Religion*. Albany: SUNY Press, 1998.

Poynton, John. "What survives? An essay review of Goswami's *Physics of the Soul*." *Journal for the Society of Psychical Research* 871, no. 67.2 (2003): 143–54.

Price, H. H. "Survival and the Idea of 'Another World.'" *Proceedings of the Society for Psychical Research* 50, no. 182 (1953): 1–25.

Quirke, Stephen. *Ancient Egyptian Religion*. London: Dover, 1992.

Raglan, Lord *Death and Rebirth: A Study in Comparative Religion*. London: Watts, 1945.

Reat, N. Ross, and Edmund. F. Perry. *A World Theology: The Central Spiritual Reality of Humankind*. Cambridge: Cambridge University Press, 1991.

Ring, Kenneth. *Life at Death: A Scientific Investigation of the Near-Death Experience*. New York: Coward, McCann, and Geohegan, 1980.

Robinson, Peter. "As for Them Who Know Them, They Will Find Their Paths: Speculations on Ritual Landscapes in the "Book of Two Ways." In *Mysterious Lands*, edited by D. O'Connor and S. Quirke. London: UCL, 2003.

Rock, Adam J., Peter B. Baynes, and Paul J. Casey. "Experimental Study of Ostensibly Shamanic Journeying Imagery in Naïve Participants I: Antecedents." *Anthropology of Consciousness* 15, no. 2 (2005): 72–92.

———. "Experimental Study of Ostensibly Shamanic Journeying Imagery in Naïve Participants II: Phenomenological Mapping and Modified Affect Bridge." *Anthropology of Consciousness* 17, no. 1 (2006): 65–83.

Roebuck, Valerie J. *The Upanishads*. New Delhi: Penguin, 2000.

Roux, Georges. *Ancient Iraq*. Harmondsworth: Penguin, 1964.

Roys, Ralph. L. *The Book of Chilam Balam of Chumayel*. Norman: University of Oklahoma Press, 1933. Reprinted 1967.

Russell, J. B. *A History of Heaven*. Princeton: Princeton University Press, 1997.

Sahagún, Bernardino. *The Florentine Codex*. Translated by A. I. O. Anderson and C. E. Dibble. 13 vols. Santa Fe: Monographs of the School of American Research, 1950–1982. First published 1547.

———. ed. *Primeros Memoriales*. Translated by T. D. Sullivan. Norman: University of Oklahoma Press, 1997.

Sartori, Penny. "A Prospective Study to Investigate the Incidence and Phenomenology of Near-Death Experiences in a Welsh Intensive Therapy Unit." Unpublished Ph.D. thesis, University of Wales, Lampeter, 2005.

———. *The Near-Death Experiences of Hospitalized Intensive Care Patients: A Five- Year Clinical Study*. Lewiston, Queenston, and Lampeter: Edwin Mellen Press, 2008.

Schaffer, J. G., and D. A. Lichtenstein. "South Asian Archaeology and the Myth of Indo-Aryan Invasions." In *The Indo-Aryan Controversy*, edited by E. F. Bryant and L. L. Patton, 75–104. London: Routledge, 2005.

Schumann-Antelme, Ruth, and Stéphane Rossini. *Becoming Osiris*. Rochester: Inner Traditions, 1998.

Seidel, Anna. "Tokens of immortality in Han graves." *Numen* 29 (1982), 79–87.

———. "Traces of Han Religion in Funeral Texts Found in Tombs." In *Taoism and Religious Culture*, edited by Akizuki Kan'ei, 21–57. Tokyo: Shuppan, 1987.

Séjourné, Laurette. *Burning Water: Thought and Religion in Ancient Mexico*. London: Thames & Hudson, 1957.

Serdahely, William. J. "Pediatric Near-Death Experiences." *Journal of Near-Death Studies* 9 (1990): 33–9.

———. "Variations from the Prototypic Near-Death Experience." *Journal of Near-Death Studies* 13, no. 3 (1995): 185–96.

Sheils, Dean. "A Cross-Cultural Study of Beliefs in Out-of-the-Body Experiences." *Journal of the Society for Psychical Research* 49, no. 775 (1978): 697–741.

Shushan, Gregory. *Conceptions of the Afterlife in Early Civilizations: Universalism, Constructivism, and Near-Death Experience*. London: Bloomsbury, 2009.

———. "Rehabilitating the Neglected 'Similar': Confronting the Issue of Cross-Cultural Similarities in the Study of Religions." *Paranthropology: Journal of Anthropological Approaches to the Paranormal* 4, no. 2 (Spring 2013): 48–53.

———. *Near-Death Experience in Indigenous Religions*. New York and Oxford: Oxford University Press, 2018.

———. *The Next World: Extraordinary Experiences of the Afterlife*. Guildford: White Crow, 2022.

Simpson, William. K., ed. *The Literature of Ancient Egypt*. 3rd Ed. New Haven: Yale, 2003.

Sladek, William R. *Inanna's Descent to the Netherworld*. Ann Arbor: University Microfilms International, 1974.

Smart, Ninian. *Dimensions of the Sacred: Anatomy of the World's Beliefs*. Berkeley: University of California Press, 1996.

Smith, Huston. *Forgotten Truth*. New York: Harper, 1977.

———. "Methodology, Comparisons, and Truth." In *A Magic Still Dwells: Comparative Religion in the Postmodern Age*, edited by K. C. Patton and B. C. Ray, 172–81. Berkeley: University of California Press, 2000.

Smith, Jonathan Z. "Wisdom's Place." In *Death, Ecstasy, and Other Worldly Journeys*, edited by J. J. Collins and M. A. Fishbane, 3–14. Albany: SUNY Press, 1995.

Smith, Mark. *Following Osiris: Perspectives on the Osirian Afterlife from Four Millennia*. Oxford: Oxford University Press, 2017.

Smith, Wilfred. C. *Towards a World Theology*. London: Macmillan, 1981.

Spronk, Klass. *Beatific Afterlife in Ancient Israel and in the Ancient Near East*. Alter Orient und Altes Testament 219. Neukirchen-Vluyn: Butzon & Bercker, 1986.

Stevenson, Ian., and Bruce. Greyson. "NDEs: Relevance to the Question of Survival after Death." In *The Near-Death Experience: A Reader*, edited by L. W. Bailey and J. Yates, 199–206. London: Routledge, 1996.

Stroebe, Wolfgang S., and Margaret Stroebe. *Bereavement and Health: The Psychological and Physical Consequences of Partner Loss*. Cambridge: Cambridge University Press, 1987.

Tedlock, Dennis. *Popol Vuh*. Rev. ed. New York: Simon and Schuster, 1996.

Thompson, Laurence. G. "On the Prehistory of Hell in China." *Journal of Chinese Religions* 17 (1983): 27–41.

———. *Chinese Religion*. Rev. ed. Encino: Dickensen, 1992.

Thompson, Stith. *Motif-Index of Folklore Literature*. 6 vols. Rev. ed. Bloomington: Indiana University Press, 1955–1958.

Trigger, Bruce. G. *Early Civilizations: Ancient Egypt in Context*. Cairo: American University in Cairo Press, 1993.

———. *Understanding Early Civilizations*. Cambridge: Cambridge University Press, 2003.

Tylor, Edward. B. *Primitive Culture*. London: Murray, 1873.

Ucko, Peter. (1969) "Ethnography and the archaeological interpretation of funerary remains." *World Archaeology* 1, 262-90.

Ullmann, Montague, Stanley Krippner, and Alan Vaughan. *Dream Telepathy: The Landmark ESP Experiments*. 3rd ed. Santa Fe: Afterworlds Press, 2023.

Veldhuis, Nick. "Entering the Netherworld." *Cuneiform Digital Library Bulletin* 2003:6 (2 September 2003).

Vicente, Raul., Michael Rizzuto, Can Sarica, Kazuaki Yamamoto, Mohammed Sadr, Tarun Khajuria, and Mostafa Fatehi, et al. "Enhanced Interplay of Neuronal Coherence and Coupling in the Dying Human Brain." *Frontiers in Aging Neuroscience* 14 (2022).

Wach, Joachim. *Types of Religious Experience*. Chicago: University of Chicago Press, 1951.

Wade, Jenny. "In a Sacred Manner We Died: Native American Near-Death Experiences." *Journal of Near-Death Studies* 22, no. 2 (2003): 83–115.

Waley, Arthur. *The Book of Songs*. 2nd ed. London: Allen & Unwin, 1954.

———. *The Nine Songs*. London: Allen & Unwin, 1955.

Walsh, Roger N. *The Spirit of Shamanism*. Los Angeles: Tarcher, 1990.

Ward, Keith. *Images of Eternity*. London: Dartmon Longman & Todd, 1987.

Wasson, R. Gordon. "The Divine Mushroom of Immortality." In *Flesh of the Gods: The Ritual Use of Hallucinogens*, edited by P. T. Furst, 185–200. Prospect Heights: Waveland, 1972. Reprinted 1990.

———. "What Was the Soma of the Aryans?" In *Flesh of the Gods: The Ritual Use of Hallucinogens*, edited by P. T. Furst, 201–13. Prospect Heights: Waveland, 1972. Reprinted 1990.

Watson, Burton. *Hsün Tzu: Basic Writings*. New York: Columbia University Press, 1963.

Weber, Max. *The Sociology of Religion*. Boston: Beacon Press, 1922. Revised 1963.

Werner, Karel. "The Vedic Concept of Human Personality and its Destiny." *Journal of Indian Philosophy*, 5, no. 3 (1978): 275–89.

Winkelman, Michael. "Shamanism as the Original Neurotheology." *Zygon* 39, no. 1 (2004): 193–217.

Whitney, William. D. *The Atharva Veda*. Cambridge: Harvard Oriental Series VII–VIII, 1905.

Witzel, Michael. "Indocentrism: Autochthonous Visions of Ancient India." In *The Indo-Aryan Controversy*, edited by E. F. Bryant and L. L. Patton, 341–404. London: Routledge, 2005.

———. "Vala and Iwato: The Myth of the Hidden Sun in India, Japan, and Beyond." *Electronic Journal of Vedic Studies* 12, no. 1 (2005): 1–69.

Yandell, Keith. E. *The Epistemology of Religious Experience*. Cambridge: Cambridge University Press, 1993.

Yü, Ying-shih. "O Soul, Come Back: A Study of the Changing Conceptions of the Soul and Afterlife in Pre-Buddhist China." *Harvard Journal of Asiatic Studies* 47 (1987): 363–95.

Zaleski, Carol. *Otherworld Journeys: Accounts of Near-Death Experiences in Medieval and Modern Times*. Oxford: Oxford University Press, 1987.

Zandee, Jan. *Death as an Enemy, According to Ancient Egyptian Conceptions*. Leiden: Brill, 1960.

Zhi-ying, Feng, and Liu Jian-xun. "Near-Death Experiences among Survivors of the 1976 Tangshan Earthquake." *Journal of Near-Death Studies* 11, no. 1 (1992): 39–48.

Index